CLASSICAL COMICS
TEACHING RESOURCE PACK

Making Shakespeare accessible
for teachers and students

Suitable for teaching ages 10–17

Written by: Kornel Kossuth

William Shakespeare

CLASSICAL COMICS TEACHING RESOURCE PACK
A Midsummer Night's Dream

First printed: May 2011
Reprinted: May 2015

Published by: Classical Comics Ltd

Copyright ©2011 Classical Comics Ltd.
All rights reserved. No part of this book may be reproduced in any form or incorporated into any information retrieval system without the written permission of Classical Comics Ltd.

Copyright notice: This book is protected by international copyright law and cannot be copied in any way until it has been purchased. Teachers are free to reproduce these pages by any method without infringing copyright restrictions, provided that the number of copies reproduced does not exceed the amount required in the school of purchase.

Written by:	Kornel Kossuth
Script Adaptation:	John McDonald
Characters & Artwork:	Kat Nicholson & Jason Cardy
Design & Layout:	Carl Andrews
Editor in Chief:	Clive Bryant

The rights of Kornel Kossuth, Kat Nicholson and Jason Cardy to be identified as the artists of this work have been asserted in accordance with the Copyright, Designs and Patents Act 1988 sections 77 and 78.

Acknowledgments: Every effort has been made to trace copyright holders of material reproduced in this book. Any rights not acknowledged here will be acknowledged in subsequent editions if notice is given to Classical Comics Ltd.

All enquiries should be addressed to:
Classical Comics Ltd
PO Box 16310
Birmingham
B30 9EL, UK

education@classicalcomics.com
www.classicalcomics.com

ISBN: 978-1-907127-06-9

Printed in the UK

CONTENTS

INTRODUCTION 4

BACKGROUND
The Background of *A Midsummer Night's Dream* 5
Shakespeare's Times 6
Puck's Epilogue 8
The Ending of *A Midsummer Night's Dream* 9

UNDERSTANDING THE PLAY
Scene-by-Scene Synopsis 11
Comprehension 14
The Different Worlds of *A Midsummer Night's Dream* 19

CHARACTER
Exploring Character 21
Character Activities 24
Character Sheets 26
Venn Diagrams 32
Blank Comic Grid 35
Spot the Difference 36
Dukedom and Kingdom 37
The Mechanicals Rehearse 38
Hippolyta the Huntress 40
Egeus – the Luckless Father 41

LANGUAGE
Shakespeare's Language 42
The Rhythm of Shakespeare's Language 44
Quince Speaks the Prologue 45
The Groups and Their Language 46
Antithesis 49
Bottom's "Bottomisms" 50
Imagery in *A Midsummer Night's Dream* 51
The Lovers' (and Others') Insults 53

THEMES
Exploring Themes in *A Midsummer Night's Dream* 54
Exploring Act I Scene 1 55
Love and Marriage 56
Happy Ever After? 57
Lysander Loves and Dotes 58
Love and Reason 59
Star-crossed Lovers 61
Obedience 62
Who Must Obey Whom? 63
Dreams and Imagination 64
I Spy With My Little Eye 65
Who is Dreaming What? 66
The Moon – Madness and Chastity 68
Chaste Diana 69
Theseus's Speech on Lovers, Poets and Madmen 70
Theme Exploration Sheet 72
Essay Writing Frame 73
Possible Essay Titles 74

DRAMA AND DISCUSSION
Drama Activities 75
Characteristic One-Liners 77
Developing Relationships 78
Acting Out Scenes from the Play 79

GAMES & ACTIVITIES
Word Jumble 81
Crossword 82
Word search 83

TEACHERS' NOTES, ANSWERS & EXPANSIONS 84

INTRODUCTION

WELCOME TO *A MIDSUMMER NIGHT'S DREAM* TEACHING RESOURCE FROM CLASSICAL COMICS.

This resource has manifold aims, which I hope it achieves:

- It is designed to be easy to use, giving teachers who have never worked with *A Midsummer Night's Dream* an in-depth guide on a range of activities they can deploy. The approach is therefore comprehensive, and this resource gives you a set of ready-to-teach lessons that need little preparation.

- The division of activities into chapters allows teachers more familiar with the text and its teaching to pick and choose the activities they want. A brief introduction to each topic, designed to kick-start thoughts on the theme, helps teachers re-cap their knowledge.

- Most importantly, this resource aims to provide a variety of activities that stimulate enjoyable learning for pupils aged 10-17. Each topic contains lesson ideas and photocopiable worksheets. For those tasks that involve a more closed response, teacher answer sheets are provided at the back of the book. Of course, the answers provided are mostly suggestions only and by no means exhaustive. Where there is no teacher sheet, the task is designed to be more exploratory, with the emphasis on pupils being able to explain their findings rather than guessing what the pre-fabricated "right" answer might be.

Although designed with the Classical Comics version of *A Midsummer Night's Dream* in mind, this resource can be used successfully with the traditional text.

If you would like to send feedback or suggest ways to improve this book, please email **education@classicalcomics.com** – your thoughts and input are always appreciated.

Kornel Kossuth

THE BACKGROUND OF A MIDSUMMER NIGHT'S DREAM

INTRODUCTION

Each Shakespeare play is enjoyable in its own right, either as a performance or as a text. However, a closer look at the background of a play, and in particular the era in which it was written, can be useful to find out what themes are present within it. In this context, a look at Shakespeare's life and what was happening at the time he wrote his plays can yield interesting information.

A Midsummer Night's Dream is of particular interest as its main plot-line is not based on any one definite source (although some parts of the play are based on other stories), while its theme is similar to that of *Romeo and Juliet* – a play Shakespeare almost certainly wrote around the same time.

There are a number of ways pupils can engage with the life and times of Shakespeare and the background of *A Midsummer Night's Dream*:

- A number of people contend that *A Midsummer Night's Dream* was written for an aristocratic wedding that Queen Elizabeth I herself may have attended. There are a number of clues in the text that could support this point of view. Based on textual evidence and using the essay framework, pupils might argue that the play was first performed at a private wedding.

- The pupils can also use the theme essay framework to explore how historical and sociological events may have influenced the plot and themes of the play.

- It was traditional at the end of a play, especially comedies, to ask for the audience's approval and to apologise for any shortcomings. In *A Midsummer Night's Dream* Puck does this in the epilogue, but with a marked difference: Puck expressly states that if the audience didn't enjoy the play they should imagine they had dreamt it. To what extent is this an original ending when compared to other epilogues, and in what way does it continue the play's preoccupation with dreams?

- In its plot-line of the Mechanicals, Shakespeare gives us a behind-the-scenes glimpse of how theatre worked in his day. Pupils could research the limitations of theatre in the Elizabethan and Jacobean era and how plays were performed in those days (costumes, scenery and props). A good place to start is the New Globe Theatre in London.

Of course, any work done on the play's background should tie in with work done in lessons and serve to enrich the pupils' understanding of the play.

SHAKESPEARE'S TIMES
HISTORICAL AND SOCIOLOGICAL INFLUENCES

A Midsummer Night's Dream is one of the few plays whose main plot-line is not based on a specific source. While Shakespeare was definitely influenced by Ovid's *Metamorphoses*, North's *Life of Theseus*, Seneca's *Hippolytus* and Chaucer's *Canterbury Tales*, none is a sufficient source in itself for the whole of the play's action. A number of the play's themes are rooted in contemporary events and preoccupations. Love and marriage are central, which would make sense if the play was originally written to be performed at a wedding, as many historians believe.

Love and Marriage

In Elizabethan England, marriage was very much a social contract entered into between two people of equal standing, with the purpose of producing an heir and thus securing the family name and wealth for another generation. This was true mainly of the aristocracy, but it was also true of other classes. Although marriage had to be entered into of one's own free will, love was not usually of primary concern. If anything, it was a bonus.

Parents and friends would have had a large influence in selecting a prospective partner. Indeed, parents would have to consent to a marriage. However, if there were no financial or social obstacles, this consent was rarely withheld. In this sense, Egeus is not typical of the Elizabethan era, especially as Lysander and Demetrius are of equal standing.

While society frowned on single men and women meeting unless they were "a couple", there were certain ritualised meetings to help youths come together (people usually married in their twenties). A number of celebrations, like "maying", allowed young people to get to know one another in group situations. At such festivals the youths would sing, dance and play games of varying intimacy. Shakespeare suggests that the play, as far as the lovers are concerned, may be an extended form of "maying", and by the end of it (at the end of Act IV), the lovers have paired off into their couples and are ready for marriage that is now based on love.

Stagecraft

Although a number of Shakespeare's plays have a play within a play, *A Midsummer Night's Dream* is the only one that allows us to look behind the scenes. Admittedly, the performance is not a professional one, but it is hard not to see parallels between how Shakespeare presents the Mechanicals and actual Elizabethan theatre troupes. There is one specific reference to a true stage event in the play: when discussing Snout's part as lion (III.1), the Mechanicals are afraid the lion might scare the ladies in the audience. In Edinburgh, in 1594, plans to have a chariot drawn in by lions at a pageant marking the baptism of Prince Henry were abandoned because the beasts might strike fear in the onlookers. So it is probably safe to say that when writing about the Mechanicals, Shakespeare was at least satirising his contemporaries and competitors.

Plays in Shakespeare's days were performed in costume of the period with very little scenery. It was up to the language of the play to recreate the world and make the audience "see" the scenery that wasn't there. In this respect, the Mechanicals' insistence on bringing in a real wall and real moonshine is out of keeping with Elizabethan stage practice, and thus is ludicrous.

We do get a sense of the confusion a rehearsal could bring. Actors did not have the whole play in front of them, but only their parts and their cues. Before the first run through or without the help of the director, they would have had very little idea what the play was about *. Therefore Quince has to explain the play not only for the audience's benefit, but also the players'. While Flute can, in his nervousness, read the whole of his part without noticing that he is reading past his own cues.

What is also unusual here is a group of laymen amateurs performing in front of aristocracy. Theatre was either performed by professional companies, such as Shakespeare's, or as pageants by amateur aristocrats in front of other aristocrats. This may be Shakespeare telling us precisely what he thinks about his competitors, or simply a device to heighten the comedy.

* for a truly superb insight into how plays were rehearsed in Shakespeare's day, get a copy of *Secrets of Acting Shakespeare* by Patrick Tucker of the Original Shakespeare Company.

Dreams

For a play that has "dream" in its title, there is remarkably little dreaming going on. Although dreams are often mentioned and many characters at various stages believe they must have been dreaming (at the end the audience is asked to make believe the whole play was "but a dream"), there is only one actual dream in *A Midsummer Night's Dream* – the one dreamt by Hermia after Lysander has left her at the end of Act II.2.

Elizabethan England differentiated between two different types of dreams. The first were those that presented hopes or fears, like a lover dreaming of her loved one, or a hunter dreaming of killing a prize animal. These dreams presented what we would now call "day residue" and are, as such, unspectacular and of no further interest or significance. The second category were predictive dreams that contained some message about future events. What makes prediction tricky is that often the visions are metaphorical rather than literal (so, instead of dreaming of a murder, the dreamer might dream that a certain animal that represents the victim is killed).

As Hermia was not worried when she lay down to sleep, her dream must be rated as predictive. While metaphorical, it is not difficult to interpret. But what about all the other references to dreams? You might explore what kinds of dreams they are, and the meaning behind them.

Fairies, the Moon and the Weather

When Oberon and Titania meet for the first time, Titania explains that the current turmoil in nature is due to the conflict between them. While fairies are not customarily responsible for the weather, there were a number of years in which the weather was considered abnormal. The years 1594-1596 all had extraordinary summers: wet and cold like winter, with regular flooding, pointing to a dislocation of the seasons just as Titania laments.

With the exception of their influence on the weather, Shakespeare's fairies (and Puck in particular) are very much creatures of rural folklore. Apart from a penchant for causing mischief, they are inherently neither good nor evil. Puck will help those who are kind to him, even though he plays pranks on others. The types of prank point to things going inexplicably wrong in an agricultural community requiring some unseen being – such as a fairy – to be invented as scapegoat. Their size seems to vary, as Titania has no problem embracing the transformed Bottom, but at the same time they battle with bats and bees, and can hide in acorns.

If fairies are considered to be demons (as many pagan gods were believed to be), then they would be able to influence the weather, as ruining crops was a prime occupation of witches and demons. Indeed, many of Puck's pranks could be seen as the work of a witch. While King of Scotland, James VI (who became James I of England when Queen Elizabeth died) wrote a book on witches, *Daemonologie* (1597). In it he expressly stated that fairies were a type of demon. He also specified that they followed Diana, the goddess of the moon. This keys in directly to the countless references to the moon and the strange, magical goings-on in the moonlit woods.

PUCK'S EPILOGUE
"No epilogue, I pray you"

In a number of plays, mostly the comedies, Shakespeare adds an epilogue at the end of the action. The epilogue is usually delivered by one of the characters, and its purpose is to apologise for the insufficiencies of the play, seeking the audience's goodwill and approval through its applause. As such, it is quite a standard piece.

However in *A Midsummer Night's Dream*, Shakespeare manages to provide an interesting variation on this idea. While the epilogue sounds conventional enough, its affinity with the content of the play itself led Shakespeare to provide in it a brilliant *coup de théâtre*. In a play in which dreams are so often mentioned, but seldom dreamt, the playwright asks the audience to imagine the play was "but a dream" if they didn't like it. This is a significant shift from other epilogues.

With the aid of other Shakespearean epilogues, and the comparison chart, pupils can explore the ending of *A Midsummer Night's Dream* before comparing it to those of the other plays. Although three other epilogues are presented, it is suggested that pupils compare the epilogue of *A Midsummer Night's Dream* with two other epilogues of their choice.

THE ENDING OF *A MIDSUMMER NIGHT'S DREAM*

TASK:
Compare two of the following epilogues to Puck's epilogue.

From *The Tempest*

PROSPERO
Now my charms are all o'erthrown,
And what strength I have's mine own,
Which is most faint: now, 'tis true,
I must be here confin'd by you,
Or sent to Naples. Let me not,
Since I have my dukedom got,
And pardon'd the deceiver, dwell
In this bare island, by your spell;
But release me from my bands,
With the help of your good hands.
Gentle breath of yours my sails
Must fill, or else my project fails,
Which was to please. Now I want
Spirits to enforce, art to enchant;
And my ending is despair,
Unless I be reliev'd by prayer,
Which pierces so, that it assaults
Mercy itself, and frees all faults.
As you from crimes would pardon'd be,
Let your indulgence set me free.

From *All's Well That Ends Well*

KING
The king's a beggar now the play is done:
All is well ended, if this suit be won,
That you express content; which we will pay,
With strife to please you, day exceeding day:
Ours be your patience then, and yours our parts;
Your gentle hands lend us, and take our hearts.

From *As You Like It*

ROSALIND
It is not the fashion to see the lady the epilogue; but it is no more unhandsome than to see the lord the prologue. If it be true that good wine needs no bush, 'tis true that a good play needs no epilogue; yet to good wine they do use good bushes, and good plays prove the better by the help of good epilogues. What a case am I in then, that am neither a good epilogue nor cannot insinuate with you in the behalf of a good play? I am not furnished like a beggar, therefore to beg will not become me: my way is to conjure you; and I'll begin with the women. I charge you, O women! for the love you bear to men, to like as much of this play as please you: and I charge you, O men! for the love you bear to women -- as I perceive by your simpering, none of you hates them -- that between you and the women, the play may please. If I were a woman, I would kiss as many of you as had beards that pleased me, complexions that liked me and breaths that I defied not: and, I am sure, as many as have good beards, or good faces, or sweet breaths, will, for my kind offer, when I make curtsy, bid me farewell.

Prospero from Classical Comics' *The Tempest*.
Artwork by: Jon Haward and Gary Erskine

THE ENDING OF *A MIDSUMMER NIGHT'S DREAM*

TASK:
Use the following table first to examine Puck's epilogue and then to compare it with two others.

Question	*A Midsummer Night's Dream*	*The Tempest*	*All's Well That Ends Well*	*As You Like It*
Who delivers the Prologue?				
Is the actor in character?				
How is the character trying to persuade the audience to clap?				
How does the epilogue relate to the rest of the play?				

SCENE-BY-SCENE SYNOPSIS

Act I Scene 1
Theseus, Duke of Athens, is impatient to marry Hippolyta, the conquered Queen of the Amazons, but he still has to wait four more days.
Egeus comes to the duke to complain that his daughter, Hermia, does not want to obey him and marry Demetrius. Instead, she loves Lysander. According to Athenian law, Hermia must either marry her father's choice of husband, be executed, or live the life of a nun, away from all men. Theseus gives Hermia four days to decide.

Seeing that matters are against them, Lysander and Hermia decide to flee Athens the next night. They agree to meet in the woods nearby. However Helena, Hermia's friend, is dejected because she loves Demetrius, who no longer loves her (as he now loves Hermia). Lysander and Hermia tell Helena of their plan to escape, so she will have Demetrius all to herself. Helena decides to betray her friend and to tell Demetrius of Hermia's planned escape in order that she might receive his thanks and be able to keep him company as he seeks out Hermia in the woods (and possibly to win his affection).

Act I Scene 2
Quince, Bottom, Snug, Flute, Snout and Starveling (the so-called "Mechanicals"), all simple workmen of Athens, meet to discuss a play they want to perform for the Duke's wedding. Although Quince is their leader, Bottom keeps taking over; in particular, he wants to play every part of their chosen play, *Pyramus and Thisbe*, although his role is to be that of Pyramus, an unfortunate lover. Flute plays Thisbe, his lady-love. The other workmen are to play the lovers' parents, with the exception of Snug the joiner, who will play the lion.
The workers agree to meet in the woods to rehearse the next night.

Act II Scene 1
A fairy and Robin Goodfellow, or "Puck", meet in the woods as both are preparing the arrival of their respective rulers, Titania and Oberon, queen and king of the fairies. Oberon and Titania have fallen out over an Indian boy whom Titania has adopted, and whom Oberon wants as a page. Because of their quarrel, nature is in turmoil and all the seasons are muddled up. Titania refuses to give up the boy or to rejoin Oberon. The fairy king decides to make her pay and asks Puck to find a magical flower. When the juice of the flower is dripped into the eyes of someone asleep, it makes them fall in love with the first thing they see when they wake. Oberon plans to use this to make Titania fall in love with some horrible creature.

While Puck is gone, Helena and Demetrius pass through the woods, searching for Hermia and Lysander. Oberon watches Demetrius spurn Helena and makes a promise that Demetrius will love her soon. Puck returns with the magical flower, and Oberon tells him to find the Athenian and administer the flower juice while he sleeps, so that he may fall in love with the girl he is with.

SCENE-BY-SCENE SYNOPSIS

Act II Scene 2

Titania, surrounded by her fairy court, goes to sleep. While asleep, Oberon puts some of the juice from the flower in her eyes. Hermia and Lysander appear in the woods, having lost their way. They decide to wait till dawn before proceeding further. Instead of sleeping close together, Hermia asks Lysander to sleep further from her, as modesty requires. While they are asleep, Puck happens upon the two. He thinks these are the two Athenians Oberon talked about, and he squeezes the juice of the flower into Lysander's eyes. When Helena comes along, having been abandoned by Demetrius, Lysander wakes to see her and, under the flower's magical power, falls in love with her. Helena thinks Lysander is mocking her and leaves. Lysander follows, leaving Hermia asleep alone. She wakes and finds she is alone, having had a nightmare in which a snake eats her heart.

Act III Scene 1

The Mechanicals meet in the woods to rehearse their play. They begin by discussing whether their play might frighten the ladies before rehearsing their lines. Puck watches the labourers make a mess of things and decides to have some fun with them. While Bottom is sent "off stage" and away from the others, Puck conjures a donkey's head onto him. When his fellow workers see him they flee, leaving him alone, singing to keep himself company. His singing wakes Titania, who has been sleeping nearby, and because of the flower juice administered by Oberon, she falls in love with him. She orders her fairies to wait on him and then leads him to her bed.

Act III Scene 2

Puck tells Oberon all that has happened. Oberon is pleased, but when Demetrius and Hermia enter, Oberon realises that Puck has bewitched the wrong man. Hermia believes Demetrius has killed Lysander, but he denies bringing harm to him. She leaves Demetrius, and, exhausted, he lies down to sleep. Oberon applies the flower to his eyes and orders Puck to bring Helena to him. Helena enters, followed by a lovesick Lysander. When Demetrius awakes, he too is now in love with Helena. Helena thinks the two men are mocking her. Hermia then arrives, and Lysander tells her that he no longer loves her. Helena thinks that Hermia is also out to make fun of her, but Hermia accuses her friend of having bewitched Lysander. Lysander and Demetrius decide to fight over their right to Helena and leave. The two women leave, too (separately). Oberon reprimands Puck and orders him to set things right by dripping the antidote into Lysander's eye. Puck casts a dense fog over the woods and separates the two men, who are trying to find each other so that they might fight. He leads both astray until, exhausted, they separately fall asleep. The two women also find their way to the area and fall asleep in the woods, exhausted by the night's events. Puck anoints Lysander's eyes with the antidote.

SCENE-BY-SCENE SYNOPSIS

Act IV Scene 1
Titania continues to dote on Bottom with his ass's head. They fall asleep together. Oberon, who has meanwhile received the changeling boy from Titania, frees her from the spell, and she wakes. She sees Bottom with the donkey's head and realises what has happened. Titania and Oberon are reconciled and decide to bless Theseus's wedding together (although we never learn the fate of the changeling boy!).

A short while later, while out hunting, Theseus, Hippolyta and Egeus stumble upon the four lovers, who are sleeping in close proximity, unbeknownst to them due to the dense fog the previous night. As best they can, they tell the Duke what has happened. Demetrius is now in love with Helena (either genuinely, or possibly due to the juice from the magical flower). Although Egeus still wants Demetrius to marry Hermia, Theseus overrules him and decides that the two happy couples shall marry together with him and Hippolyta.

After all have left, Bottom wakes up as his normal self (with his human head) but at a complete loss to say what has happened.

Act IV Scene 2
Without Bottom, the Mechanicals despair as they cannot hope to stage the play without their leading actor. All their hopes for fame and honour are dashed. Then, suddenly, Bottom arrives and urges them to prepare for their performance.

Act V Scene 1
Hippolyta and Theseus marvel at the story of the four lovers. When presented with the choice of plays to while away the time until the night, Theseus – despite the protests of his master of revels, Philostrate – chooses the Mechanicals' play of *Pyramus and Thisbe*.

During the play, the Athenian youths mock the labourers, who overact and misread their lines. In the play, Pyramus and Thisbe are two lovers whose parents don't approve of their love. They communicate through a chink in the wall and agree to meet outside the town. Thisbe is first there and is surprised by a lion. She runs away, but leaves her scarf in its maw. Pyramus then arrives and, seeing the mauled scarf, thinks Thisbe is dead and kills himself. When Thisbe returns she sees the dead Pyramus and kills herself out of grief. Theseus is pleased with the play, and all retire. The play over, the celebrations ended for the day, and everyone in bed, Oberon, Titania and their fairies fly through the house, blessing it and the couples within it.

Epilogue
Puck remains alone and asks that the audience, if displeased, imagine that what they saw was just a dream. If, however, they are pleased, he asks for their approval through clapping.

COMPREHENSION
ACT I

Fill in the blanks using the words provided.
You may use a word once only, and you may not need to use them all.

Theseus, the _____ of Athens, can hardly wait to get married to _____, the Queen of the _____, whom he conquered in _____. Egeus disrupts their preparations and complains that his daughter, _____, will not obey his instructions and marry _____ because she loves _____ instead. Theseus tells Hermia that, on the day of the royal wedding, she must decide either to marry as her father wishes, be executed, or become a _____ for ever. Lysander and Hermia bewail their bad fortune and decide to _____ from _____. They tell Hermia's friend Helena all about their intentions. _____ was once loved by Demetrius, before he loved Hermia. She still loves Demetrius and secretly decides to tell him of the lovers' _____ to leave the town, in the hope of receiving some _____ .

Meanwhile, a group of simple _____ from Athens are planning to perform a _____ for the Duke's _____ celebrations. They plan on staging *Pyramus and* _____, with Bottom as _____ and _____ as Thisbe, although _____ wants to play all the parts in the play. They decide to meet in the _____ the next night to rehearse.

King	Helena	woods	city	Lysander
Pyramus	Syracuse	thanks	Duke	Bottom
flee	wanderers	kisses	Centaurs	nun
Amazons	workmen	Athens	Egeus	dance
Flute	priestess	plan	wedding	Thisbe
Hermia	play	Hippolyta	Demetrius	battle

COMPREHENSION
ACT II

Fill in the blanks using the words provided.
You may use a word once only, and you may not need to use them all.

Robin Goodfellow, otherwise known as _____ , meets a _____ in the woods. Both Titania and Oberon, the Queen and the King of the fairies, plan to be in the _____ that night. However, the two are in conflict because _____ has an Indian child that _____ wants, and she _____ to give it up. As a result of their _____ , nature is in _____ . Oberon is prepared to end the fight if Titania gives him the child. Her refusal makes Oberon vow to make her pay for her _____ .

He orders Puck to search out a _____ , the juice of which makes people fall in love with the next thing they _____ when they wake, after it has been applied to the _____ . Oberon wants to make sure that Titania wakes up when something _____ is near.

While Puck is gone, Oberon watches Demetrius and _____ walk through the woods in search of _____ and Hermia. Demetrius continues to push Helena away. When Puck comes back to Oberon with the flower, in an attempt to set things right between Demetrius and Helena, he tells Puck to _____ the Athenian's eyes with the flower juice so that he will _____ the girl he _____ .

Elsewhere, Titania falls asleep, surrounded by her _____ . While asleep, Oberon smears some of the flower's _____ onto her eyes.

In another part of the wood, Hermia and Lysander have lost their way; tired, they decide to sleep where they are. As they are not yet _____ , Hermia insists that they sleep _____ . Puck, seeing them, thinks these are the two his master talked about, and he applies the juice onto _____ eyes. Helena stumbles into the area and wakes him. The magic of the flower has its effect, and he falls in love with her. Helena runs off, but Lysander _____ her. After dreaming that a _____ was eating her heart, Hermia wakes up alone.

city	hate	see	old enough	quarrel
disobedience	flower	eyes	anoint	vile
juice	turmoil	Puck	woods	Oberon
Demetrius	Lysander	together	fairy	spurned
snake	follows	love	married	Demetrius's
Hermia	Titania	refuses	apart	fairy-court
potion	Lysander's	harmony	thought	Helena

COMPREHENSION
ACT III

Fill in the blanks using the words provided.
You may use a word once only, and you may not need to use them all.

Puck watches the _____ rehearse their play and decides to have some fun with them. He puts a spell on _____ so that his head becomes a _____ . When his friends see him, they run away. Left by himself, he _____ to cheer himself up. The noise wakes _____ , who _____ with him.

Puck reports all he has done to _____ , who is _____ . _____ and Hermia enter, Hermia accusing him of having killed _____ . Oberon realises Puck has made a _____ . While Demetrius sleeps, exhausted from the night's events, Oberon puts the love juice on his eyes.

_____ enters, followed by Lysander. Waking under the power of the potion, Demetrius sees Helena and falls in love with her; now both men _____ over her. _____ returns to the scene and accuses Helena of having _____ Lysander. The two men go off to fight, and the two women leave separately.

Oberon is _____ at Puck and tells him to set things right. Puck conjures up a dense _____ in the wood and leads the two men _____ . When they both fall asleep from _____ , Puck drips an _____ into _____ eyes. The two women, also tired from the night's happenings, arrive at the scene and, thinking they are alone, fall _____ , too.

Oberon	bewitched	asleep	elephant	astray
down	killed	delighted	falls in love	Titania
Hermia	talks	Flute	potion	angry
mistake	antidote	Demetrius	fight	Lysander's
Bottom	Demetrius's	Mechanicals	Helena	sings
donkey's	exhaustion	fog	Theseus	Lysander

COMPREHENSION
ACT IV

Fill in the blanks using the words provided.
You may use a word once only, and you may not need to use them all.

_____ continues to be in love with the donkey-headed Bottom and asks her fairies to pander to his every _____. Oberon, who has meanwhile _____ the Indian child from Titania, releases her from her _____. Titania wakes to see Bottom with the _____ head and realises she has not been _____. The two make up and decide to _____ Theseus's wedding.

_____ and his court are out _____ in the morning, when they stumble upon the four lovers, who wake up to find that while _____ loves _____ again, _____ now loves _____. _____ still wants Hermia to marry Demetrius, but Theseus overrules him, seeing as the four are now _____. Theseus decides that the two _____ will _____ together with him and Hippolyta.

After they have left the scene, _____ also wakes up, returned to his normal state and as _____ again; but he cannot say what happened to him.

Back in Athens, the Mechanics are _____ without Bottom as they cannot _____ the play without him. Suddenly he bursts in, and they are _____ and have _____ again that their performance will go ahead.

Helena	overjoyed	taken	spell	wish
Egeus	matched	Oberon	Demetrius	couples
marry	live	ruin	Theseus	Lysander
bless	Puck	donkey	hunting	hope
dreaming	himself	given	sleeping	Hermia
Titania	distraught	Bottom	perform	Hippolyta

COMPREHENSION
ACT V

Fill in the blanks using the words provided.
You may use a word once only, and you may not need to use them all.

Theseus and _____ are not sure what to make of the lovers' _____ of the night's happenings. Philostrate, the master of the Duke's _____ and entertainment, presents Theseus with a number of plays to _____ away the evening until bedtime. He chooses the Mechanicals' play of *Pyramus and Thisbe*.

All through the _____, the Athenians make fun of the _____ and poor acting of the Mechanicals. Peter Quince, as prologue, gets his _____ all wrong in his lines, saying the _____ of what he means. In the play, _____ (played by _____) and Thisbe (played by _____) live next to each other and love one another, although their _____ are against their love. They _____ through a chink or hole in the great wall that separates them, played by Snout. They agree to meet in secret outside the _____. Thisbe arrives _____ at their meeting place and is _____ by a _____ (played by Snug). She flees but leaves her scarf, which is _____ by the lion. When Pyramus arrives, he sees the mauled scarf and, believing that his beloved has been killed, _____ himself. Thisbe _____ and sees the _____ Pyramus; distraught, she kills herself, too.

_____ is _____ with the play and gives praise to the actors. After the play, they all go off to their _____.

When all have left, Oberon, Titania and their _____ fly through the house and _____ its inhabitants.

Finally, at the end of the play, Puck enters, alone, and asks for _____ or, if the audience did not enjoy the play, for them to imagine it was only a _____.

parents	Pyramus	antics	revels	while
killed	applause	fairies	rooms	performance
Hippolyta	frightened	Flute	kills	bless
opposite	city	lion	Egeus	Bottom
punctuation	pleased	mauled	returns	Theseus
account	dead	dream	communicate	first

THE DIFFERENT WORLDS OF A MIDSUMMER NIGHT'S DREAM

"In the wood, a league without the town"

In *A Midsummer Night's Dream*, Shakespeare brings together three different worlds and three different plot-lines. First are the Athenian court and the lovers in a plot revolving around love, marriage and finding the perfect partner. Set against this is the second world, that of the Mechanicals staging a story of tragic love. Finally, Shakespeare also presents us with the fairy world, with its troubled king and queen.
The diagram below shows how Shakespeare structures and interweaves the three worlds into a coherent whole. Fill in the squares, briefly detailing the events that take place. The first one is done for you.

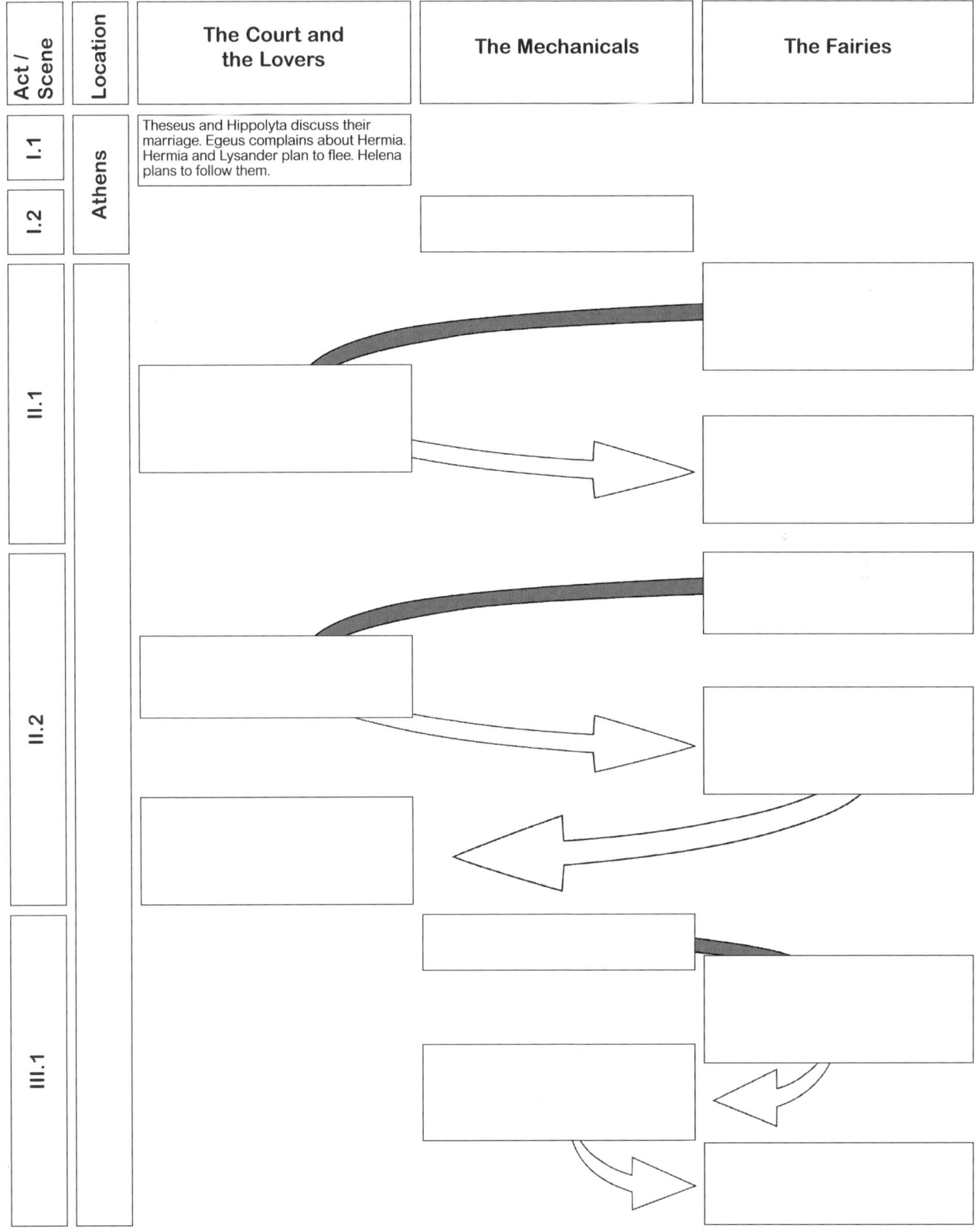

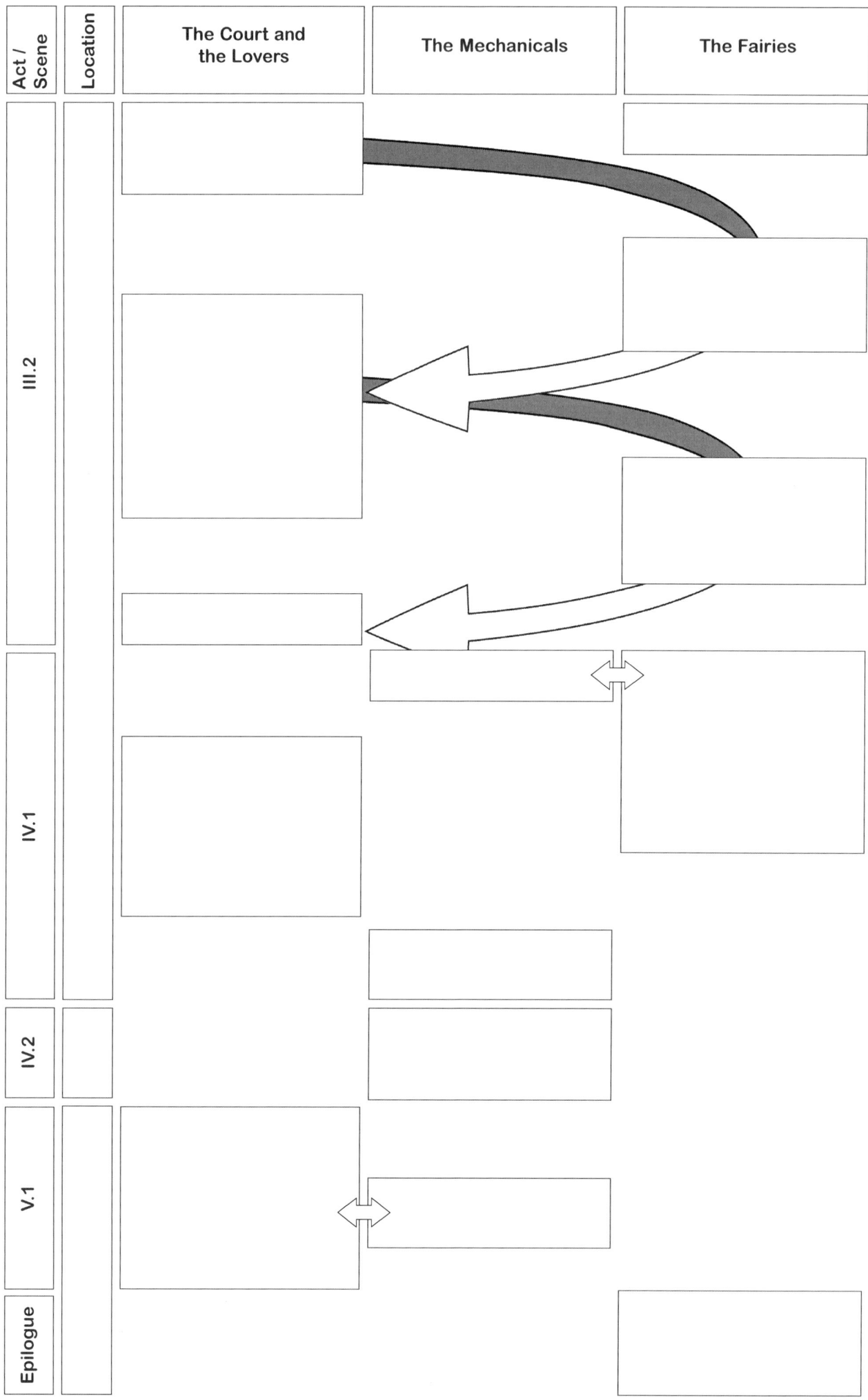

EXPLORING CHARACTER

A Midsummer Night's Dream is an interesting play, as it has no real central or lead character(s). Theseus, for example, although marginal to the main plot-line, has the second largest part in the play when judged by the number of lines spoken (233). Bottom, the character with the largest part, has 261 lines. The other leading characters all have a similar amount of lines: Helena (229), Oberon (226), Puck (209), Lysander (178), Hermia (166), Titania (158), and Demetrius (134).

As a result of this equality of roles, the characters are usually looked at and analysed in groups: thus there are the lovers, the Athenian court, the fairies, and the Mechanicals. Grouping the characters like this does not suggest those in one group are all the same, but it can help to highlight the differences. Many people, for example, have difficulty telling the lovers apart, just as Puck did. Although this is Shakespeare's intention, there are subtle differences between them.

The Mechanicals provide comic relief in most performances although, as characters, they are sincere. While Bottom is the main role and star here and the others (with the exception of Peter Quince) do not have a lot to say, they are nevertheless all different character types that contribute in their own way to the play. Titania and Oberon can be seen as mirrors of Hippolyta and Theseus. Their fairy world in the woods poses a threat to the mortals as the fairies interfere with their lives. However, the fairies have their own troubles to sort out, too. While Titania seems to be more passive, Oberon and Puck drive the plot forward and engage themselves actively in complicating life for the lovers.

The Athenian court (Theseus, Hippolyta and Egeus) serves to start the plot-line of the lovers but has no other plot-related function. However, a number of the themes of the play are highlighted in these characters.

THE MAIN CHARACTERS
"Call forth your actors by the scroll"

THE ATHENIAN COURT
Theseus

Theseus is the Duke of Athens and the ruler of all the people we meet in the play. He has had many lovers and conquered many lands. In the play, he recently conquered the Amazons and intends to marry their queen, Hippolyta.

As a ruler, Theseus is law-abiding, though he will try to mitigate the law when he believes it to be too harsh (he converts the death sentence threatening Hermia into eternal isolation). However, he will not have authority questioned and backs Egeus's initial claim. His treatment of the Mechanicals shows him to be fair and magnanimous – he appreciates the effort they have made and the difficulties they have had, as simple workmen, to produce the play. He seems rational, driven by thought rather than feelings. His speech in V.1 suggests that he looks down upon dreamers and poets, thus denying the emotional side of his character. It is interesting to note that he intends to win Hippolyta over "with pomp, with triumph, and with revelling" (I.1) – there is no talk of love. So, although a great leader and fair judge, it seems his emotional side is lacking.

Hippolyta

Although Hippolyta has a minor role, she seems to have a profound influence on Theseus for the better, becalming him. She has little to say, but Theseus's frequent references to her suggest he is trying to please her. She appears to be quite straightforward in her comments to the Mechanicals' performance of the play, but gentle. She is obviously thrilled by the hunt – a true warrior queen.

Although she echoes Theseus's longing for the moon to change at the end of the play, we never know for sure whether she actually wants to marry Theseus, or perhaps she realises that, as a captive, she must make the best of a bad situation – hence her silence. If only she would speak more…

THE MAIN CHARACTERS

(cont'd)
Egeus

Egeus's complaint about his daughter Hermia sets off the action in the lovers' plot. Although Lysander and Demetrius are of equal worth and Hermia loves the former, he is intent on marrying his daughter to the latter – even after Demetrius no longer wants Hermia, but Helena again (IV.1). Thus (as we never know why he prefers Demetrius) his wish represents parental arbitrariness in its most extreme form. His wishes are overruled by Theseus; from then on he is silent and we never know what Egeus thinks of the outcome.

THE FAIRIES
Oberon

Like Theseus, Oberon is a ruler who expects absolute obedience. In this respect he is not only jealous, but zealous too. When Titania goes against his bidding he refuses to forgive her until he has punished her. He therefore seems to be yet another male who subdues women.

However, he appears to be genuinely concerned about the fate of mortals and willing to help them in their troubles, as his attempts to ensure the lovers receive their "correct" partner show. It is Helena's futile love of Demetrius that spurs him into action. While his methods (using magic) may be questionable, the result certainly isn't. Thus he can be seen as the archetypal ruler who is not interested in the means, so long as the goal is achieved. As a protector of "damsels in distress" but a harsh husband, he is typically an "old-school" gentleman.

Puck

Puck is one of the most versatile characters in the play. He is jester to Oberon and never far from mischief. When he is introduced to us, the fairy says he will help people who treat him kindly, although we never witness this on stage. He is full of energy and enthusiasm and seems genuinely eager to please Oberon, his master. There is a childish joy rather than malevolence in all his doings, and he relishes the success of his pranks; Puck only seems to want to entertain – even if that is at the expense of others. Although Puck's mistake in his dealing with the lovers is understandable and seems accidental, the audience cannot help but think that Puck may actually know more than he is letting on, confusing the male lovers on purpose.

Interestingly, it is Puck who solicits the audience's approval in the epilogue, rather than Oberon or another, more powerful figure. As prime origin of mischief, as the one who has been the root of the various misunderstandings and transformations, it is almost as if he is promising the audience that he will better himself.

Titania

Titania shares womanly bonds with her Indian priestess, which makes her want to look after the changeling herself. Although she appears to dominate Oberon in their first encounter, taking control of the altercation, she has to submit to his will, even though this submission is gained through magic rather than persuasion or force of will. Oberon's victory is therefore not complete.

Titania is ridiculed into submission, and she is very much aware of the indignity of her passion for Bottom. She is able to set this aside though, recognising Oberon as her lord. This is rather troubling, as her emotions cannot have suddenly been wiped away. She must be aware that Oberon tricked her into giving up the changeling, and so it comes as a surprise that she is willing to forget her previous vehemence and accept Oberon as her lord. Maybe her fairy nature has something to do with this, or maybe she is reconciling for the good of humanity to stop the quarreling. We shall never know.

THE MAIN CHARACTERS

(cont'd)

THE LOVERS

Hermia

Hermia is the smaller of the women, about which she has a slight inferiority complex. She is passionate in her defence of what she believes in and is not afraid to speak out in front of the Duke. She is also prepared to follow Lysander out of Athens so they can marry, displaying great dedication to her lover.

When attacked by Helena, she reacts sharply and seems more willing to let the argument develop into a physical fight. Being loyal herself, she does not understand the changing attachments of the male lovers.

Helena

Helena is tall and fair (at least compared to Hermia). She is similar to Hermia in many ways, possibly to show how the lovers are interchangeable, but also possibly because the two women grew up together.

Helena seems to be more devious and manipulative. When Lysander and Hermia confide in her, she betrays her friend's trust for the chance to indulge her lovesickness. Although she later evokes images of their youth spent in harmony when she believes Hermia to be mocking her, she is the one who first forgets the bands that bind the two women. Also, when Hermia threatens her, Helena seeks the protection of the men, showing her to be more scheming.

Lysander & Demetrius

If the two female lovers are almost indistinguishable, the men are even more so: Lysander even admits that they are of equal standing and riches. The differences are slight, but audiences tend to prefer Lysander to Demetrius. This is because Lysander remains true to Hermia and only switches his object of affection under the influence of the love potion. Demetrius, however, originally loved Helena but then loves Hermia, even though Lysander loves her and she him. We do not know why Demetrius switched (did Egeus have anything to do with it?). Another fact that makes Demetrius less amiable is the way he treats Helena when she follows him into the woods. He threatens her and we believe he could carry out his threat – a sense of menace we never have with Lysander.

THE MECHANICALS

Bottom

Bottom is convinced of his abilities as an actor. He is enthusiastic to the point of being a nuisance. In the eyes of the other Mechanicals, he is a star who alone can ensure the success of their performance. He strives to use more select language but usually ends up using malapropisms – a sign of someone acting above their station.

He can be seen as an annoying know-it-all who is not even scared of lecturing his Duke, and who wants to ensure everyone shares his vision. However, he can also be portrayed more gently, as someone whose only chance to develop himself and escape the squalor of his life is the stage, even though he is no great actor. His childish enthusiasm for escapism sometimes gets the better of him, but there is nothing patronising about him. Puck's view of him is obviously that he is a pompous ass, which he exemplifies most effectively. His experience in the woods superficially does not seem to change him, but his speech alone, before he returns to Athens, suggests that some residue remains with him and may yet work upon him. After all, being beloved of the fairy queen cannot leave such a man unaffected.

CHARACTER ACTIVITIES
"I in this affair do thee employ"

Character work can focus either on one group of characters, or on comparing characters from different groups. One important way to explore a character is to see how they react to other people: what they do and say in response to the lines of other characters. Indeed, in a play script, with the exception of any soliloquies, this is the only way to deduce character.

The Lovers
Work here could focus on the constancy of the female lovers, set against the changing affections of the men. Another possible focus is the relationship between Hermia and Helena, which is referred to by both of them as a good and long-lasting friendship, but which, under the strain of the shifting loves of the men, comes under severe pressure.

- The way affections are transferred between the lovers due to the intervention of Puck and the juice of the love-in-idleness flower has often been compared to a dance. There are four distinct stages of this roundel: the opening constellation, two steps between, depending on which male is under the influence of the potion, and then the end constellation, where "Jack has Jill".

- People often notice how similar the lovers are. Indeed, Shakespeare seems to have made the lovers interchangeable on purpose, to show how ridiculous their antics are and how strange love itself is. To explore to what extent the lovers are alike, the pupils can do a "spot-the-difference" exercise that focuses on what the characters share in common, and what separates them. This can be a first step to acting out the characters or to an essay on the lovers.

- Pupils could be asked to write a stream of consciousness piece as either Helena or Hermia in the heat of the conflict of Act III Scene 2. What does she make of the changing affections of the men? Why does she turn against her friend of old? Obviously, the text of the play must be the starting point, but pupils can develop their own thoughts from there.

The Mechanicals
The Mechanicals are the most homogeneous group: they all work together to stage the play, and there is little antagonism between them – save possibly between Bottom and Quince. Bottom, of course, is the main character, but the other Mechanicals are by no means colourless, as their interactions show.

- Taking the rehearsal of the Mechanicals in Act III Scene 1, pupils could analyse what they learn about each labourer from this interaction, also taking their names and professions into account.

- Much of the play's comedy stems from the obvious incapability of the Mechanicals to act their chosen play. Not only do they overact, they often get words wrong and have no sense of the suspension of disbelief that is so vital an ingredient in all theatre. But to what extent are the Mechanicals really bad actors, or mis-cast in their roles? Their view of acting may be wrong, but does that mean they are all wrong in their roles? Using their names, occupations and what we know about them from the play, pupils could explore how each might act and how that fits within the play they intend to perform.

- We learn a lot about Bottom's thoughts and ideas, but what does Peter Quince think of his star? Pupils could write a stream of consciousness piece showing Quince's thoughts about Bottom either after Act I Scene 2 or after Bottom has been "translated" in Act III Scene 2. The only opinions he shares about Bottom appear in Act IV Scene 2.

The Fairies
The most active of the fairies and the one most worth exploring is Robin Goodfellow, or Puck. He is something of a free agent, bringing chaos into the lives of both the lovers and the Mechanicals. His impish nature seems intent on causing mischief – a fun aspect for pupils to explore.

- Pupils can take a close look at Puck's pranks, as described by the fairy and himself at the beginning of Act II Scene 1. Pupils can be asked to visualise them in an illustration and to find common features. Based on these, they can then be asked to invent their own pranks and act them out.

- The fairy king and queen are often regarded as subconscious doubles of Theseus and Hippolyta. Taking this approach as a starting point, pupils could explore to what extent the human dukedom is similar to the fairy kingdom. Of particular interest here is to what extent the fairy court lives out latent desires of the Athenian court.
- Titania reconciles herself very quickly with the fact that Oberon enchanted her to gain the Indian boy in Act IV Scene 1. What might move her to do this is an interesting topic for a stream of consciousness piece in the character of Titania.

The Athenian Court

The Athenian court frames the main plot-line and also starts the action of the lovers. Additionally, it is the background for the plot of the Mechanicals. As characters, Theseus and Hippolyta are not very developed, although the former is certainly more so than the latter. As has been said above, the relationship between Theseus and Hippolyta can be compared to the relationship between Oberon and Titania.

- We never know to what extent Hippolyta loves Theseus. How does she feel about the wedding? Pupils can explore her thoughts and feelings after Act I Scene 1 using stream of consciousness writing.
- Hippolyta's most extended speech is about hounds, while out hunting with Theseus (Act IV Scene 1). Pupils can explore what this tells us about her and her view of her marriage, future husband, and their life together.
- Egeus starts the main complication of the lovers' plot by forbidding his daughter to marry the man she loves. He still insists she marry Demetrius, even after events have turned against him. Theseus overrules him, and he has no further speech in the play. What does he think about events? How might he react to the triple wedding? Pupils can explore this using stream of consciousness or by examining his character based on what he says in the play.

Character Sheets

There are a number of questions or issues that are central to each character. These can be given to the pupils in the form of a worksheet. Pupils should start on different questions and then be asked to work clockwise around the worksheet. After a set time, pupils can work in groups to compare the worksheets, and fill in any missing information or sections. This resource provides character sheets for Bottom, Oberon, Puck, Titania, Helena and Theseus.

Blank Comic Sheets

Pivotal moments of the play can also be used to explore emotions (and thus character) using blank comic pages (page 35). Instead of filling in what the characters are saying (Shakespeare tells us this already), pupils can be asked to fill in what the characters are thinking, using thought bubbles and conforming to comic book layout rules (e.g. order of reading from top left to bottom right, bold writing to emphasise words in the text). The drawing can be rudimentary "stick-men" – anything as long as some essence of mood and/or story is captured.

Venn Diagrams

Venn diagrams are used in logic and mathematics to show what various sets have in common. This technique can also be used to explore the similarities and differences (which can be as simple or complex as the pupils like) of any three characters.

One way to use Venn diagrams is to split the class into groups and give each group a different set of three characters to analyse. Using a template or anything circular, the Venn diagrams should be drawn on large paper or card. Each group should be given some time to fill in its diagram. Afterwards, each group moves so that they are in front of the Venn diagram of a different group. Give them some time to look at this diagram and to make comments on it. The comments can then be discussed and resolved in class.

BOTTOM CHARACTER SHEET

Do you think Bottom is happy with his lot in life?

Is Bottom too domineering?

Is Bottom a good actor?

In what way might the time with Titania have changed Bottom?

PUCK CHARACTER SHEET

Why does Puck play his pranks?

How does Puck see his Queen, Titania?

Does Puck like Oberon?

What age do you think Puck is? In what way might Puck's age influence our view of him?

OBERON CHARACTER SHEET

Is Oberon a just ruler of fairyland?

Do you think Oberon thinks only of himself?

Why does Oberon want the changeling boy so much?

Why does Oberon help the lovers?

TITANIA CHARACTER SHEET

Is Titania right to withhold the changeling boy from Oberon?

Why do you think Titania sleeps so often?

What kind of a ruler is Titania?

Why does Titania give in to Oberon so easily?

HELENA CHARACTER SHEET

How does Helena feel about loving Demetrius?

Do you think Helena would really want to be Hermia?

Why does Helena think that everyone is mocking her?

What makes Helena change her mind and believe Demetrius loves her?

THESEUS CHARACTER SHEET

Will Theseus manage to get Hippolyta to love him?

Is Theseus a good Duke?

Is Theseus fair in overruling Egeus?

In what way do you think Hippolyta influences Theseus?

VENN DIAGRAMS

Example (incomplete)

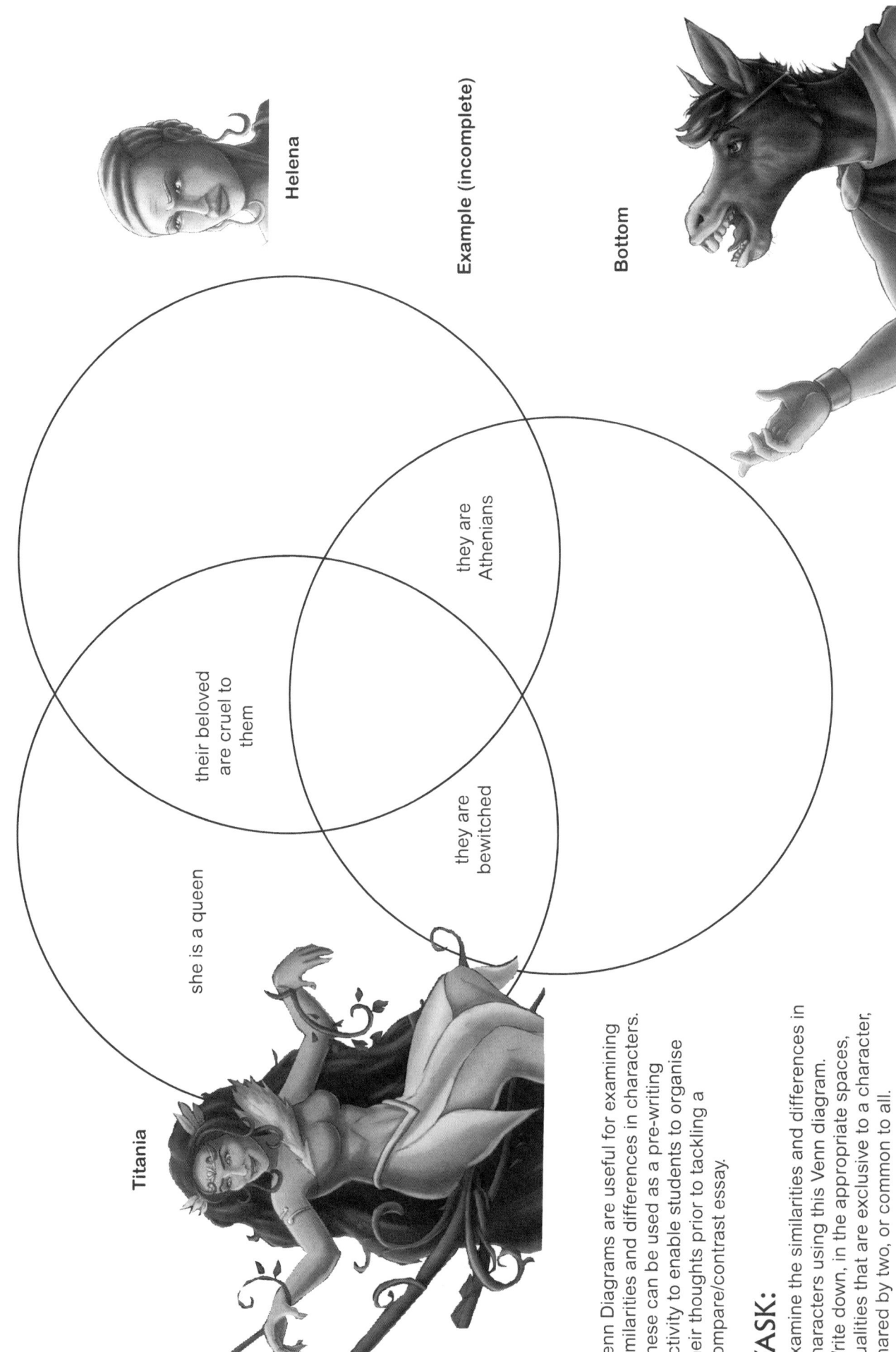

Helena

Bottom

Titania

- she is a queen
- their beloved are cruel to them
- they are Athenians
- they are bewitched

Venn Diagrams are useful for examining similarities and differences in characters. These can be used as a pre-writing activity to enable students to organise their thoughts prior to tackling a compare/contrast essay.

TASK:

Examine the similarities and differences in characters using this Venn diagram. Write down, in the appropriate spaces, qualities that are exclusive to a character, shared by two, or common to all.

VENN DIAGRAMS

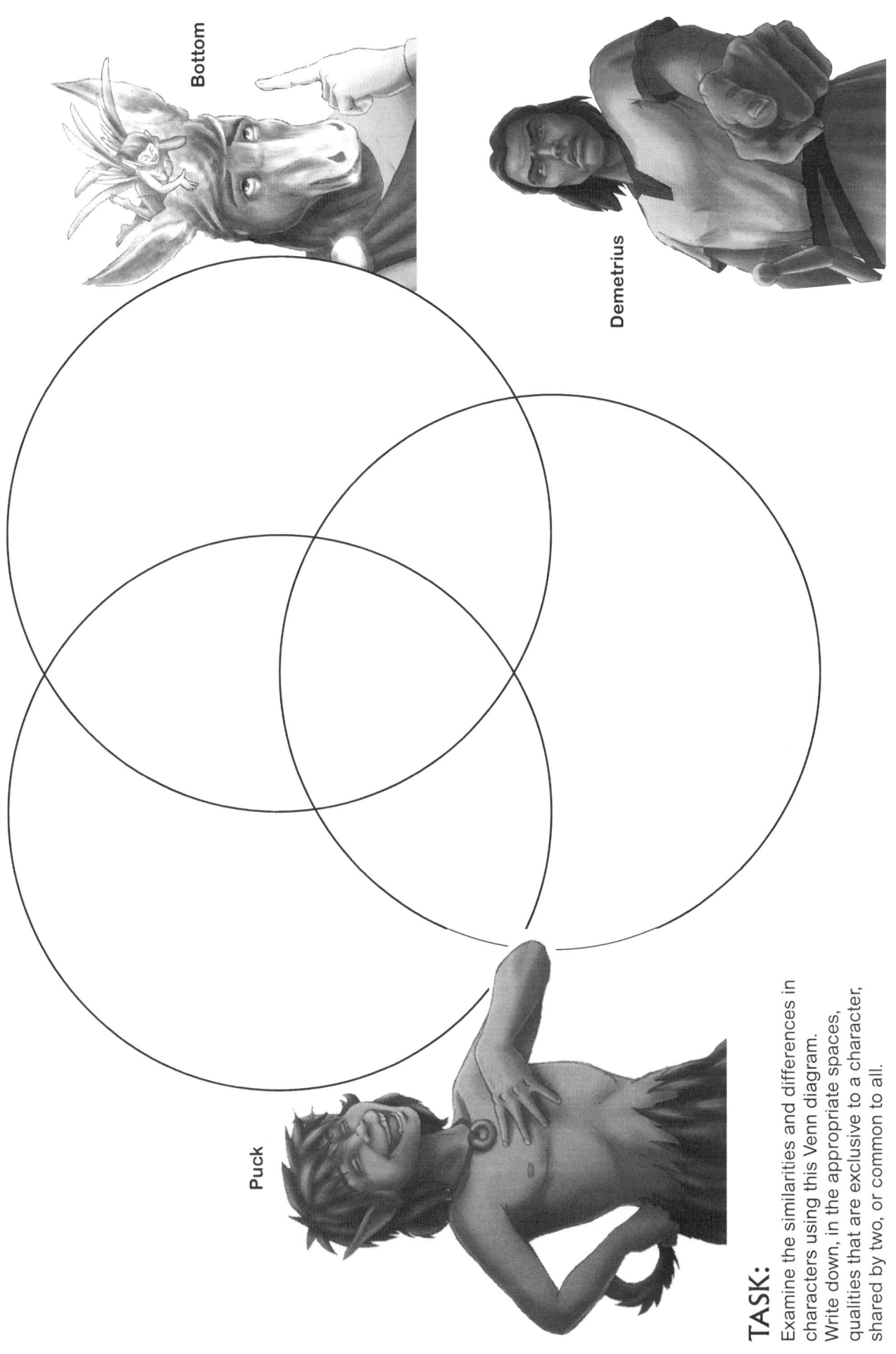

TASK:
Examine the similarities and differences in characters using this Venn diagram. Write down, in the appropriate spaces, qualities that are exclusive to a character, shared by two, or common to all.

VENN DIAGRAMS

TASK:

Examine the similarities and differences in characters using this Venn diagram. Write down, in the appropriate spaces, qualities that are exclusive to a character, shared by two, or common to all.

BLANK COMIC GRID

SPOT THE DIFFERENCE
"I am, my lord, well deriv'd as he, as well possess'd"

TASK:
Use the following charts to explore to what extent the lovers are similar and different. For the men you might want to differentiate between when they are under the influence of the love juice and when they are not (particularly for Lysander). Compare the number of differences between the men and the number between the women. What does this say about Shakespeare's portrayal of each gender?

HELENA   HERMIA

short →

aggressive

fair

lacking confidence

cautious, wary

assertive

dark

tall

loyal to her beloved

lacking dignity

passive

selfless

loyal

rash

trusting

DEMETRIUS   LYSANDER

← affluent →

courageous

inconstant

aristocratic

eager to prove he's right

assertive

cruel

confident

aggressive

proactive

humorous, mocking

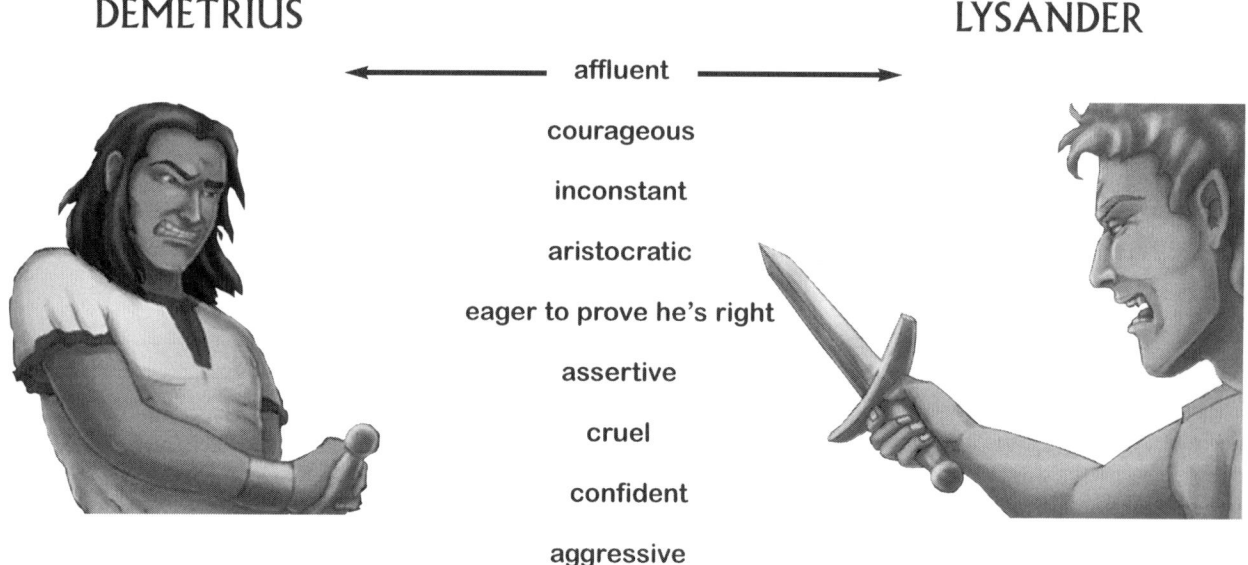

DUKEDOM AND KINGDOM
"Come, my queen, take hands with me"

In many modern productions of the play, as they never appear on stage at the same time, the roles of Titania and Oberon are doubled up with Hippolyta and Theseus, respectively – meaning one actor plays both Oberon and Theseus, while another plays both Titania and Hippolyta. In what way does the fairy court mirror the Athenian court? Use this sheet to help you explore the issue.

	The Athenian Court	The Fairy Court
What is the relationship between the rulers like?		
What problem(s) do they have?		
How does Theseus / Oberon intend to solve the problem(s)		
How are Theseus / Oberon's spirits lifted?		
How do they behave towards their subjects?		
What might the Athenian Court learn from the Fairy Court?		
What might the Fairy Court learn from the Athenian Court?		

THE MECHANICALS REHEARSE
(from Act III Scene 1)

BOTTOM
Are we all met?

QUINCE
Pat, pat; and here's a marvellous convenient place for our rehearsal. This green plot shall be our stage, this hawthorn-brake our tiring-house; and we will do it in action as we will do it before the duke.

BOTTOM
Peter Quince,--

QUINCE
What sayest thou, bully Bottom?

BOTTOM
There are things in this comedy of "Pyramus and Thisbe" that will never please. First, Pyramus must draw a sword to kill himself; which the ladies cannot abide. How answer you that?

SNOUT
By'r lakin, a parlous fear.

STARVELING
I believe we must leave the killing out, when all is done.

BOTTOM
Not a whit: I have a device to make all well. Write me a prologue; and let the prologue seem to say, we will do no harm with our swords, and that Pyramus is not killed indeed; and, for the more better assurance, tell them that I, Pyramus, am not Pyramus, but Bottom the weaver: this will put them out of fear.

QUINCE
Well, we will have such a prologue; and it shall be written in eight and six.

BOTTOM
No, make it two more; let it be written in eight and eight.

SNOUT
Will not the ladies be afeard of the lion?

STARVELING
I fear it, I promise you.

BOTTOM
Masters, you ought to consider with yourselves: to bring in – God shield us! – a lion among ladies, is a most dreadful thing; for there is not a more fearful wild-fowl than your lion living, and we ought to look to it.

Side questions:

- In what way are both Bottom and Quince trying to take charge?
- Why do you think Bottom might be trying to test Quince?
- With whom do the others side and why?
- If Bottom has a solution, why did he mention it as a problem above?
- How would they say this? Are Bottom and Quince fighting or is Bottom just correcting Quince?
- What does this line suggest about Snout?
- Surely Bottom knows they won't bring on a real lion. So why is he saying this?

SNOUT
Therefore, another prologue must tell he is not a lion.

BOTTOM
Nay, you must name his name, and half his face must be seen through the lion's neck; and he himself must speak through, saying thus, or to the same defect,– "Ladies,"– or, "Fair ladies, I would wish you," – or, "I would request you,"– or, "I would entreat you, not to fear, not to tremble: my life for yours. If you think I come hither as a lion, it were pity of my life: no, I am no such thing; I am a man as other men are;" and there, indeed, let him name his name, and tell them plainly, he is Snug the joiner.

QUINCE
Well it shall be so. But there is two hard things: that is, to bring the moonlight into a chamber; for, you know, Pyramus and Thisbe meet by moonlight.

SNOUT
Doth the moon shine that night we play our play?

BOTTOM
A calendar, a calendar! look in the almanac; find out moonshine, find out moonshine.

QUINCE
Yes, it doth shine that night.

BOTTOM
Why, then may you leave a casement of the great chamber-window, where we play, open; and the moon may shine in at the casement.

QUINCE
Ay; or else one must come in with a bush of thorns and a lantern, and say he comes to disfigure, or to present, the person of Moonshine. Then, there is another thing: we must have a wall in the great chamber; for Pyramus and Thisbe says the story, did talk through the chink of a wall.

SNOUT
You can never bring in a wall. What say you, Bottom?

BOTTOM
Some man or other must present Wall: and let him have some plaster, or some loam, or some rough-cast about him, to signify wall; and let him hold his fingers thus, and through that cranny shall Pyramus and Thisbe whisper.

QUINCE
If that may be, then all is well. Come, sit down, every mother's son, and rehearse your parts. Pyramus, you begin. When you have spoken your speech, enter into that brake; and so every one according to his cue.

Sidebar questions:
- Why does Bottom not agree with Snout?
- Why does Quince highlight these problems?
- Does Snout want to be like Bottom?
- Why does Quince say "Ay" when he then disagrees with Bottom?
- Why does Snout ask Bottom rather than Quince, the director?
- Why does Bottom copy the idea Quince had for the moon?

HIPPOLYTA THE HUNTRESS
"The bouncing Amazon, your buskin'd mistress and your warrior love"

Hippolyta's longest speech is in Act IV Scene 1 when she talks about hunting hounds. Theseus has just praised his own hounds, and she responds as below. What does this speech tell us about Hippolyta?

> Theseus has just mentioned his hounds – why does she mention these (possibly more famous) hounds here?

> Why does Hippolyta mention two such outstanding heroes in front of Theseus?

I was with Hercules* and Cadmus* once,

When in a wood of Crete they bay'd the bear

With hounds of Sparta*: never did I hear

Such gallant chiding; for, besides the groves,

The skies, the fountains, every region near

Seem'd all one mutual cry. I never heard

So musical a discord, such sweet thunder.

> She calls the barking of the hounds "sweet thunder". What does this tell us about her?

> Twice Hippolyta says she "never" heard such noise. What does this suggest?

*__Hercules__: a mythological hero who was the strongest man alive
*__Cadmus__: another mythological figure; the founder of Thebes
*__Sparta__: a region in Greece renowned for its warriors and hunting hounds

EGEUS – THE LUCKLESS FATHER
"I beg the law, the law, upon his head"

Act I Scene 1

    Full of vexation come I, with complaint
    Against my child, my daughter Hermia.
    Stand forth, Demetrius. My noble lord,
    This man hath my consent to marry her.
    Stand forth, Lysander; and, my gracious duke,
    This man hath bewitch'd the bosom of my child;
    [...]
    With cunning hast thou filch'd my daughter's heart,
    Turn'd her obedience, which is due to me,
    To stubborn harshness. And, my gracious duke,
    Be it so she will not here before your grace
    Consent to marry with Demetrius,
    I beg the ancient privilege of Athens:
    As she is mine, I may dispose of her;
    Which shall be either to this gentleman,
    Or to her death, according to our law
    Immediately provided in that case.

> What kind of a father is Egeus? Is his point of view right? Are his directives fair? practical? reasonable?

Act IV Scene 1

EGEUS

    Enough, enough! my lord, you have enough.
    I beg the law, the law, upon his head.
    They would have stol'n away; they would, Demetrius,
    Thereby to have defeated you and me;
    You of your wife, and me of my consent,
    Of my consent that she should be your wife.
    [...]

> Is Egeus being sensible here, considering the situation?

THESEUS

    Egeus, I will overbear your will;
    For in the temple, by and by, with us
    These couples shall eternally be knit;

> How might Egeus react to this?

SHAKESPEARE'S LANGUAGE

Introduction

Apart from Shakespeare's wide and diverse vocabulary and somewhat unusual diction or word order, the two main issues that pupils find difficult with Shakespeare are the prosody (verse structure) of his writing and the imagery.

The vocabulary issue can only be tackled with a glossary or dictionary, although some knowledge of foreign languages (especially French and Latin) may help. The difficulty students have with the word order is more baffling, especially as most pupils have no difficulty comprehending what Yoda (of *Star Wars* fame) says. Patience the answer here must be.

Prosody:

In *A Midsummer Night's Dream*, Shakespeare uses a variety of different verse forms to bring out the character of the various groups. Thus the Athenian court usually speaks in blank verse, the lovers in rhymed couplets, and the Mechanicals in prose (Shakespeare often used prose/verse and rhyme to denote class).

Although prosody can be technically difficult, it is worthwhile for the pupils to examine the effect of the different kinds of verse form, using the number of stresses per line to guide them. Before examining the various types of verse used in the play, pupils should be confident with identifying iambic pentameter – Shakespeare's predominant metre.

A line of iambic pentameter contains five iambs. An iamb consists of two syllables, the first one being unstressed, the second stressed (ti-TUM). So the basic line of Shakespearean poetry has ten syllables with every second syllable stressed as follows (each "x" representing a syllable):

x	>X<	x	>X<	x	>X<	x	>X<	x	>X<

e.g.,

Now,	fair	Hi-	ppol-	y-	ta,	our	nup-	tial	hour

Lines of iambic pentameter that don't rhyme are called blank verse.

Also, Shakespeare's lines aren't always pure iambic pentameter; there are sometimes extra, unstressed syllables added in.

Some ideas for work on the structure of Shakespeare's language:

- To discover the rhythm of Shakespeare's lines, the pupils can practise splitting the lines up into syllables and then discovering where the stresses are, using pure iambic pentameter as a guideline. Once they have understood the concept, they can write a few lines of their own in iambic pentameter.

- Pupils could be asked to analyse typical speech for each group and try to explain the effect achieved by using different types of verse forms. Pupils should look at rhythm, rhyme, and word choice.

- After having examined various styles of versification, pupils could write their own short verse speech, using a style befitting their chosen character.

- Another frequent problem pupils have with verse is that they tend to read it to the end of a line rather than from punctuation mark to punctuation mark. Peter Quince's prologue is an excellent example of how lines of verse can be misread by stopping in the wrong place.

SHAKESPEARE'S LANGUAGE

Imagery:
Some of the beauty of Shakespeare's language (as well as its difficulty) stems from his daring and original use of imagery. The main techniques used are similes and metaphors. It is important to bear in mind that both are images, and both are comparisons that derive their effectiveness and strength from the degree to which the first element is similar to the second. The more effective the image, the more levels it will work on, and also the more it will challenge received opinion or cliché.

Some ideas for work on language are:

- Examine some stylistic elements that are either typically Shakespearean (like antithesis) or peculiar to a character like Bottom's malapropisms.

- Use one of Shakespeare's more descriptive passages to kick-start a descriptive piece, if possible using some of Shakespeare's techniques.

- After pupils have discovered the main features of a character's speech, they could try their own hand at writing some dialogue for that character, staying true to their personality. This could also be in iambic pentameter if this has already been discussed, to provide a real challenge.

- For more focused work on imagery, pupils can be asked to search for a number of similes and metaphors and explain their effect, first analysing what the second element means, and then how this relates to the first element. This should be a good starting point to then explain why the image is effective or why/how it fails.

- Shakespeare is also famous for his unusual and inventive insults. *A Midsummer Night's Dream* contains a small helping of these, mainly when the lovers are at loggerheads. For a more fun activity, pupils can search these out (in III.2) and then hurl them at each other, using different tones of voice (menacing, mocking, sarcastic, hurt, etc.).

THE RHYTHM OF SHAKESPEARE'S LANGUAGE
"It is not enough to speak, but to speak true"

Use the grid below to help you highlight the iambic pentameter in the following lines of Theseus's speech in Act V Scene 1. The basic rhythm for this is written down at the top of the table. Each syllable should occupy one box. Remember that not every line has to be pure iambic pentameter, and some word groups can be pronounced as one or two syllables (such as "poet").

> The lunatic, the lover, and the poet,
> Are of imagination all compact:
> One sees more devils than vast hell can hold;
> That is the madman: the lover, all as frantic,
> Sees Helen's beauty in a brow of Egypt:
> The poet's eye, in a fine frenzy rolling,
> Doth glance from heaven to earth, from earth to heaven;
> And as imagination bodies forth
> The forms of things unknown, the poet's pen
> Turns them to shapes, and gives to airy nothing
> A local habitation, and a name.

X The	>X< lun-	X a-	>X< tic,	X the	>X< lov-	X er,	>X< and	X the	>X< poet,		

QUINCE SPEAKS THE PROLOGUE
"This fellow doth not stand upon points"

Quince, in his nervousness, mixes up the punctuation of his prologue in front of the Duke. Printed below is the piece as he delivers it, as well as the same prologue without punctuation. See if you can work out where the punctuation should belong.

Prologue
If we offend, it is with our good will.
That you should think, we come not to offend,
But with good will. To show our simple skill,
That is the true beginning of our end.
Consider then, we come but in despite.
We do not come as minding to content you,
Our true intent is. All for your delight
We are not here. That you should here repent you,
The actors are at hand; and, by their show,
You shall know all, that you are like to know.

TASK:
Punctuate this correctly:

if we offend it is with our good will
that you should think we come not to offend
but with good will to show our simple skill
that is the true beginning of our end
consider then we come but in despite
we do not come as minding to content you
our true intent is all for your delight
we are not here that you should here repent you
the actors are at hand and by their show
you shall know all that you are like to know

THE GROUPS AND THEIR LANGUAGE
"Tongue-tied simplicity in least speak most"

First of all determine the rhyme and rhythm (if applicable) of each group's speech, and then explain what effect this has on how the characters in the group are perceived.

The character's words	What does the poetic form tell us about the character?
ATHENIAN COURT	
THESEUS (talking to Hippolyta in Act I Scene 1) Now, fair Hippolyta, our nuptial hour Draws on apace: four happy days bring in Another moon; but, O, methinks, how slow This old moon wanes! she lingers my desires, Like to a step-dame, or a dowager, Long withering out a young man's revenue.	What can you say about the rhythm and rhyme? What effect does this mode of speaking have?
FAIRIES	
TITANIA (rebuking Oberon in Act II Scene 1) And never, since the middle summer's spring, Met we on hill, in dale, forest or mead, By paved fountain or by rushy brook, Or in the beached margent of the sea, To dance our ringlets to the whistling wind, But with thy brawls thou hast disturb'd our sport.	What can you say about the rhythm and rhyme? What effect does this mode of speaking have?
TITANIA (talking to her fairies in Act III Scene 1) Come, wait upon him; lead him to my bower. The moon, methinks, looks with a watery eye; And when she weeps, weeps every little flower, Lamenting some enforced chastity. Tie up my love's tongue, bring him silently.	What can you say about the rhythm and rhyme? What effect does this mode of speaking have?

THE GROUPS AND THEIR LANGUAGE
(cont'd)

The character's words	What does the poetic form tell us about the character?
PUCK (alone in Act II Scene 2) Through the forest have I gone, But Athenian found I none, On whose eyes I might approve This flower's force in stirring love. Night and silence – who is here? Weeds of Athens he doth wear: This is he, my master said, Despised the Athenian maid; And here the maiden, sleeping sound, On the dank and dirty ground.	What can you say about the rhythm and rhyme? What effect does this mode of speaking have?
PUCK (talking to Oberon in Act III Scene 2) Near to her close and consecrated bower, While she was in her dull and sleeping hour, A crew of patches, rude Mechanicals, That work for bread upon Athenian stalls, Were met together to rehearse a play, Intended for great Theseus' nuptial day.	What can you say about the rhythm and rhyme? What effect does this mode of speaking have?
MECHANICALS	
PETER QUINCE (talking to the Mechanicals in Act I Scene 2) Here is the scroll of every man's name, which is thought fit, through all Athens, to play in our interlude before the duke and the duchess, on his wedding-day at night.	What can you say about the rhythm and rhyme? What effect does this mode of speaking have?

Classical Comics Teaching Resource: *A Midsummer Night's Dream*

THE GROUPS AND THEIR LANGUAGE
(cont'd)

The character's words	What does the poetic form tell us about the character?
BOTTOM (as Pyramus in the play, Act V Scene 1) But stay, O spite! But mark, poor knight, What dreadful dole is here? Eyes, do you see? How can it be? O dainty duck! O dear! Thy mantle good, What! stain'd with blood? Approach, ye Furies fell! O Fates, come, come; Cut thread and thrum; Quail, crush, conclude, and quell!	What can you say about the rhythm and rhyme? What effect does this mode of speaking have?
LOVERS	
HERMIA (talking to Lysander in Act I Scene 1) I swear to thee, by Cupid's strongest bow, By his best arrow with the golden head, By the simplicity of Venus' doves, By that which knitteth souls and prospers loves, And by that fire which burn'd the Carthage queen, When the false Trojan under sail was seen, By all the vows that ever men have broke, In number more than ever women spoke: In that same place thou hast appointed me, To-morrow truly will I meet with thee.	What can you say about the rhythm and rhyme? What effect does this mode of speaking have?

… Language

ANTITHESIS
"Merry and tragical? Tedious and brief?"

One of Shakespeare's favourite figures of speech is antithesis – putting opposites next to each other. There are a number of instances of this in *A Midsummer Night's Dream*. For example in Act III Scene 2, Lysander says to Demetrius,

> Thou canst compel no more than she entreat:
> Thy threats have no more strength than her weak prayers.

"compel" (force) and "entreat" (beg) are opposites, as are "strength" and "weak", but "threats" and "prayers" are also opposites.

TASK:

Now explore the opposites in these two short extracts from Act I Scene 1. Each underlined word has an opposite – find the opposite from the words at the bottom and fill it in the correct place of the speech (without referring to the play)

LYSANDER
    The course of true love never did run smooth;
    But, either it was different in blood,--

HERMIA
    O cross! too _____ to be enthrall'd to low!

LYSANDER
    Or else misgraffed in respect of years,--

HERMIA
    O spite! too _____ to be engag'd to young!

HELENA
    O, that your _____ would teach my smiles such skill!

HERMIA
    I give him curses, yet he gives me _____ .

HELENA
    O, that my prayers could such affection move!

HERMIA
    The more I _____ , the more he follows me.

HELENA
    The more I _____ , the more he hateth me.

love   hate   high   old   love   frowns

Classical Comics Teaching Resource: *A Midsummer Night's Dream* — Language

BOTTOM'S "BOTTOMISMS"
"There is not one word apt"

Part of the comedy the Mechanicals offer in *A Midsummer Night's Dream* is that they are trying to act a "lofty" (as Bottom would call it) play, but they are themselves rough and ready labourers without a broad vocabulary – which doesn't mean they don't try! Unfortunately for them, and fortunately for the audience, they are not usually successful; and often they, and in particular Bottom, use malapropisms: wrong words that sound similar to the words that should be used.

TASK:
Use the following grid to explore what word the Mechanical wants to say, and what the word he uses actually means.

	What word should he have used?	What does the word he has used mean?
You were best to call them generally, man by man (I.2)		
but I will aggravate my voice so, that I will roar you as gently as any sucking dove (I.2)		
and there we may rehearse, most obscenely and courageously (I.2)		
he himself must speak through, saying thus, or to the same defect, (III.1)		
or else one must [...] and say, he comes to disfigure, or to present, the person of Moonshine (III.1 – Quince)		
I have an exposition of sleep come upon me (IV.1)		
Since lion vile hath here deflower'd my dear (V.1)		

Based on your findings, you might now like to consider in what way malapropisms are funny.

IMAGERY IN *A MIDSUMMER NIGHT'S DREAM*
"His speech was like a tangled chain"

Shakespeare often uses similes (comparisons using "like" or "as [attribute] as a [something]") and metaphors (images) to convey his message and to make his language more effective and interesting. Both techniques rely on the two elements of the image having something in common.

For example: "His speech was like a tangled chain" (simile), where the effectiveness of the simile depends on the "speech" being similar to a "tangled chain". This can be displayed using a Venn diagram:

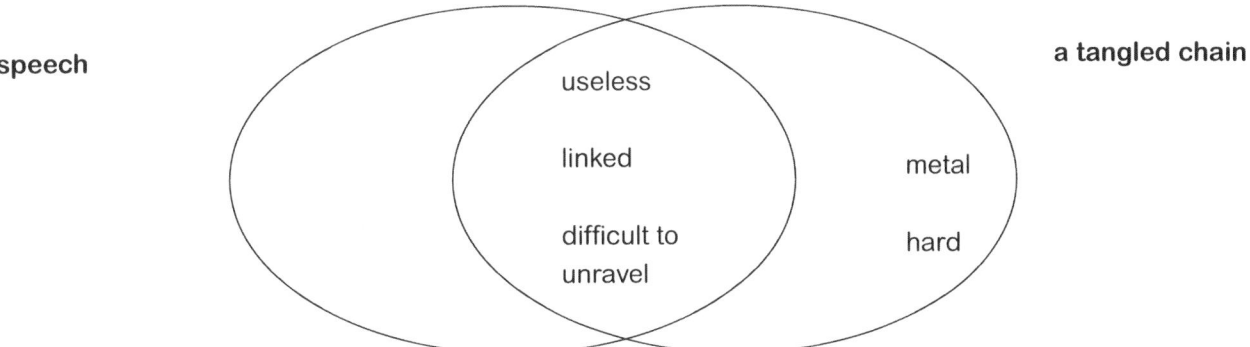

As can be seen, "speech" (depending on what kind of speech it is; here it refers to Quince's mixed up prologue) can be like a "tangled chain". It is linked, because the words work together to make sense, but if spoken incorrectly they become difficult to unravel and no longer make sense, making them useless. Good images (as with this image), be they similes or metaphors, will usually have a number of things in common and also provide some new and startling insight into the object being described.

TASK:

Now that you know how imagery works, try it out for yourself and analyse the imagery Shakespeare uses in *A Midsummer Night's Dream*. Go through the play and find instances of imagery. There are plenty of them to choose from. Use the framework below for your analysis.

Image: _____
Is it a simile or a metaphor?

first element   **second element**

_____   _____

_____
_____
_____
_____

IMAGERY IN *A MIDSUMMER NIGHT'S DREAM*
"Lysander riddles very prettily"

Now that you know how imagery works, try it out for yourself and analyse the imagery Shakespeare uses in *A Midsummer Night's Dream*. Go through the play and find instances of imagery. There are plenty of them to choose from. Use the framework below for your analysis.

Image: _____
Is it a simile or a metaphor?

first element   **second element**

_____
_____
_____
_____

Image: _____
Is it a simile or a metaphor?

first element   **second element**

_____
_____
_____
_____

Classical Comics Teaching Resource: *A Midsummer Night's Dream* — Language

THE LOVERS' (AND OTHERS') INSULTS
"Curs'd be thy stones for thus deceiving me!"

Use the following grid to jot down the insults the lovers exchange in Act III Scene 2. Can you find any other insults in the play?

Once you have collected a number of insults, you can try them out in pairs – but rather than just shout the insults at each other, try to be in character. How would Hermia and Helena say their insults to each other? How Lysander to Hermia?

Hermia vs. Demetrius

Lysander vs. Hermia

Hermia vs. Helena

Helena vs. Hermia

Demetrius vs. Lysander

Use this grid to jot down any other insults you come across in *A Midsummer Night's Dream*.

Who is insulting whom?	The insult

EXPLORING THEMES IN A MIDSUMMER NIGHT'S DREAM

Introduction

This chapter focuses on the main themes of *A Midsummer Night's Dream*.
They are (in order of presentation):
- Love and Marriage
- Obedience
- Dreams and Imagination
- The Moon – madness and chastity

There are, of course, areas where these overlap: work on marriage will also have to examine issues of obedience, as one of the marital conflicts presented in the play (between Titania and Oberon) revolves around their disobedience to each other. Similarly, the moon pervades all themes – but in particular the theme of dreams and imagination. These similarities are invitations to explore the themes and their interconnections further. Some themes also interlink with character work – once again, this is an invitation to work broadly and approach one topic from a number of different angles.
At the end of the chapter is a general section that focuses primarily on writing an analytical essay involving one of the themes presented.

SETTING THE THEMES

The beginning of a play – much like the beginning of any story, novel or film – has to fulfil a number of functions. First and foremost it must, of course, grab the attention of the audience. Usually, the main characters are presented at the beginning, or at least near the beginning. Main themes are also habitually introduced in the opening scene.

With its three different groups of characters who inhabit three different worlds, *A Midsummer Night's Dream* obviously cannot present all of the main characters in its opening scene – in fact it only presents one group of characters: the Athenian court. However, it does introduce a number of the main themes that will concern all the groups: the theme of love and marriage, which is equally a theme of the fairy realm (with Oberon and Titania's quarrel) and of the Mechanicals (through their play of *Pyramus and Thisbe*).

A number of themes are listed in the grid opposite. Pupils should be asked to find evidence of these themes in the opening scene of the play. Two rows have been left blank to enable pupils to note down their own ideas and thus take more control of their learning. It is suggested that pupils work in pairs or groups for this activity.

EXPLORING ACT 1 SCENE 1

TASK:
Use the following table to explore to what extent the themes of *A Midsummer Night's Dream*, listed on the left of the page, are present in the opening scene of the play. Remember to back up your thoughts with evidence from the play, and to explain in what way the quotation you have selected involves the theme.

Themes	Evidence from the text	Explain relevance of evidence
Love & Marriage		
Obedience		
Dreams		
Imagination (the mind's eye)		

LOVE AND MARRIAGE
"Reason and love keep little company together now-a-days"

A Midsummer Night's Dream is, above all, a play about love and marriage. Throughout the play, love is the dominant theme and the driving force, and it is highlighted in its various aspects, from adolescent folly to more mature conjugal love.

We are introduced to the theme of marriage in the opening lines of the play – but to what extent this marriage is backed by love, we can never really discern. Hippolyta seems to be freedom-loving, and from Theseus's words, it appears that she does not necessarily love him (although he expresses a desire to win her heart). Despite that, he does seem to feel love for her; beyond that, all else is conjecture. What we do know is that the marriage is a state affair, possibly with the intention of knitting together the recently conquered Amazons with Theseus's realm. Hippolyta seems to accept this state of affairs and is prepared to make the best of the situation.

The other "mature" couple of the play is very different. Titania and Oberon have obviously been together for quite some time. We see them at odds with each other over the issue of the changeling boy; however, they are quick to point out their shortfalls prior to that catalyst. From the events prior to the play and recounted in the text, it seems they did not have the best of relationships; and this current quarrel is having repercussions in nature, affecting the whole world. It is obvious that Oberon desires Titania – how he speaks of her is laden with voluptuousness, and his revenge is equally corporeal. It seems that physicality is a key ingredient to their relationship.

The lovers represent young love, which is portrayed as a mixture of intense emotions, besottedness, of being "in love", and changing one's emotional attachments. There is a lot of dynamic in this youthful love, a reflection of the fact that theirs is an age when people test each other's emotions and commitment prior to marriage. The women stay true to their loves throughout: Helena never ceases loving Demetrius, and Hermia never loves anybody but Lysander. In addition, Hermia at no point believes that Lysander would willingly or knowingly betray her love.

A distinction often made in the play is between doting and loving. The former is a strong but superficial and usually transient passion, not open to reflection or reason, while the latter is a more mature feeling based on an intimate knowledge of the partner's character.

Mixed into this cocktail of lovers and various forms of love is the story of *Pyramus and Thisbe*, a tragic story of love that is reminiscent of *Romeo and Juliet* (which Shakespeare was writing at the same time as *A Midsummer Night's Dream*). *Pyramus and Thisbe* shows how the plot of the play – lovers forbidden to stay together – could have developed, if not for the crazy happenings in the wood.

Some ideas for activities:

- At the end all the couples are (happily) married. To what extent do the pupils think they will live "happily ever after"? Students can use the text as a basis for exploration. For one, Demetrius is never officially cured from the effect of the flower juice. Maybe that is something that will wear off?

- To discover the difference between doting and loving, pupils can compare Lysander's words when he is in love with Hermia with when he is under the influence of the love juice.

- A lot of the confusion of the lovers is due to love-in-idleness. Pupils could write a poem about what is in the juice of that flower, making sure the poem is metaphorical (saying what induces the "doting").

- Pupils could write a stream of consciousness piece in the character of either Lysander or Demetrius about waking up under the influence of the love potion.

- One aspect of love explored in the play is its relationship to reason. Those under the influence of the love potion try to explain their change of heart in different ways. Pupils could explore these passages and draw conclusions on what extent love and reason do or do not mix.

- Compare the main plot elements of the lovers' plot in *A Midsummer Night's Dream*, *Pyramus and Thisbe* and *Romeo and Juliet*. The idea here is to not only see how the plots are similar, but also to discover how similar starting positions can lead to a tragic outcome just as easily as a happy one. How does this realisation reflect on our notions of the possibility of a happy ending?

HAPPY EVER AFTER?
"All shall be well"

Use the grid below to explore to what extent you think the couples – all married off or reconciled at the end of the play – will have a happy marriage. Use evidence from the play to support your points.

Couple	Will they live on happily?	Evidence from the text
Theseus & Hippolyta		
Lysander & Hermia		
Demetrius & Helena		
Oberon & Titania		

LYSANDER LOVES AND DOTES
"By all the vows that ever men have broke"

Lysander's true love to Hermia is converted by the love potion into doting on Helena. In what way does this affect his language? Use the grid below to help you explore the difference between loving and doting.

Lysander loves Hermia	Lysander dotes on Helena
How does he address each woman?	
Comparison:	
What imagery does he use? What for?	
Comparison:	
Are there any differences in emotion? Explain how you can tell.	

LOVE AND REASON
"Reason becomes the marshal to my will"

In the course of the play, a number of characters fall unexpectedly in love with others thanks to the workings of love-in-idleness. The reactions of the bewitched to their change of heart is often to try to rationalise the sudden shift in their emotions. Examining their arguments and reactions is a good way to explore the theme of love, and also to find out whether love and reason are irreconcilable, as Bottom suggests.

Titania I pray thee, gentle mortal, sing again: Mine ear is much enamour'd of thy note; So is mine eye enthralled to thy shape; And thy fair virtue's force, perforce, doth move me, On the first view to say, to swear, I love thee. **Bottom** Methinks, mistress, you should have little reason for that: and yet, to say the truth, reason and love keep little company together now-a-days; the more the pity, that some honest neighbours will not make them friends. Nay, I can gleek upon occasion.	What characteristics of Bottom does Titania say she is in love with?
Titania Thou art as wise as thou art beautiful. **Bottom** Not so, neither: but if I had wit enough to get out of this wood, I have enough to serve mine own turn.	What tells us that she realises he is not quite a fit companion?
	How do we know Titania – though besotted – is still a powerful queen, not to be crossed?
Titania Out of this wood do not desire to go: Thou shalt remain here, whether thou wilt or no. I am a spirit of no common rate: The summer still doth tend upon my state; And I do love thee: therefore, go with me; I'll give thee fairies to attend on thee; […] And I will purge thy mortal grossness so, That thou shalt like an airy spirit go.	Why is Titania's love unreasonable?

LOVE AND REASON

(cont'd)

Lysander The will of man is by his reason sway'd, And reason says you are the worthier maid. Things growing are not ripe until their season: So I, being young, till now ripe not to reason; And touching now the point of human skill, Reason becomes the marshal to my will, And leads me to your eyes; where I o'erlook Love's stories, written in love's richest book.	How does Lysander explain his change of feelings?
	Why do you think he uses reason as an argument?
	What could you say against this argument?
Demetrius But, my good lord, I wot not by what power,– But by some power it is,– my love to Hermia, Melted as the snow, seems to me now As the remembrance of an idle gaud, Which in my childhood I did dote upon; And all the faith, the virtue of my heart, The object and the pleasure of mine eye, Is only Helena. To her, my lord, Was I betroth'd ere I saw Hermia: But, like a sickness, did I loathe this food; But, as in health, come to my natural taste, Now I do wish it, love it, long for it, And will for evermore be true to it.	How does Demetrius explain that he loves Helena once again?
	Why is the image of "sickness" particularly apt?
	What could you say against his argument?

STAR-CROSSED LOVERS
"The course of true love never did run smooth"

In Act I Scene 1, Lysander and Hermia bewail their fate – to love one another, but to have Hermia's father against that union. This set-up is reminiscent of *Pyramus and Thisbe*, which the Mechanicals perform in Act V, and *Romeo and Juliet*, a drama Shakespeare was working on at the same time as *A Midsummer Night's Dream*. Use the grid below to compare the fate of these ill-fated lovers.

Question:	Hermia & Lysander	Pyramus & Thisbe	Romeo & Juliet
Who is against their marriage and why?			
How do they attempt to overcome the opposition to their love?			
Does the plan work?			
What is the outcome?			
What is the main reason for this outcome?			

OBEDIENCE
"As she is mine, I may dispose of her"

In Shakespeare's time, society was much stricter, revolving around a number of bonds of kinship as well as obedience. Depending upon who they were and where they lived, different people had different duties and responsibilities. While the feudal system had come to an end, lords would still have a huge staff of servants who were required to be obedient and loyal.

In society, the position of women was not strong, and they were expected to look after the household (staff) and support their husbands. In all things they were expected to obey their husbands, who had total control over them. While there are examples of independent women (Queen Elizabeth I being the most remarkable one), this was the exception and not the rule. The male dominance is obvious in the play: Egeus can dispose of his daughter as he sees fit, even put her to death – a right that Theseus upholds; Theseus is preparing to marry a warrior woman, turning her from a figure of female power into a calm and silent housewife, waiting upon his pleasure; in the final Act, after marriage, all the women (with the sometime exception of Hippolyta) have fallen strangely (and uncomfortably) silent.

At the time the play was written (1595), all people were expected to be loyal to the sovereign and to obey her. The sovereign was at the top of society and therefore claimed the highest of all the various duties and loyalties that bound society. Thus, in the world of the play, Theseus is the person who holds all bonds of obedience together: the Mechanicals perform for him (and wish to please him), the lovers are subject to his will and law, as is Egeus, who has to accept that his will concerning his daughter has been overruled.

Some ideas for activities:

- Pupils can be asked to draw a chart showing bonds of obedience. Characters in this would be grouped in a pyramid, showing allegiances and how they affect the characters in the play.
- In Act IV Scene 1, Bottom thoroughly enjoys his role as lover of the fairy queen, and he commands various fairies to carry out duties for him. Pupils could be asked to write a playscript containing some further instructions, detailing how the fairies wait on him and react to the mortal's strange wishes.
- Pupils can be asked to draw two pictures of Hippolyta: one before her defeat by Theseus, showing her as an independent warrior, the other after her marriage, emphasising how she has been turned into an obedient queen. The clothing as well as her posture should show the change.

WHO MUST OBEY WHOM?
"Your servant shall do so"

Fill in the names of the following characters in the chart below and show how obedience and dominance are displayed in the play.

Hermia, Puck, Lysander, Demetrius, Titania, Hippolyta, Theseus, Oberon, Egeus

The Athenians

The Fairies

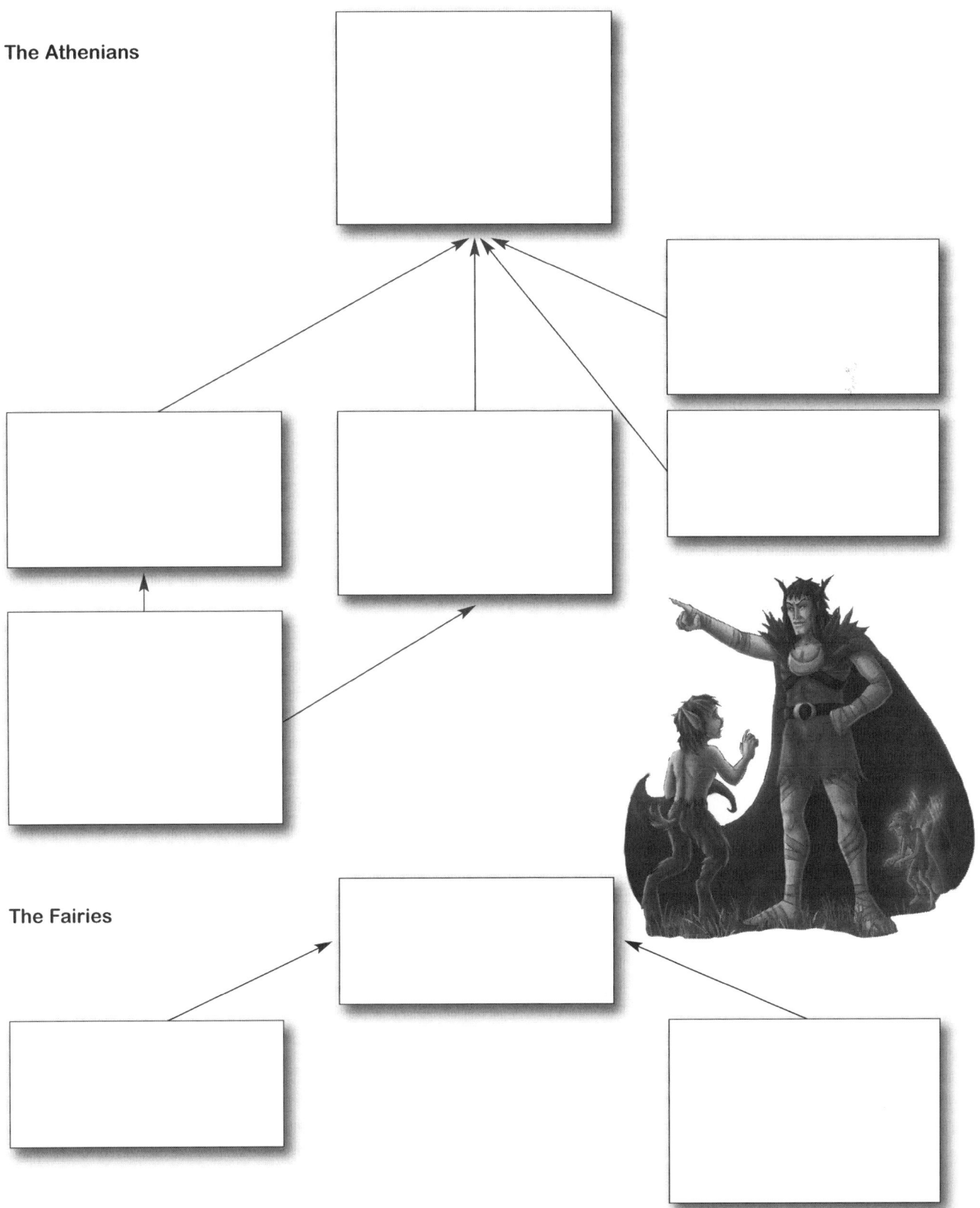

DREAMS AND IMAGINATION
"What visions have I seen!"

Dreams are another major preoccupation of *A Midsummer Night's Dream*. Indeed, with such a title, it would be strange if the play did not deal with dreams to a certain degree. Having said that, although the play contains numerous references to dreams and dreaming, there is only one real dream in it: Hermia's in Act II Scene 2 of having a serpent eating her heart.

Dreams, it seems, were something that preoccupied Shakespeare throughout his life, particularly at the time of writing *A Midsummer Night's Dream*. *Romeo and Juliet*, in the famous Queen Mab speech of Mercutio, contains a detailed description of the "fairies' midwife" that brings humans their dreams. Here the themes of fairies and dreams combine.

Although there is only one dream in *A Midsummer Night's Dream*, a number of characters at various times in the play profess to having dreamt, or of their experience resembling a dream. Thus, wide stretches of the play can be seen as having a dreamlike quality – at least for the characters involved. But we, as audience, also share in this dreamlike quality, as we are instructed by Puck to suppose the whole play was "but a dream" if we didn't like it.

Linked to the idea of dreams, understood as "wishful thinking", is the notion of the imagination – what we see with our mind's eye. *A Midsummer Night's Dream* is the play in which Shakespeare most often uses the word "eye" – surely no coincidence. Cupid is blind, and the love juice is smeared on the eyes. With their direct connection to the brain, the eyes to a large degree control what we think and desire.

Some ideas for activities:

- The word "dream" keeps cropping up at important stages of the play. The pupils could be asked to analyse what the dream imagery in each case suggests.
- Similarly, the ideas of "eyes" and looking with someone else's eyes recur again and again. Students can be asked to analyse who sees with whose eyes at certain stages, and how the vision is "restored" (if at all).
- In the epilogue, the audience is asked to think the whole play was "but a dream" if they didn't like it. To what extent could the play be seen as a dream? What elements of a dream appear in the play? And is a dream something positive or negative? (the epilogue seems to suggest a dream is not to be taken seriously). The pupils could also examine what positive and negative aspects a dream might have, and how those tie in with the play.
- Hermia's dream seems to warn her of Lysander's leaving her. What dream might Egeus have on the night of Hermia fleeing the house? Pupils who are particularly gifted could try writing the dream in iambic pentameter.

I SPY WITH MY LITTLE EYE
"Your eyes must with his judgment look"

In the play, a number of characters are either asked to see things differently (i.e. through the eyes of another) or they have a view that conflicts with another's. Use the chart below to note whose eyes each character looks with (or is asked to see the world with) and what the effect of this is, or should be.

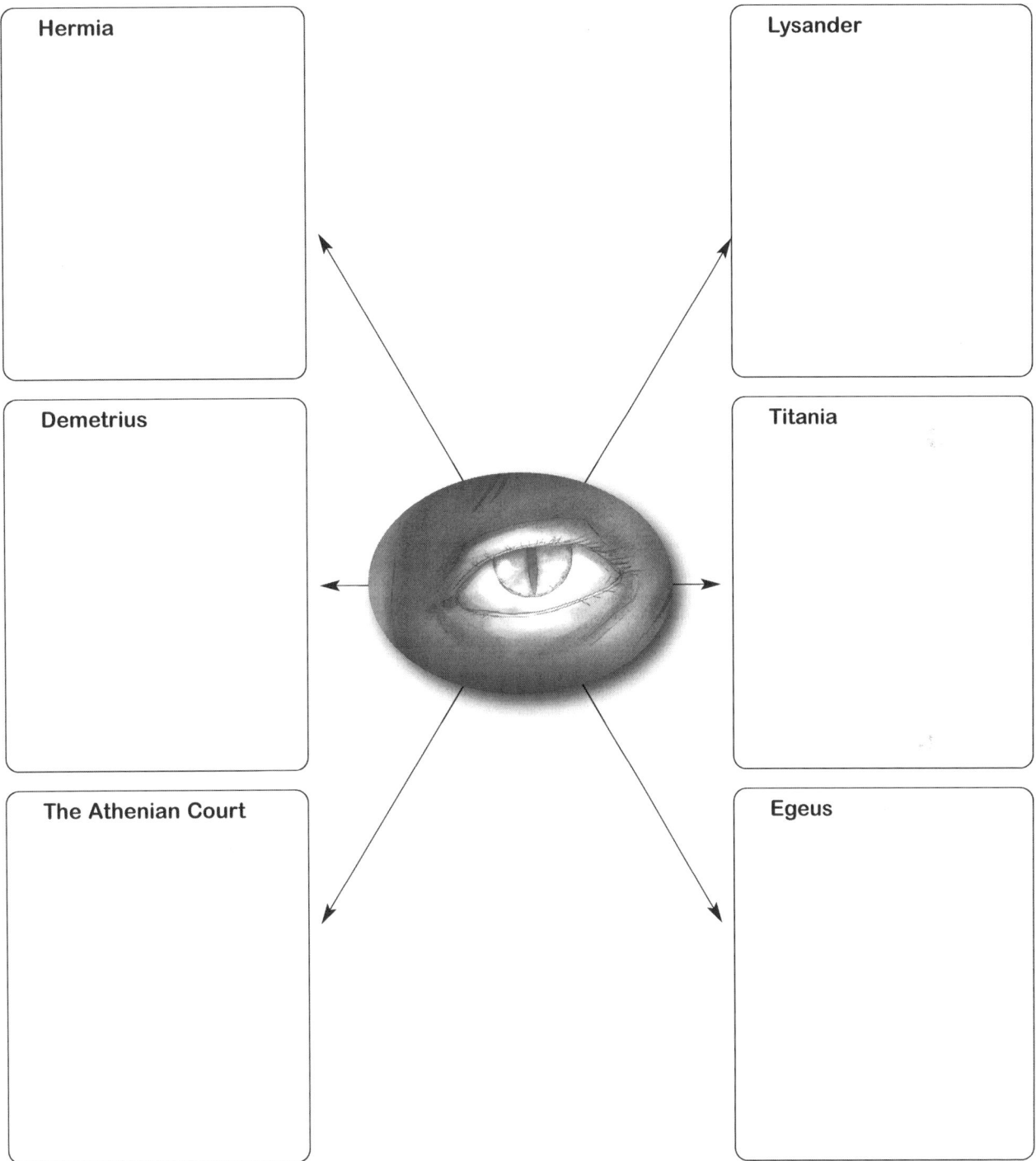

- Hermia
- Lysander
- Demetrius
- Titania
- The Athenian Court
- Egeus

WHO IS DREAMING WHAT?

"Four nights will quickly dream away the time"

In *A Midsummer Night's Dream*, a number of characters refer to dreams they thought they had or actually did have – which underlines the dreamlike quality of the whole play. Why all these references to dreams? Use the grid below to help you explore the various dreams.

Who does the dream apply to?	Evidence from the text & content of the dream	Relevance of the dream
Theseus (I.1)		
Hermia (II.2)		
Lovers (IV.1)		

WHO IS DREAMING WHAT?

(cont'd)

Who does the dream apply to?	Evidence from the text & content of the dream	Relevance of the dream
Bottom (IV.1)		
Titania (IV.1)		
Audience (epilogue)		

THE MOON – MADNESS AND CHASTITY
"The moon, methinks, looks with a wat'ry eye"

As one would expect of a play with "dream" in the title, a lot of the action takes place at night. This might explain why there are frequent references to the moon. However, the moon is not only mentioned when the characters talk about meeting in the woods – a large number of the references to the moon pertain to the Mechanicals staging *Pyramus and Thisbe* and the difficulties they have of credibly showing moonshine on stage. The remaining references deal with the more troubling aspects of the moon and its goddess, Diana. In a play that revolves mainly around love and marriage, Shakespeare uses moon imagery to show the opposite side: celibacy and chastity.

As Shakespeare wrote the play during the reign of Elizabeth I, widely known as the Virgin Queen, he could not paint too negative a picture of chastity. Indeed, while chastity is presented as undesirable to the male dominated court and the young Hermia, Titania (though not chaste) is linked more closely to the ideas and ideals of chastity, both through the episode of her votaress and the fact that Oberon restores her sight to a more chaste view of the world (although, unlike suggested of Elizabeth I, she is not immune to the power of the love-in-idleness, nor to Cupid's arrow).

Another aspect of the moon that is briefly explored is its affinity to lunacy. This name for madness stems from the belief that the moon and its varying phases could influence people's behaviour. Indeed, the play somehow suggests that the chaotic goings-on of the night are more akin to madness than anything else. The characters involved all believe they have been dreaming, but Theseus insists it must be some form of madness; we, the audience, know it is the folly of being in love.

Some ideas for activities:
- Pupils can be asked to explore the references to the moon that are more than mere references to night-time or the Mechanicals' staging difficulties. The idea here should be to find out what each quotation signifies and how it fits in with the themes of the play.

- Theseus's speech on poets, madmen and lovers (in V.1) is central to the idea of lunacy and is worth exploring in detail. Particular emphasis should be placed on how Theseus means to disparage all three but somehow gives them a positive spin, especially when referring to poets.

CHASTE DIANA
"Chanting faint hymns to the cold fruitless moon"

Use the following grid to explore some of Shakespeare's moon-related imagery.

Extract	What does the extract mean?
Theseus, bewailing the fact that time passes too slowly until his wedding day (I.1) but, O, methinks, how slow This old moon wanes! She lingers my desires, Like to a step-dame, or a dowager, Long withering out a young man's revenue.	
Theseus, describing to Hermia what fate awaits her, should she disobey her father (I.1) For aye to be in shady cloister mew'd, To live a barren sister all your life, Chanting faint hymns to the cold fruitless moon.	
Oberon, describing how the flower "love-in-idleness" gained its power from Cupid's arrow (II.1) And loos'd his love-shaft smartly from his bow, As it should pierce a hundred thousand hearts. But I might see young Cupid's fiery shaft Quench'd in the chaste beams of the wat'ry moon	
Titania, enamoured, before she retires with Bottom (III.1) The moon, methinks, looks with a watery eye; And when she weeps, weeps every little flower, Lamenting some enforced chastity.	
Oberon, applying the cure for the love potion into Titania's eyes (IV.1) Be, as thou wast wont to be; See, as thou wast wont to see: Dian's bud o'er Cupid's flower Hath such force and blessed power.	

THESEUS'S SPEECH ON LOVERS, POETS AND MADMEN
"But man is but a patched fool"

Theseus, commenting on the strange story of the lovers, delivers an important speech about lovers, madmen, poets and the imagination. Use this sheet to explore what Theseus is saying, and how his criticism somehow sounds positive.

> Why would a madman see devils? What connotation does this give to the madman?

> Note the many references to eyes and seeing – how does this relate to the rest of the play?

> Does "cool reason" sound positive or negative? Explain.

Lovers and madmen have such seething brains,
Such shaping fantasies, that apprehend
More than cool reason ever comprehends.
The lunatic, the lover, and the poet,
Are of imagination all compact:
One sees more devils than vast hell can hold;
That is the madman: the lover, all as frantic,
Sees Helen's beauty in a brow of Egypt:
The poet's eye, in a fine frenzy rolling,
Doth glance from heaven to earth, from earth to heaven;
And, as imagination bodies forth
The forms of things unknown, the poet's pen
Turns them to shapes, and gives to airy nothing
A local habitation, and a name.
Such tricks hath strong imagination,
That, if it would but apprehend some joy,
It comprehends some bringer of that joy:
Or, in the night, imagining some fear,
How easy is a bush suppos'd a bear?

> Who is the Helen being referred to here? The one from the play, or another? Why Egypt?

> What does the poet do with his pen?

> Is the poet more like the lover or the madman?

> Do these last lines refer to poets only, or to all three? Explain.

> What do the words "frantic" and "frenzy" suggest?

ANALYTICAL ESSAYS

Writing an analytical essay on a theme involves looking at the whole play and discovering how the theme develops, including any build-up and resolution.

To write an analytical essay successfully, it is suggested that pupils use the P-E-E-L structure.
PEEL stands for:

P-oint   Stating the argument.
E-vidence   The evidence for the point, using quotations where applicable.
E-xplain   A deeper explanation of the argument, taking the evidence into account, relative to the theme and the essay title.
L-ink   Reinforce the Point at the end, linking all arguments back to the beginning.

To prepare an essay using this technique, isolate key scenes that deal with the theme and explore each scene with reference to the essay title. These scenes, using quotations where appropriate, will form the backbone of your essay, as they provide the evidence for the arguments.
In order to avoid rambling, it is important that the analysis of the scenes is geared solely towards the title. Similarly, no more than three scenes should be explored in any depth.
The scenes selected do not have to prove the same point – indeed, it is often better to present different views, all of which support (or contradict) the argument, bringing the points together in the conclusion of the essay.

The following worksheets are presented to aid in the preparation of analytical essays:

- Charting the development of a theme throughout the play;
- Exploring a theme by briefly analysing a number of key scenes generally (not bound to an essay title);
- Planning sheet for an analytical essay, including the deeper analysis of three scenes.

THEME EXPLORATION SHEET

Use the following worksheet to help order your thoughts on the theme of your choice.

THEME:	
Select a scene in which the theme is central	
Summarise the scene briefly, using quotations where appropriate, focusing on how the theme is present.	What does the scene tell us about the theme? Note down all observations that are connected to the theme.
If possible, select another scene in which the theme is central or present.	
Summarise the scene briefly, using quotations where appropriate, focusing on how the theme is present.	What does the scene tell us about the theme? Note down all observations that are connected to the theme.
If possible, select a third scene in which the theme is central or present.	
Summarise the scene briefly, using quotations where appropriate, focusing on how the theme is present.	What does the scene tell us about the theme? Note down all observations that are connected to the theme.
If possible, select a fourth scene in which the theme is central or present.	
Summarise the scene briefly, using quotations where appropriate, focusing on how the theme is present.	What does the scene tell us about the theme? Note down all observations that are connected to the theme.

ESSAY WRITING FRAME

Use the framework to help you organise your ideas for an essay on the theme of your choice.

TITLE OF ESSAY (the statement)	
First paragraph: **Introduction**	
Briefly discuss the statement. What are the main points? Link the statement to the play.	
Second paragraph: Illustrate the statement with an example.	
Find a passage in the play that can be used as an example for the point you're trying to make.	What does this passage show in relation to the statement?
Third paragraph: illustrate the statement with a second example.	
Find a scene in the play that can be used as an example for the point you're trying to make.	What does this passage show in relation to the statement?
Fourth paragraph: Use a third example to illustrate the statement.	
Find a part in the play that can be used as an example for the point you're trying to make.	What does this passage show in relation to the statement?
Fifth paragraph: **Conclusion** – your opinion.	
Does the statement hold true or not? Perhaps it is only occasionally true?	Briefly re-cap the main points and finish with your own opinion.

POSSIBLE ESSAY TITLES

Based on the main themes in *A Midsummer Night's Dream*, the following is a selection of possible essay titles centred around each theme.

Love and Marriage

1. In what way is the love between Theseus and Hippolyta, Titania and Oberon and the lovers different?
2. To what extent does reason govern the choice of marriage partner in *A Midsummer Night's Dream*? Focus also on Egeus's choice of husband for Hermia.
3. Lysander says, "The course of true love never did run smooth." To what extent is this exemplified in *A Midsummer Night's Dream*?
4. If not for the love potion, *A Midsummer Night's Dream* would not have a happy ending. Discuss this statement, making reference to either the *Pyramus and Thisbe* story or *Romeo and Juliet*.
5. Based on the evidence of *A Midsummer Night's Dream*, what is Shakespeare's idea of the role of women in marriage?
6. The "roundel" of the lovers in the woods shows how fickle love can be. Do you think that the lovers can be happy after all that has happened to them in the woods?

Obedience

1. Why does Titania cease her strife with Oberon after he has removed the enchantment from her?
2. What lessons about obedience and duty can we learn from Egeus? Think not only about his obedience to Theseus, but also about Hermia.
3. Puck and Oberon are servant and master. What kind of a relationship is it exactly? What does it tell us about obedience and servitude generally?
4. Both Theseus and Oberon rule their respective kingdoms strictly, expecting absolute obedience. Discuss.

Dreams

1. What does *A Midsummer Night's Dream* with its multiple (supposed) dreams suggest about the nature of dreams?
2. In what way is Hermia's dream of the snake prophetic, and why is she the only person to have a warning dream?
3. In what way might it be helpful, as an audience, to imagine that the whole play was just a dream?
4. In what way does the fact that they think the happenings in the wood were just a dream affect the lovers and also Theseus and Hippolyta?

Imagination

1. Do you agree that sight is the most important sense in love? Use evidence from *A Midsummer Night's Dream* in your answer.
2. In what way is the Mechanicals' use of props and roles in their play ironic? You might wish to focus on their thoughts regarding killing and lions on stage as well as the wall and the moon.
3. To what extent might the audience believe that the whole fairy realm is nothing but a figment of the imagination? And if so, whose imagination?
4. To what extent do you think that Puck can be seen as an embodiment of the imagination?

The Moon (Madness and Chastity)

1. In what ways does *A Midsummer Night's Dream* suggest that marriage is preferable to chastity?
2. To what extent can the female characters in the play be regarded as embodiments of chastity?
3. The moon is generally seen as a symbol of women. To what extent does *A Midsummer Night's Dream* reflect this idea?
4. Love is a form of madness. Discuss.
5. Although the mad goings-on in the wood are due to the juice of the flower, it is equally possible that they could have happened without any magical intervention. Argue for and against this proposition.
6. In what way can writing poetry or plays be seen as "a fine frenzy"? In your answer, you should also discuss the connotations of the phrase, relating your arguments to *A Midsummer Night's Dream*.

DRAMA ACTIVITIES

Introduction
Because *A Midsummer Night's Dream* is a play, any intense involvement with the text – to be successful – must involve acting of some sort. Pupils don't need to act out the whole play or even entire scenes to get a flavour of the piece. Short, focused drama exercises can help engage with the play as it was intended.
There are a number of general drama techniques that can be used in various circumstances and adapted to suit the focus of the lesson. The most important of these are:

Freeze Framing
A group of pupils are asked to recreate a scene. They are given some time to work out where to position the characters, what expression their faces should show, and what gestures to make. Then, when the teacher says "freeze", they must get into the correct positions and hold the freeze, basically forming a three-dimensional photo (rather like a panel in the graphic novel).
Pupils can be unfrozen a group at a time to give them a chance to look at what other pupils have done. This allows a brief discussion / peer review about what makes a particular freeze effective.
You may wish to extend this technique by allowing frozen characters to briefly describe what they are thinking.

Hot-Seating
This is a drama technique particularly suited to exploring character and motivation. One pupil is chosen to play the part of a character from the text (e.g. Demetrius), and the rest of the class asks questions, which the pupil has to answer as he/she believes that character would.
The questions should be fired quite quickly, much like at a news conference, challenging the hot-seated pupil's thinking as well as their ability to build up a credible character around the information contained in the play.

Repetition of Phrases
A very good way of gauging the effectiveness of language and the pitch of a delivery is to take a short phrase and repeat it in as many different ways as possible, e.g. angrily, joyfully, spitefully, worriedly, doubtfully. This will help the pupils to listen to their voices and modulate them according to mood, as well as discover which mood suits a certain line best. Recording this in audio only, or even video with audio, provides valuable feedback to the pupil.

Short Interchanges
Similar to extended freeze-frames, this is a great method for some very basic character acting. Pupils are paired up, and each is assigned a character and a small number of lines for an interaction. From those lines, each pupil selects one line that they feel best represents the main message from that character. The pupils then say their lines in turn, trying to put as much emphasis as possible into their selected lines, using gestures and facial expressions. In that way, they distil their given character into one line and a gesture. Developments of relationship can also be explored using this technique, by choosing lines that follow the play's development.

Short Speech
Asking pupils to prepare a short speech (e.g. Egeus's or Hippolyta's) is an ideal way of developing speaking skills. Ideally, pupils would memorise the extract so that they can give a good delivery (without a sheet obstructing their connection with the audience). This would also enable them to add more

DRAMA ACTIVITIES

(cont'd)

gestures and facial expression to their delivery, deepening their character acting. It is a great idea to record the pupils as they speak, using video equipment. Playing this back to them and discussing what they did well and what they need to work on, based on the impartial evidence of a recording, is one of the best ways to improve speaking skills.

More advanced techniques include:

Mime
Pupils often struggle with how to act without talking; how to behave when on stage but not actually delivering any lines. Exercises that involve mime are a great way to help overcome this difficulty. It is possible to mime simple emotions and even act out a whole scene without saying a word. Alternatively, a teacher or a pupil could read the lines, with the other pupils acting along without saying a word.

Improvisation
This technique requires courage and a detailed knowledge of the characters. It is therefore best combined with character work. The technique involves putting the characters into a scene and asking them to act the scene out straight away, with no preparation. Harrowing as this experience can be for some pupils, it encourages quick thinking, staying in role, and character study.

Some ideas for activities involving drama techniques include:

- Hot-seat Egeus after I.1. Questions should revolve around why he is so eager for his daughter to marry Demetrius, what he has against Lysander, and why he would be willing to have his daughter killed if she disobeys him.
- Hot-seat Oberon after his resolve to make Titania pay for her disobedience in II.1. Questions should revolve around why he wants the Indian boy so much, why he does not accept Titania's explanation, why he wishes to punish her so cruelly, and why he thinks he is in the right.
- Hot-seat the lovers after they have woken from their experience in the woods (IV.1). They should be questioned on what they remember, how they view the events, and how they can explain them.
- Select a number of opposing characters (Helena – Demetrius, Titania – Oberon) or characters in dialogue (Oberon – Puck, Bottom – Quince) and give each character only one line to say. Split the class into two groups and assign each group one of the roles. Each pupil is to say their line emphatically, with one gesture.
- Egeus does not have a lot to say. In particular at the end, he is overruled and is not allowed to plead his case. This makes the scene a good test-piece to explore mime and other forms of non-verbal reaction to what is being said.
- Freeze-frame the ten most important scenes. Pupils can either make up their own list of ten, or the list could be drawn up together in class (which also allows for a comparison of freezes). After the pupils are given sufficient time to prepare, freeze all ten moments in succession. Keep the best freeze each time for other pupils to see and (when unfrozen) to comment on the freeze's effectiveness.

It is often useful to group pupils for drama activities and to have one pupil as "director" or coach, helping the other pupils to achieve their shared vision.

CHARACTERISTIC ONE-LINERS
"There is not one word apt"

TASK:
Below is a selection of one-liners from various characters. First match up the lines to the characters, and then try to capture that person's characteristics in how she or he says the line.

Characters	Lines
Theseus	The fairy land buys not the child of me
Hippolyta	If I do it, let the audience look to their eyes
Egeus	I love thee not, therefore pursue me not
Oberon	Nay, faith, let me not play a woman; I have a beard coming
Titania	Have you the lion's part written? pray you, if it be, give it me, for I am slow of study
Puck	You can never bring in a wall
Bottom	I am, my lord, as well deriv'd as he
Quince	But, O, methinks, how slow this old moon wanes
Flute	I know not by what power I am made bold
Starveling	I will fawn on you: use me but as your spaniel
Snout	I never heard so musical a discord, such sweet thunder
Snug	I am that merry wanderer of the night
Helena	All that I have to say, is, to tell you that the lantern is the moon; I, the man i' the moon
Hermia	Thou shalt not from this grove, till I torment thee for this injury
Lysander	But, masters, here are your parts
Demetrius	I beg the ancient privilege of Athens

DEVELOPING RELATIONSHIPS
"Some true love turn'd, and not a false turn'd true"

One-liners can also be used to chart how a relationship between two characters develops. The following one-liners trace the relationship between Oberon and Titania, and Demetrius and Helena. Apart from acting them out and seeing how the relationship changes, you can also analyse who says what, and who usually starts the dialogue, discerning what this might tell you about the characters and their relationship.

Oberon: Ill met by moonlight, proud Titania	**Titania:** What, jealous Oberon! Fairies, skip hence
Titania: And this same progeny of evils comes From our debate, from our dissension	**Oberon:** Why should Titania cross her Oberon?
Oberon: I do but beg a little changeling boy	**Titania:** The fairy land buys not the child of me
Oberon (to himself): thou shalt not from this grove, Till I torment thee for this injury	(no response from Titania)
Oberon: What thou seest, when thou dost wake, Do it for thy true-love take	**Titania (to herself, about Bottom):** What angel wakes me from my flowery bed?
Oberon (spoken to Puck): And now I have the boy, I will undo This hateful imperfection of her eyes	**Titania:** My Oberon! what visions have I seen! Methought, I was enamour'd of an ass
Oberon: Sound, music! Come, my queen, take hands with me	**Titania:** Come, my lord; and in our flight, Tell me how it came this night
Titania: Hand in hand, with fairy grace, Will we sing, and bless this place	**Oberon:** Now, until the break of day, Through this house each fairy stray

Helena (spoken to Hermia): O, teach me how you look, and with what art You sway the motion of Demetrius' heart	(no response from Demetrius)
Demetrius: I love thee not, therefore pursue me not	**Helena:** Use me but as your spaniel, spurn me, strike me
Demetrius: I'll run from thee, and hide me in the brakes	**Helena:** We cannot fight for love, as men may do; We should be woo'd, and were not made to woo
Demetrius: O Helen, goddess, nymph, perfect, divine!	**Helena:** O spite; O hell! I see you all are bent To set against me for your merriment
Helena: I pray you, though you mock me, gentlemen, Let her not hurt me	**Demetrius:** She shall not
Demetrius: The object and the pleasure of mine eye, Is only Helena	**Helena:** I have found Demetrius, like a jewel, Mine own, and not mine own

Classical Comics Teaching Resource: *A Midsummer Night's Dream* — Drama and Discussion

ACTING OUT SCENES FROM THE PLAY
"Say, what abridgement have you for this evening?"

Acting out scenes in class is always a challenge – in a variety of ways. Discipline can be an issue (especially as excitement mounts), so it is important to establish clear rules and procedures for when pupils need to pay attention. The greatest problems will probably be the amount of space and keeping all pupils involved.

Three scenes (or part-scenes) in *A Midsummer Night's Dream* are particularly suited to being acted out in class. These are the meeting of Titania and Oberon (II.1), Titania doting on Bottom (IV.1), and the performance of the Mechanicals' play (V.1). All these scenes can be staged in a way that involves all pupils (if necessary in two parallel groups), and they each present different challenges. Act II Scene 1 has two very strong characters clashing, while their respective fairy trains have nothing to say but must contribute in some way to the atmosphere of conflict and unclear loyalty; Act IV Scene 1 has a host of fairies either attending to Bottom's wishes or commenting on the situation through miming; Act V Scene 1 has the Mechanicals presenting their play with the court of Athens looking on – while the Mechanicals speak, the whole court must react to what they see.

Act II Scene 1:
Two things should be borne in mind here. Firstly, while only Titania and Oberon speak, they enter with their servant fairies, who need to do something while the two main characters fight it out. Secondly, Titania talks of nature being in discord, and this could be represented in some way to underline her case. The atmosphere that should be brought across is one of turmoil and upheaval.

Some ideas on how to stage the scene:
- The fairies in each train could support their ruler and act as though they would pick a fight with any fairy of the other ruler's train – much like gangs sizing each other up. Alternatively, they could act surprised and at a loss of how to deal with this sudden and heated argument between their rulers.
- Some pupils could be dressed as trees or flowers, and their contortions could mirror the turmoil in nature.
- Make use of the music department to find percussion instruments that can simulate a storm (drums, cymbals etc.). Lighting will be more difficult, but darkening the room and using torches with a flash function would be effective.
- There should be real venom between the two actors playing Oberon and Titania – lovers' spats are usually ugly, and this one is no exception. Remember Titania is not a lightweight, but a commanding queen who actually gets the better of Oberon in this encounter.

ACTING OUT SCENES FROM THE PLAY

(cont'd)

Act IV Scene 1:

In this scene, Bottom, who does not know he has a donkey's head on his neck, feels more at home as the fairy queen's lover and orders the fairies around. They obey him, of course, but one wonders whether they do this freely or grudgingly. Once again, we have two main characters and a host of fairies in attendance with silent parts.

Some ideas on how to stage the scene:

- Bottom calls for music. What kind of music might the fairies play him? Here you could use the resources of the music department to create fairy sounds.

- Titania is obviously in love with Bottom. How does she express this? We know she strokes him, but how else might she show her total adulation for the "translated" Bottom?

- How does Bottom act in all this? He sends four fairies on various missions – how does he ask them to do this? Is he full of his power and exercising it just to show he can? Or is he only asking the fairies for help?

- How do the fairies being asked to do chores react? Are they eager to please their queen and thereby also Bottom? Or do they resent having to work for a donkey-headed mortal and show this, as far as they dare?

- What do the other fairies make of their mistress's new love? How do they show what they think of this liaison?

Act V Scene 1:

Here the entire Athenian court, which has celebrated the triple wedding, watches the play staged by the Mechanicals. This is a key comic scene; if it is to be effective, not only must the Mechanicals act well and their timing be impeccable, but all other onlookers must add to the atmosphere of hilarity.

Some ideas on how to stage the scene:

- For this scene you have to think about where the Mechanicals act and how the court will watch them, at the same time ensuring that the real audience can see both groups.

- Only the Athenian men (Theseus, Lysander and Demetrius) and Hippolyta comment on the play. All other onlookers (in particular Hermia and Helena) do not speak. Does this mean they have to be silent? How could they show their reaction to the Mechanicals?

- How do the Mechanicals react to the mockery of the court, which they can hear? Does it make them say their lines more quickly, to get it over and done with, or more emphatically, in a bid to win the audience over? Or are they so lost in their own performance that they do not react to it?

- What do the Mechanicals that are not "on stage" do? Do they immerse themselves in the performance of their colleagues? Or do they groan and realise how bad their play is?

- Both Pyramus's and Thisbe's final speeches are full of linguistic humour. Does this transfer onto the actors? Or does one of the Mechanicals manage to evoke real feelings for his character?

These are suggestions on these three scenes, but any scene can be adapted for acting out in the classroom. The more time and effort you put into a "mini-production", the more rewarding it will be; and the more pupils will gain from the experience of exploring playscripts for themselves and bringing their own personal slants to a text.

WORD JUMBLE

Solve the following anagrams to find the names of characters or things to do with *A Midsummer Night's Dream*.

Jumbled Spelling	Correct Spelling
Slay nerd	
Tiered Sum	
She Suet	
Happy Toil	
He I Mar	
An Heel	
She Tan	
Hotplate Sir	
Ron Beo	
I At A Nit	
Wool Go Fled	
To Tomb	
Nic Que	
Grist V Lane	
Guns	
Not Us	
Clang Hinge	
Seated Drums	
Lame Boss Pose	
Ebb Cow	
DI Puc	
Ms Mire Mud	
Things	
Armed	
She Peaks Ear	

CROSSWORD

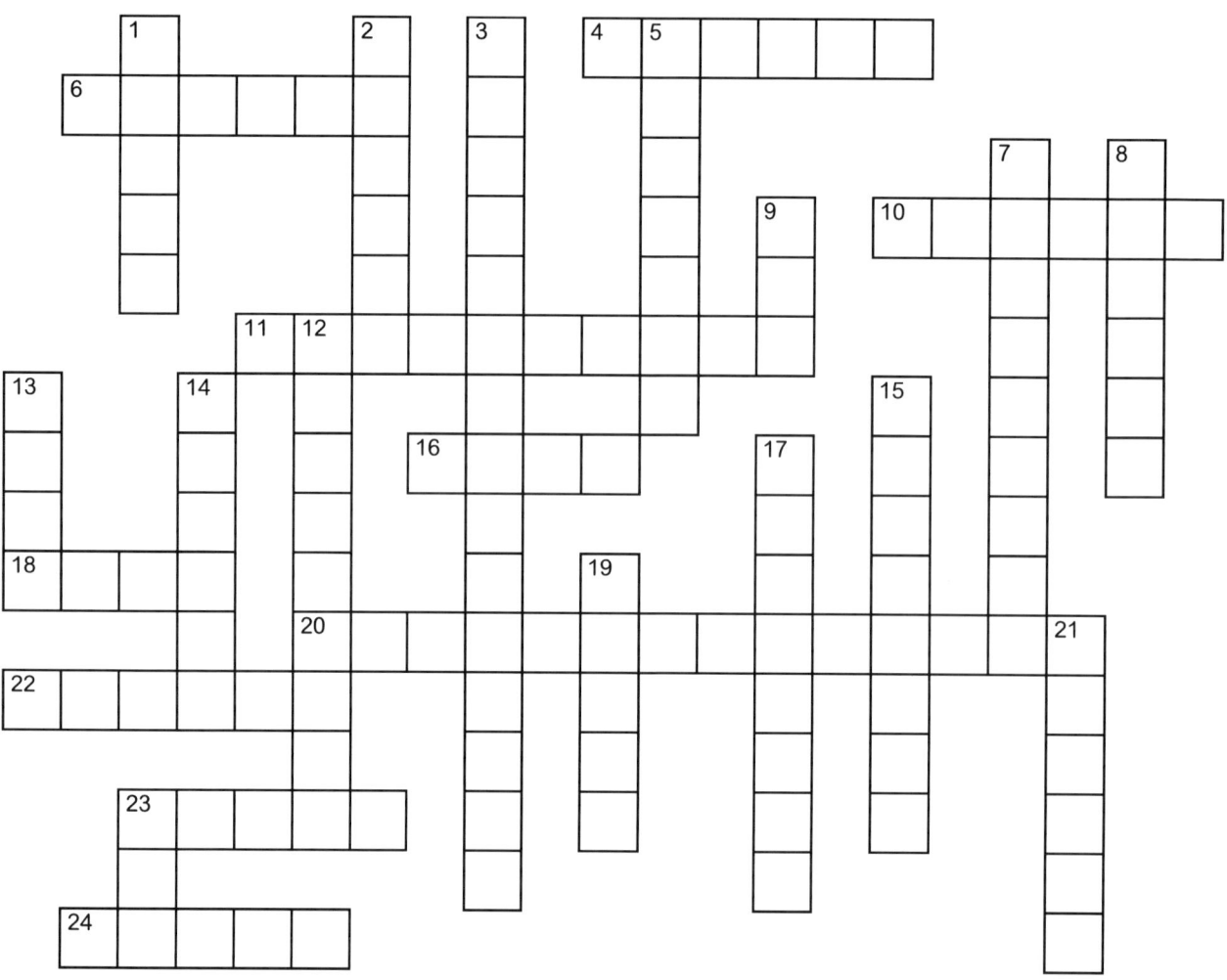

ACROSS
4 Theseus is Duke of this (6)
6 The leader of the acting group: Peter _____ (6)
10 The fairy king (6)
11 The _____ boy, whom the Fairy King and Queen argue about (10)
16 An Act I Scene 1, how many days until the wedding? (4)
18 Snug's role in the Mechanicals' play (4)
20 The name of the magical flower (4,2,8)
22 The play performed for the Duke: Pyramus and _____ (6)
23 The name of the song that Bottom will ask to be written: Bottom's _____ (5)
24 Hermia's father (5)

DOWN
1 The "god" whose arrow hit the flower (5)
2 Hermia's friend and occasional love-rival (6)
3 Puck's real name (5,10)
5 The fairy queen (7)
7 The boy whom Hermia's father wants her to marry (9)
8 The type of head put on Bottom by Puck (6)
9 The weather element created by Puck so that the lovers become lost in the forest (3)
12 Theseus's fiancee, who was Queen of the Amazons
13 The part played by Snout, separating the lovers in the Mechanicals' play (4)
14 Duke Theseus hunts with these (6)
15 Hermia's true love (8)
17 Theseus opts not to hear this at the end of the Mechanicals' play (8)
19 What Hermia dreams eats away her heart (5)
21 "The course of true love never did run_____" (6)
23 Canine companion to the man in the moon (3)

WORD SEARCH

The following words are hidden in the grid below. Words can be horizontal, vertical, or diagonal, and they may run in any direction (forwards or backwards).

ATHENS	SNOUT	MUSTARDSEED	HELENA
HOBGOBLIN	COBWEB	THESEUS	PHILOSTRATE
QUINCE	MOONSHINE	FAIRY	WALL
BOTTOM	SNUG	OBERON	HERMIA
HOUNDS	DEMETRIUS	THISBE	PUCK
ROBINGOODFELLOW	MOTE	FLUTE	HIPPOLYTA
CHANGELING	STARVELING	PEASEBLOSSOM	PYRAMUS
LYSANDER	EGEUS	TITANIA	

```
Z U I K Z B C M A O J O S A T H E N S Q W P
G P T P G E V K C U P A I M R E H S X E N X
W H Y I B E N F T B J H H P I Q L O K D F S
Y I G H N S F S G F L D Q T E B X G P J N E
W L S C O B W E B V E B R N P E I T O L T
L O U R Z O V U N E A X M O A J I S U S J C
L S E X L N M I S C R T B O F E P T T A V N
W T G N J J L D H Z D I Y X T S V A O V T W
B R E P Y B R A L U N S D L A E R E S A Q A
N A Y L O A N E H G F I D I O V A N F G J P
E T F G T G N S O K V T N M E P U B P F E Y
Y E B S E M U O L E H A H L O G P E F S N R
M O U L T M D Y T E T I I I X O A I N N O I
H M I E A F Y U S I B N Q R S S N O H H R A
P N F R E C L E T X G E Z Q E B N S L I E F
G F Y L H F U N M W V O H B I D E X H M B E
N P L C F S C H G M F E L R P A N C P I O F
I O X V Z A M E O Z L O C S B G U A W L N J
W H O U N D S T S E S C C X Y U L F S A F E
A A O E E Z T T N S G V K Z R E R I D Y L R
W O C A T O M A O D E M E T R I U S I Q L L
F R X A B H L M Q U I N C E W Q W J S U M O
```

83

THE ENDING OF *A MIDSUMMER NIGHT'S DREAM*
TEACHERS' VERSION

Solution (page 10)

Question	*A Midsummer Night's Dream*	*The Tempest*	*All's Well That Ends Well*	*As You Like It*
Who delivers the Prologue?	Puck, a minor character of mischief	Prospero, the main character	King, a minor character	Rosalind, a female, the main character
Is the actor in character?	Yes, but aware that he is talking to an audience.	Debateable – at the beginning he seems to be in character; when addressing audience mixture of Prospero and actor.	no, he speaks as an actor who is no longer the king but a "beggar".	no, philosophises about the structure of plays and the worth of epilogues.
How is the character trying to persuade the audience to clap?	No persuasion, more argument: if the audience is dissatisfied, it was all a dream, if they are satisfied, they should clap.	Imploring them to release him from island through the clapping as he has no more magic. Wind produced by hands will propel his sails.	Title of the play is not true until audience claps; actors at mercy of audience.	Appealing to men and women to persuade each other; the promise of a kiss from her.
How does the epilogue relate to the rest of the play?	Puck says that if audience didn't like the play they should imagine it was a dream – epilogue thus keys in to the main theme and calls the whole experience of the play into question.	Prospero, who has controlled the whole plot of the play, is now powerless as he has renounced his magic. As he has become a normal man, so the play must end and he must rely on the audience to "save" him.	Not really – this is a stock epilogue. It only relates to title of the play that the play can't really end well (although it has) unless the audience approve of it.	Throughout the play Rosalind has been gently steering the play to its happy resolution. It is therefore fitting that she is also the one to solicit approval. Additionally, she plays upon all people being happily married in the play by appealing to women's and men's love.

COMPREHENSION TESTS
TEACHERS' VERSION

Solution (pages 14-16)

Act I

Theseus, the **Duke** of Athens, can hardly wait to get married to **Hippolyta**, the Queen of the **Amazons**, whom he conquered in **battle**. Egeus disrupts their preparations and complains that his daughter, **Hermia**, will not obey his instructions and marry **Demetrius** because she loves **Lysander** instead. Theseus tells Hermia that, on the day of the royal wedding, she must decide either to marry as her father wishes, be executed, or become a **nun** for ever. Lysander and Hermia bewail their bad fortune and decide to **flee** from **Athens**. They tell Hermia's friend Helena all about their intentions. **Helen** was once loved by Demetrius, before he loved Hermia. She still loves Demetrius and secretly decides to tell him of the lovers' **plan** to leave the town, in the hope of receiving some **thanks**.

Meanwhile, a group of simple **workmen** from Athens are planning to perform a **play** for the Duke's **wedding** celebrations. They plan on staging *Pyramus and Thisbe*, with Bottom as **Pyramus** and **Flute** as Thisbe, although **Bottom** wants to play all the parts in the play. They decide to meet in the **woods** the next night to rehearse.

Act II

Robin Goodfellow, otherwise known as **Puck**, meets a **fairy** in the woods. Both Titania and Oberon, the Queen and the King of the fairies, plan to be in the **woods** that night. However, the two are in conflict because **Titania** has an Indian child that **Oberon** wants, and she **refuses** to give it up. As a result of their **quarrel**, nature is in **turmoil**. Oberon is prepared to end the fight if Titania gives him the child. Her refusal makes Oberon vow to make her pay for her **disobedience**. He orders Puck to search out a **flower**, the juice of which makes people fall in love with the next thing they **see** when they wake, after it has been applied to the **eyes**. Oberon wants to make sure that Titania wakes up when something **vile** is near. While Puck is gone, Oberon watches Demetrius and **Helena** walk through the woods in search of **Lysander** and Hermia. Demetrius continues to push Helena away. When Puck comes back to Oberon with the flower, in an attempt to set things right between Demetrius and Helena, he tells Puck to **anoint** the Athenian's eyes with the flower juice so that he will **love** the girl he **spurned**.

Elsewhere, Titania falls asleep, surrounded by her **fairy-court**. While asleep, Oberon smears some of the flower's **juice** onto her eyes.

In another part of the wood, Hermia and Lysander have lost their way; tired, they decide to sleep where they are. As they are not yet **married**, Hermia insists that they sleep **apart**. Puck, seeing them, thinks these are the two his master talked about, and he applies the juice onto **Lysander's** eyes. Helena stumbles into the area and wakes him. The magic of the flower has its effect, and he falls in love with her. Helena runs off, but Lysander **follows** her. After dreaming that a **snake** was eating her heart, Hermia wakes up alone.

Act III

Puck watches the **Mechanicals** rehearse their play and decides to have some fun with them. He puts a spell on **Bottom** so that his head becomes a **donkey**'s. When his friends see him, they run away. Left by himself, he **sings** to cheer himself up. The noise wakes **Titania**, who **falls in love** with him.

Puck reports all he has done to **Oberon**, who is **delighted**. **Demetrius** and Hermia enter, Hermia accusing him of having killed **Lysander**. Oberon realises Puck has made a **mistake**. While Demetrius sleeps, exhausted from the night's events, Oberon puts the love juice on his eyes. **Helena** enters, followed by Lysander. Waking under the power of the potion, Demetrius sees Helena and falls in love with her; now both men **fight** over her. **Hermia** returns to the scene and accuses Helena of having **bewitched** Lysander. The two men go off to fight, and the two women leave separately.

Oberon is **angry** at Puck and tells him to set things right. Puck conjures up a dense **fog** in the wood and leads the two men **astray**. When they both fall asleep from **exhaustion**, Puck drips an **antidote** into **Lysander's** eyes. The two women, also tired from the night's happenings, arrive at the scene and, thinking they are alone, fall **asleep**, too.

COMPREHENSION TESTS
TEACHERS' VERSION

Solution (pages 17-18)

Act IV

Titania continues to be in love with the donkey-headed Bottom and asks her fairies to pander to his every **wish**. Oberon, who has meanwhile **taken** the Indian child from Titania, releases her from her **spell**. Titania wakes to see Bottom with the **donkey** head and realises she has not been **dreaming**. The two make up and decide to **bless** Theseus's wedding.

Theseus and his court are out **hunting** in the morning, when they stumble upon the four lovers, who wake up to find that while **Lysander** loves **Hermia** again, **Demetrius** now loves **Helena**. **Egeus** still wants Hermia to marry Demetrius, but Theseus overrules him, seeing as the four are now **matched**. Theseus decides that the two **couples** will **marry** together with him and Hippolyta.

After they have left the scene, **Bottom** also wakes up, returned to his normal state and as **himself** again; but he cannot say what happened to him.

Back in Athens, the Mechanics are **distraught** without Bottom as they cannot **perform** the play without him. Suddenly he bursts in, and they are **overjoyed** and have **hope** again that their performance will go ahead.

Act V

Theseus and **Hippolyta** are not sure what to make of the lovers' **account** of the night's happenings. Philostrate, the master of the Duke's **revels** and entertainment, presents Theseus with a number of plays to **while** away the evening until bedtime. He chooses the Mechanicals' play of *Pyramus and Thisbe*.

All through the **performance**, the Athenians make fun of the **antics** and poor acting of the Mechanicals. Peter Quince, as prologue, gets his **punctuation** all wrong in his lines, saying the **opposite** of what he means. In the play, **Pyramus** (played by **Bottom**) and Thisbe (played by **Flute**) live next to each other and love one another, although their **parents** are against their love. They **communicate** through a chink or hole in the great wall that separates them, played by Snout. They agree to meet in secret outside the **city**. Thisbe arrives **first** at their meeting place and is **frightened** by a **lion** (played by Snug). She flees but leaves her scarf, which is **mauled** by the lion. When Pyramus arrives, he sees the mauled scarf and, believing that his beloved has been killed, **kills** himself. Thisbe **returns** and sees the **dead** Pyramus; distraught, she kills herself, too.

Theseus is **pleased** with the play and gives praise to the actors. After the play, they all go off to their **rooms**.

When all have left, Oberon, Titania and their **fairies** fly through the house and **bless** its inhabitants. Finally, at the end of the play, Puck enters, alone, and asks for **applause** or, if the audience did not enjoy the play, for them to imagine it was only a **dream**.

THE DIFFERENT WORLDS OF A MIDSUMMER NIGHT'S DREAM
TEACHERS' VERSION

Solution (pages 19-20)

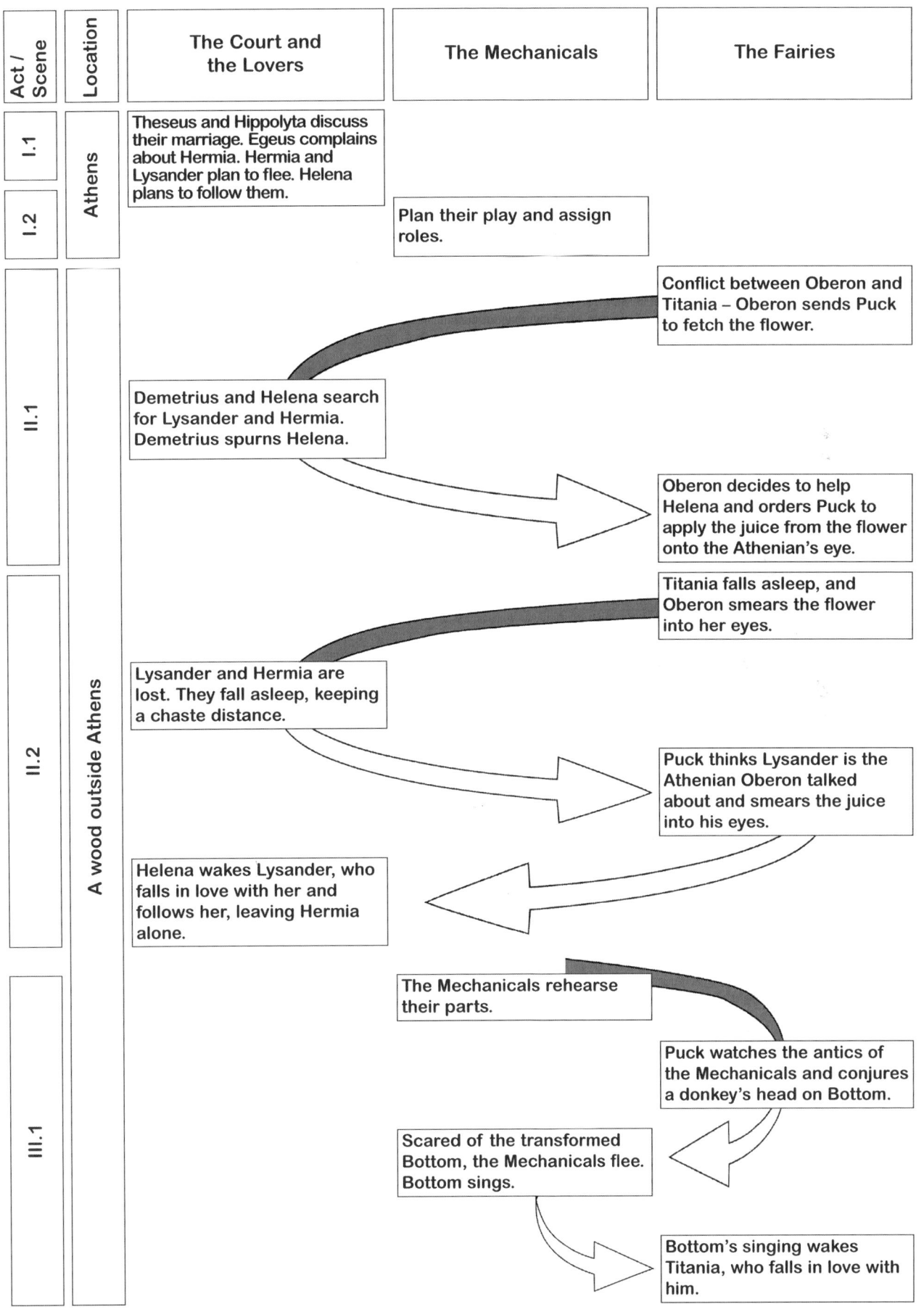

Act / Scene	Location	The Court and the Lovers	The Mechanicals	The Fairies
III.2	A wood outside Athens	Hermia believes Demetrius has killed Lysander. Demetrius lies down to sleep.		Oberon is pleased with Puck's work so far.
				Oberon realises Puck's mistake and applies the juice into Demetrius's eyes. He orders Puck to bring Helena.
		Helena, followed by Lysander, enters. Demetrius falls in love with her. Helena thinks the men are making fun of her. Lysander tells Hermia he hates her; Hermia accuses Helena of bewitching Lysander. The men go off to fight.		
				Oberon orders Puck to set things right by applying the antidote to Lysander's eyes. Puck leads the men away from each other.
		Exhausted, all fall asleep.	Bottom is the beloved of Titania.	Titania continues to love Bottom, and they fall asleep together. Oberon puts the antidote into Titania's eyes, and she realises what has happened. King and Queen make up and decide to bless the Duke's wedding.
IV.1		While out hunting, Theseus, Hippolyta and Egeus stumble upon the four lovers. Theseus overrules Egeus and decrees that all three couples will marry together.		
			Bottom wakes up and is at a loss to explain what happened.	
IV.2	Athens		The Mechanicals despair without Bottom. Bottom appears, and they prepare for the wedding.	
V.1	A wood outside Athens	Theseus and Hipolyta marvel at the lovers' story. Theseus chooses the Mechanicals' play. The Athenians interrupt the performance frequently to make witty asides. Theseus is pleased with the play, and all retire.	The Mechanicals perform *Pyramus and Thisbe*.	
Epilogue				Oberon, Titania and the Fairies fly through the house and bless it. Puck closes the play by speaking directly to the audience.

SPOT THE DIFFERENCE
TEACHERS' VERSION

Solution (page 36)

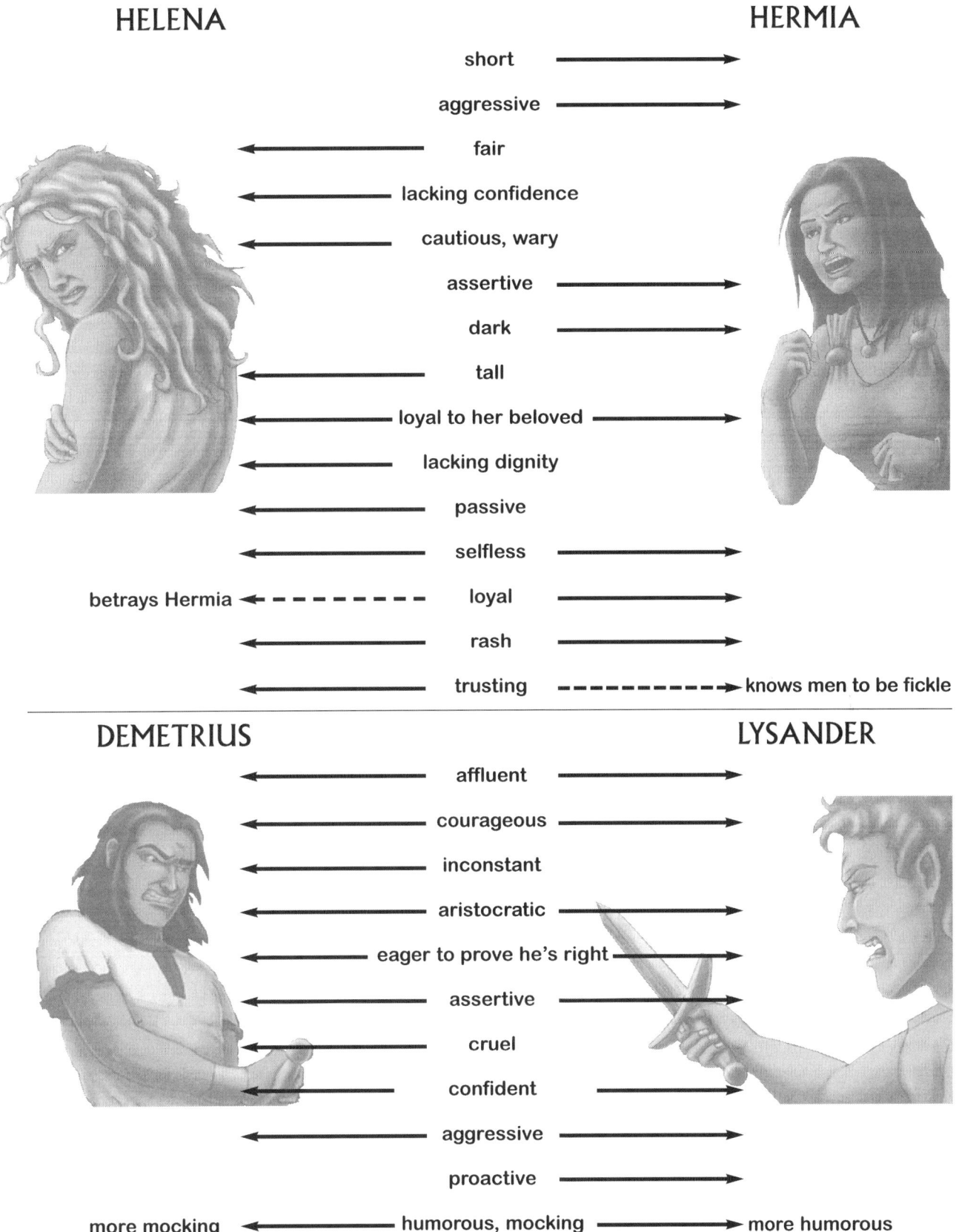

DUKEDOM AND KINGDOM
TEACHERS' VERSION

Solution (page 37)

	The Athenian Court	The Fairy Court
What is the relationship between the rulers like?	Theseus has conquered Hippolyta and seems to love her, but we do not know whether she loves him. Theseus treats her with reverence and frequently asks her how she is. But he is the ruler and dominates her, if not quite as clearly as Oberon.	Oberon wants to dominate Titania. He is obviously passionate about Titania but needs to be very clear about who rules. The two are not on equal footing.
What problem(s) do they have?	1. Egeus complains that his daughter doesn't want to marry the man he has chosen for her. 2. Theseus needs to woo Hippolyta and convince her of his love Both problems revolve around accepting male authority.	Titania has a changeling boy whom Oberon wants. Because she refuses to give him up they argue, causing nature to be in turmoil. Once again, the problem is about accepting male authority.
How does Theseus / Oberon intend to solve the problem(s)	1. Gives Hermia 4 days to reach a decision. He does not want to go against Hermia's choice, but he must uphold the law, so he changes the penalty. 2. Plans on a grand wedding to impress Hippolyta.	1. Is sure to gain the boy from Titania and plans on punishing her for her disobedience. 2. Oberon also takes on solving Theseus's problem with the lovers, which he does with the help of the magical juice from the flower.
How are Theseus / Oberon's spirits lifted?	Theseus has no court jester that we know of. Philostrate is the master of his revels, and the Mechanicals keep him entertained after his wedding. But this entertainment is after the resolution of the conflict, not during, as with the Fairy Court.	Puck, Oberon's servant and jester, not only does Oberon's bidding, but in doing it also seeks to cheer him up. He achieves this with "creating" the monster that Titania falls in love with, although Oberon is not pleased with his confusion of the lovers.
How do they behave towards their subjects?	Theseus seems to care about his subjects – he does not want to comply with Egeus's wishes (ultimately overriding him), and he cares about the effort the Mechanicals put into their play.	Oberon is on good footing with Puck but knows that he needs to keep him on a short leash. His relationship with Titania's fairies (who are surely also his subjects) is less clear, but possibly hostile.
What might the Athenian Court learn from the Fairy Court?	Theseus appears tame and rational in comparison to Oberon. If Fairyland is a subconscious reflection of Athens, then Theseus is repressing his emotions. He needs to show more passion – also to win over Hippolyta. Theseus should possibly try to find more creative solutions to the problems he faces.	
What might the Fairy Court learn from the Athenian Court?	Oberon could learn to be more magnanimous and not dominate so aggressively (if he needs to dominate Titania). He should try to rule more fairly and consistently, rather than on a whim.	

THE RHYTHM OF SHAKESPEARE'S LANGUAGE
TEACHERS' VERSION

Solution (page 44)

X	>X<	X	>X<	X	>X<	X	>X<	X	>X<		
The	lun-	a-	tic,	the	lov-	er,	and	the	poet,		
Are	of	i-	mag-	in-	a-	tion	all	com-	pact:		
One	sees	more	de-	vils	than	vast	hell	can	hold;		
That	is	the	mad-	man:	the	lo-	ver,	all	as	fran-	tic,
Sees	He-	len's	beau-	ty	in	a	brow	of	E-	gypt:	
The	po-	et's	eye,	in	a	fine	fren-	zy	ro-	lling,	
Doth	glance	from	hea-	ven	to	earth,	from	earth	to	hea-	ven;
And	as	i-	mag-	in-	a-	tion	bo-	dies	forth		
The	forms	of	things	un-	known,	the	po-	et's	pen		
Turns	them	to	shapes	and	gives	to	air-	y	no-	thing	
A	lo-	cal	ha-	bi-	ta-	tion,	and	a	name		

QUINCE SPEAKS THE PROLOGUE
TEACHERS' VERSION

Solution (page 45)

If we offend, it is with our good will
that you should think we come, not to offend,
but with good will to show our simple skill:
that is the true beginning of our end.
Consider then, we come (but in despite
we do not come) as minding to content you.
Our true intent is all for your delight.
We are not here that you should here repent you.
The actors are at hand and by their show
you shall know all that you are like to know.

THE GROUPS AND THEIR LANGUAGE
TEACHERS' VERSION

Solution (pages 46-47)

The character's words	What does the poetic form tell us about the character?
ATHENIAN COURT	
THESEUS (talking to Hippolyta in Act I Scene 1) Now, fair Hippolyta, our nuptial hour Draws on apace: four happy days bring in Another moon; but, O, methinks, how slow This old moon wanes! she lingers my desires, Like to a step-dame, or a dowager, Long withering out a young man's revenue.	What can you say about the rhythm and rhyme? **blank verse: unrhymed iambic pentameter (5 stresses per line).** What effect does this mode of speaking have? **Slow rhythm without rhyme makes it sound serious and grave. Suits a ruler. Sounds like what he says is important, like he is someone who should be listened to.**
FAIRIES	
TITANIA (rebuking Oberon in Act II Scene 1) And never, since the middle summer's spring, Met we on hill, in dale, forest or mead, By paved fountain or by rushy brook, Or in the beached margent of the sea, To dance our ringlets to the whistling wind, But with thy brawls thou hast disturb'd our sport.	What can you say about the rhythm and rhyme? **almost pure iambic pentameter ("forest or mead" has an extra unstressed syllable in it), unrhymed; blank verse again (5 stresses per line).** What effect does this mode of speaking have? **As with Theseus, this form makes Titania sound serious. As she is arguing with Oberon, this form underlines the gravity of the argument and also her strong words and position.**
TITANIA (talking to her fairies in Act III Scene 1) Come, wait upon him; lead him to my bower. The moon, methinks, looks with a watery eye; And when she weeps, weeps every little flower, Lamenting some enforced chastity. Tie up my love's tongue, bring him silently.	What can you say about the rhythm and rhyme? **5 stresses per line again (iambic pentameter), but this time the lines rhyme: some are rhyming couplets.** What effect does this mode of speaking have? **This is more lyrical, more like a song. At home and with her lover, Titania sounds softer. She is in love, which might also explain the rhyme, which adds flow and softness.**
PUCK (alone in Act II Scene 2) Through the forest have I gone, But Athenian found I none, On whose eyes I might approve This flower's force in stirring love. Night and silence – who is here? Weeds of Athens he doth wear: This is he, my master said, Despised the Athenian maid; And here the maiden, sleeping sound, On the dank and dirty ground.	What can you say about the rhythm and rhyme? **4 stresses per line, basically iambic tetrameter, but many irregularities. Lines rhyme as rhyming couplets.** What effect does this mode of speaking have? **Four feet per line make the lines faster, more racy. This is underlined by the rhyming couplets, which speed the lines along. The whole atmosphere is of jerky (due to metrical irregularities) speed and quirkiness – a good mirror of how Puck is.**

THE GROUPS AND THEIR LANGUAGE
TEACHERS' VERSION

Solution (pages 47-48)

The character's words	What does the poetic form tell us about the character?
PUCK (talking to Oberon in Act III Scene 2) Near to her close and consecrated bower, While she was in her dull and sleeping hour, A crew of patches, rude Mechanicals, That work for bread upon Athenian stalls, Were met together to rehearse a play, Intended for great Theseus' nuptial day.	What can you say about the rhythm and rhyme? **5 stresses per line – pure (with exception of "Theseus") iambic pentameter. Once again the lines rhyme as rhyming couplets.**
	What effect does this mode of speaking have? **Puck is more serious here; he is, after all, talking to his master. Although he cannot suppress his rhyme and the speeding of one line into the next, the five stresses give his lines a more serious tone.**
MECHANICALS	
PETER QUINCE (talking to the Mechanicals in Act I Scene 2) Here is the scroll of every man's name, which is thought fit, through all Athens, to play in our interlude before the duke and the duchess, on his wedding-day at night.	What can you say about the rhythm and rhyme? **There is neither rhythm nor rhyme in this – this is prose.**
	What effect does this mode of speaking have? **Prose – as a more pedestrian way of speaking – suits the Mechanicals. They are simple people, so they speak simply, in prose rather than in verse like all the other characters.**
BOTTOM (as Pyramus in the play, Act V Scene 1) But stay, O spite! But mark, poor knight, What dreadful dole is here? Eyes, do you see? How can it be? O dainty duck! O dear! Thy mantle good, What! stain'd with blood? Approach, ye Furies fell! O Fates, come, come; Cut thread and thrum; Quail, crush, conclude, and quell!	What can you say about the rhythm and rhyme? **Lines with 2 stresses alternate with lines of 3 stresses, all iambs. The lines rhyme (rhyming couplets).**
	What effect does this mode of speaking have? **The lines are so short, they cannot build meaning well and therefore sound more like bursts than real speech. In addition the rhymes are quite simple, which – together with the rhythm and line length – makes this sound quite ridiculous. This suits the Mechanicals' play, which is meant to sound ridiculous.**
LOVERS	
HERMIA (talking to Lysander in Act I Scene 1) I swear to thee, by Cupid's strongest bow, By his best arrow with the golden head, By the simplicity of Venus' doves, By that which knitteth souls and prospers loves, And by that fire which burn'd the Carthage queen, When the false Trojan under sail was seen, By all the vows that ever men have broke, In number more than ever women spoke: In that same place thou hast appointed me, To-morrow truly will I meet with thee.	What can you say about the rhythm and rhyme? **5 stresses per line: iambic pentameter (pure). Although her initial speech does not rhyme, as she professes her love for Lysander, Hermia starts to rhyme.**
	What effect does this mode of speaking have? **Depending on the subject matter, the lovers sometimes rhyme, sometimes don't. Here, the rhyme softens the gravity of the pentameter and makes the lines softer, and they cling together more. The pentameter shows she is careful in what she says and talks in a considered manner. She is therefore a lover who is intellectually in control of the situation.**

ANTITHESIS
TEACHERS' VERSION

Solution (page 49)

LYSANDER

The course of true love never did run smooth;

But, either it was different in blood,--

HERMIA

O cross! too **high** to be enthrall'd to low!

LYSANDER

Or else misgraffed in respect of years,--

HERMIA

O spite! too **old** to be engag'd to young!

HELENA

O, that your **frowns** would teach my smiles such skill!

HERMIA

I give him curses, yet he gives me love.

HELENA

O, that my prayers could such affection move!

HERMIA

The more I **hate**, the more he follows me.

HELENA

The more I **love**, the more he hateth me.

BOTTOM'S "BOTTOMISMS"
TEACHERS' VERSION

Solution (page 50)

	What word should he have used?	What does the word he has used mean?
You were best to call them generally, man by man (I.2)	individually or severally	as a whole group, involving all
but I will aggravate my voice so, that I will roar you as gently as any sucking dove (I.2)	moderate	make worse / make more harsh
and there we may rehearse, most obscenely and courageously (I.2)	seemingly (may be inspired by them acting scenes)	in an indecent or disgusting way
he himself must speak through, saying thus, or to the same defect, (III.1)	effect	shortcoming or imperfection
or else one must [...] and say, he comes to disfigure, or to present, the person of Moonshine (III.1 – Quince)	figure	spoil the appearance of
I have an exposition of sleep come upon me (IV.1)	disposition to	a full description and explanation of something; a large public showing of art
Since lion vile hath here deflower'd my dear (V.1)	devoured	to deflower is to take away the virginity of a woman, often against her will

THE LOVERS' (AND OTHERS') INSULTS
TEACHERS' VERSION

Solution (page 53)

Hermia vs. Demetrius
Out, dog! Out, cur! (III.2, 66)

Hermia vs. Helena
You juggler! You canker-blossom! You thief of love! (III.2, 284-5)
thou painted maypole (III.2, 298)

Demetrius vs. Lysander
Thou runaway, thou coward (III.2, 407)

Lysander vs. Hermia
Away, you Ethiope! (III.2, 259)
Hang off, thou cat, thou burr! Vile thing, let loose (III.2, 262)
Out, tawny Tartar, out! Out loathed medicine! O hated potion, hence! (III.2, 265-6)
Get you gone, you dwarf; you minimus, of hindering knot-grass made; you bead, you acorn. (III.2, 330-3)

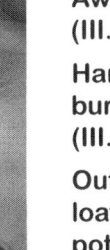

Helena vs. Hermia
Injurious Hermia! Most ungrateful maid! (III.2, 196)
You counterfeit, you puppet, you! (III.2, 290)
She was a vixen, when she went to school (III.2, 326)

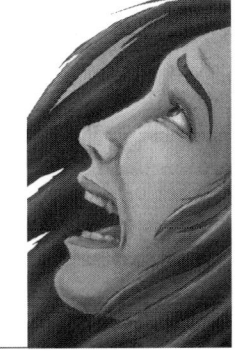

Who is insulting whom?	The insult
Egeus vs. Lysander	Scornful Lysander! (I.1, 91)
Titania vs. Oberon	What, jealous Oberon! (II.1, 61)
Oberon vs. Titania	Ill met by moonlight, proud Titania. (II.1, 60) Tarry, rash wanton. (II.1, 63)

EXPLORING ACT 1 SCENE 1
TEACHERS' VERSION

Solution (page 55)

Themes	Evidence from the text	Explain relevance of evidence
Love & Marriage	Theseus announces he will marry Hippolyta in four days; he won her in war and intends to make her love him through pomp.	The nuptials of Theseus are the backdrop for the whole play. It provides the reason for the Mechanicals' play. His marriage is one aspect of marriage – the state wedding, which has little to do with love.
Love & Marriage	Egeus wants Hermia to marry his choice of husband although she is in love with someone else.	Marriage here seems to run counter to love, and we have here the makings of a tragedy (cf. *Romeo & Juliet* and *Pyramus & Thisbe*) if not for the events in the wood.
Obedience	Theseus, as ruler of Athens, expects obedience from his subjects, and Egeus reinforces this: "with duty and desire we follow you".	Theseus eventually overrules Egeus – but is also prepared to do what he must. Obedience goes both ways. Without strict obedience the world would end in chaos, as shown by the quarrel of Titania and Oberon.
Obedience	Hermia is not prepared to submit to her father and actually wishes him to obey her: "I would my father looked but with my eyes"	Love is stronger than any other bonds. That she is willing to risk everything for love leads to the lovers being in the woods. She is obedient to love (once again this could lead to tragedy as in *Pyramus & Thisbe*).
Obedience	Lysander and Hermia plan to escape the laws of Athens and thus the need to obey Theseus's injunction.	Obedience cannot be given when it goes against fundamental personal feeling. The only solution seems to be to flee.
Dreams	Hippolyta says about the wait till they are married, "Four nights will quickly dream away the time".	Dreams are entertaining and while away the time – the whole play can be seen as a dream (cf. the epilogue).
Dreams	Dreams belong to love, as do thoughts and sighs.	Suggests that lovers and dreamers are connected – as we shall see: the antics of the lovers seem to be dreams to them.
Imagination (the mind's eye)	Hermia wants her father to see Lysander with her eyes (and Theseus tells her she must see Demetrius with her father's eyes).	That beauty is in the eye of the beholder is a cliché that is particularly relevant to the play. The flower's juice has to be smeared into the eye, underlining how eyesight is altered by love.
Imagination (the mind's eye)	Helen wishes she were "Hermia's fair" rather than her own fair, as Demetrius is attracted to the former.	Once again shows there is no impartiality in love and that beauty is subjective. This will be played out in detail in the woods as both men's perceptions are altered by the flower.
Imagination (the mind's eye)	Helena muses on love and the fact that Cupid is blind.	This is true not only of the lovers, but in particular of Titania, who does not truly see whom she has fallen in love with.

HAPPY EVER AFTER?
TEACHERS' VERSION

Solution (page 57)

Couple	Will they live on happily?	Evidence from the text
Theseus & Hippolyta	They will stay married, but whether happily or not is less easy to predict. She loves her freedom, so will not enjoy the confines of marriage. Theseus seems intent on pleasing her, so the beginning should be happy. However, Theseus is a philanderer, and therefore it seems likely that in time he will wander and she will grow frustrated and go hunting on her own; maybe she will have affairs, too.	Hippolyta does not have a large role but seems to accept her situation (I.1), suggesting the marriage – as a state affair – will stay. Speech about hounds suggests she misses hunting and the freedom of it (IV.1). Theseus refers to her frequently (I.1, IV.1). Oberon lists Theseus's lovers in Act II Scene 1.
Lysander & Hermia	They will be happy as they seem devoted to each other and genuinely love one another. The episode in the woods may linger on and lead to awkward questions later, but both seem happy to accept that as a dream.	Both were prepared to run away together and build a new life away from Athens (I.1). Lysander immediately returns to Hermia and does not seem to miss Helena on waking (IV.1). Hermia never believed Lysander would forsake her of his own will (III.1 and 2), so she trusts him.
Demetrius & Helena	Possibly, but not as assured as Lysander and Hermia: Demetrius, thanks to the potion, cannot do anything but dote on her. Although Helena reciprocates this feeling, it is not clear how she will deal with a clinging Demetrius later in life. She will fall out of love and maybe learn to love Demetrius, but will she be able to put up with a continually doting Demetrius?	Demetrius can but dote (III.2 and II.1); Helena also dotes on him (I.1 and II.1). Doting (the feeling of being in love) usually gives way to more mature love; with Demetrius it can't. This could be a source of later problems, as Helena, when she dotes, is barely tolerable to ordinary humans (II.1).
Oberon & Titania	The two seem reconciled. Their love and passion for one another was never in doubt, so as king and queen they will be happy. However, it is to be expected that they will continue to have spats and disagree quite forcefully, making up again soon afterward.	Reconciliation in Act IV Scene 1. Oberon's continued passion is evident in Act IV Scene 1, too. Oberon is "jealous", and he is intent on having Titania obey him (II.1). She is independent of him and a power in her own right (II.1 and III.1). Further conflicts therefore seem inevitable.

LYSANDER LOVES AND DOTES
TEACHERS' VERSION

Solution (page 58)

Lysander loves Hermia	Lysander dotes on Helena
Act I Scene 1: Lysander plans to escape from Athens: therefore, hear me, Hermia. I have a widow aunt, a dowager Of great revenue, and she hath no child: From Athens is her house remote seven leagues; And she respects me as her only son. There, gentle Hermia, may I marry thee, And to that place the sharp Athenian law Cannot pursue us. If thou lov'st me then, Steal forth thy father's house to-morrow night, And in the wood, a league without the town (Where I did meet thee once with Helena, To do observance to a morn of May), There will I stay for thee.	Act II Scene 2: Lysander wakes to fall in love with Helena and then explains why he loves her now: And run through fire I will for thy sweet sake. Transparent Helena! Nature here shows art, That through thy bosom makes me see thy heart. [...] Content with Hermia! No; I do repent The tedious minutes I with her have spent. Not Hermia, but Helena I love. Who will not change a raven for a dove? The will of man is by his reason sway'd; And reason says you are the worthier maid. [...] Reason becomes the marshal to my will, And leads me to your eyes; where I o'erlook Love's stories, written in love's richest book.
Act II Scene 2: Lysander and Hermia are lost in the wood and they decide to rest. He tries to sleep next to Hermia: Fair love, you faint with wand'ring in the wood; And, to speak troth, I have forgot our way: We'll rest us, Hermia, if you think it good, And tarry for the comfort of the day. [...] O, take the sense, sweet, of my innocence! Love takes the meaning in love's conference. I mean, that my heart unto yours is knit. So that but one heart we can make of it: Two bosoms interchained with an oath; So then, two bosoms, and a single troth. Then, by your side no bed-room me deny; For, lying so, Hermia, I do not lie.	Act III Scene 2: Lysander is still trying to persuade Helena that he loves her more than Demetrius, who also dotes on Helena now: And yours of Helena to me bequeath, Whom I do love, and will do till my death. [...] Fair Helena, who more engilds the night Than all you fiery oes and eyes of light. [...] Stay, gentle Helena! hear my excuse: [...] Helen, I love thee; by my life, I do: I swear by that which I will lose for thee, To prove him false, that says I love thee not.

LYSANDER LOVES AND DOTES
TEACHERS' VERSION

Solution (page 58 cont'd)

Lysander loves Hermia	Lysander dotes on Helena
How does he address each woman?	
Hermia, gentle Hermia, fair love, sweet	transparent Helena, fair Helena, gentle Helena, Helen
Comparison: While the names appear to be very similar, what Lysander calls Hermia seems to focus more on character (sweet, gentle), and Helena's appellations focus more on her looks (transparent, fair). Both are called gentle, and this may be to calm them rather than as a marker of their character. Furthermore, the "fair" he calls both could in one case be applied to character (Hermia), in the other to looks (Helena), as the love potion bewitches his eyes.	
What imagery does he use? What for?	
When planning the escape he uses very straightforward language – this is administration rather than lovers' talk. When trying to persuade Hermia, his language becomes more metaphorical with images of true love: hearts knitted and chained together.	His language is exaggerated and full of imagery, mainly comparing Helena to other natural phenomena and finding them wanting. He uses a lot of comparatives and superlatives, too.
Comparison: When talking to Hermia, Lysander's language is mainly quite plain, although he does employ (quite clever, but commonplace) metaphors when trying to persuade her. This may have to do with the fact that the wooing is over and they are secure in each other's love, making 'flowery' language unnecessary. With Helena, Lysander has to try to convince her of his love, and he uses hyperbole for this and an excessive praise of her looks.	
Are there any differences in emotion? Explain how you can tell.	
This seems to be a more settled relationship with openness and honesty, with no need to impress or make compliments the whole time. He does not use complicated metaphors, and he talks very honestly when planning their escape. When he tries to persuade her to share a bed with him, he employs more intricate language, but this is not exaggerated.	His language is marked by frequent exclamations and "do or die" statements about his love and Helena's beauty. As such, the language does not ring as true as when Lysander is in love. One almost has the feeling he could be talking to any woman.

LOVE AND REASON
TEACHERS' VERSION

Solution (page 59)

Titania
I pray thee, gentle mortal, sing again:
Mine ear is much enamour'd of thy note;
So is mine eye enthralled to thy shape;
And thy fair virtue's force, perforce, doth move me,
On the first view to say, to swear, I love thee.

Bottom
Methinks, mistress, you should have little reason for that: and yet, to say the truth, reason and love keep little company together now-a-days; the more the pity, that some honest neighbours will not make them friends. Nay, I can gleek upon occasion.

Titania
Thou art as wise as thou art beautiful.

Bottom
Not so, neither: but if I had wit enough to get out of this wood, I have enough to serve mine own turn.

Titania
Out of this wood do not desire to go:
Thou shalt remain here, whether thou wilt or no.
I am a spirit of no common rate:
The summer still doth tend upon my state;
And I do love thee: therefore, go with me;
I'll give thee fairies to attend on thee; […]
And I will purge thy mortal grossness so,
That thou shalt like an airy spirit go.

What characteristics of Bottom does Titania say she is in love with?
His voice, his figure, and his wit / wisdom.

What tells us that she realises he is not quite a fit companion?
She wants to make him a fairy, to "purge" his mortal roughness. This suggests that him being a mortal somehow bothers her.

How do we know Titania – though besotted – is still a powerful queen, not to be crossed?
"Thou shalt remain here" is an imperious command. She also has a fairy train which she is willing to put at his service, but which she can equally use to keep him with her.

Why is Titania's love unreasonable?
It is quite obvious that Bottom has none of the things she says she is in love with. There is therefore no sound basis for her love, making it unreasonable.

LOVE AND REASON
TEACHERS' VERSION

Solution (page 60)

Lysander The will of man is by his reason sway'd, And reason says you are the worthier maid. Things growing are not ripe until their season: So I, being young, till now ripe not to reason; And touching now the point of human skill, Reason becomes the marshal to my will, And leads me to your eyes; where I o'erlook Love's stories, written in love's richest book.	How does Lysander explain his change of feelings? **He has grown up. With his full faculty of reason he now knows (intellectually) that Helena is the worthier woman.**
	Why do you think he uses reason as an argument? **Reason is something very difficult to dispute. If someone argues logically, it is much harder to argue against that. Also, it sounds more serious.**
	What could you say against this argument? **Lysander won't have grown up in one night. Maturing is a process that takes time and therefore cannot account for a sudden shift in affection. Also, he does not explain the reasons for Helena being "worthier". Besides, falling in love has little to do with reason.**
Demetrius But, my good lord, I wot not by what power,– But by some power it is,– my love to Hermia, Melted as the snow, seems to me now As the remembrance of an idle gaud, Which in my childhood I did dote upon; And all the faith, the virtue of my heart, The object and the pleasure of mine eye, Is only Helena. To her, my lord, Was I betroth'd ere I saw Hermia: But, like a sickness, did I loathe this food; But, as in health, come to my natural taste, Now I do wish it, love it, long for it, And will for evermore be true to it.	How does Demetrius explain that he loves Helena once again? **On the one hand he seems to suggest, like Lysander, that he has grown up and discarded his childhood folly of Hermia. On the other, he likens his loving of Hermia to a sickness that intervened in his healthy state of loving Helena (before he became "sick with Hermia" and afterwards, having been cured by the love potion)**
	Why is the image of "sickness" particularly apt? **When doting on someone, it is often said one is lovesick. As his love for Hermia was not returned, he was, in fact, lovesick (though not in the way he now maintains).**
	What could you say against his argument? **The argument brought against Lysander about growing up can be used here as well. Furthermore, loving someone cannot be described as a sickness – it is not a bodily disposition that can easily be altered. In the end, the most one can do is say – like Demetrius – that "by some power" that must remain unknown, his love has changed. It has nothing to do with reason, growing up, or convalescing, though.**

STAR-CROSSED LOVERS
TEACHERS' VERSION

Solution (page 61)

Question:	Hermia & Lysander	Pyramus & Thisbe	Romeo & Juliet
Who is against their marriage and why?	Hermia's father, Egeus, and – because Egeus evokes the law of Athens – Theseus, Duke of Athens, their ruler, too. We don't know why Egeus is against Lysander marrying Hermia, except that he wants her to marry Demetrius.	We only know of the wall, but this suggests that both their parents are against the relationship.	Both families are against them even associating with one another, as the Montagues and Capulets are sworn enemies
How do they attempt to overcome the opposition to their love?	They agree to meet in the woods at night and then flee from Athens to a rich aunt of Lysander. They will live there, as the law of Athens does not apply in that region.	They agree to meet outside the town, at Ninus' (Ninny's!) tomb. We do not know whether this was merely to be able to meet one another or whether they planned to elope.	They marry in secret and plan on leaving Verona with the help of Friar Laurence. He puts Juliet into a death-like sleep and plans on getting her to Romeo that way.
Does the plan work?	Because of Helena, they are followed into the woods by Lysander's rival in love, Demetrius. They also lose their way and are discovered the next morning by Theseus and Egeus – so superficially, the plan does not work.	Thisbe is first at the tomb and runs away as a lion is there. It mauls her mantle. Pyramus finds it and, believing Thisbe has been killed by a lion, kills himself. Thisbe finds his body and kills herself too.	Romeo is not told of the plan, and on seeing Juliet he believes her truly dead, so he kills himself. Juliet wakes up to find Romeo dead and kills herself as well.
What is the outcome?	Hermia and Lysander marry, as Demetrius gives up his claim to Hermia, and Theseus then overrules Egeus.	The lovers are both dead (both having committed suicide).	The lovers are both dead (both having committed suicide).
What is the main reason for this outcome?	Demetrius gives up his claim to Hermia as he magically falls in love with Helena, due to the magic flower juice.	The lion, forcing Pyramus to jump to the wrong conclusion.	The letter of Friar Laurence to tell Romeo of the plan did not reach him (so Friar John, the messenger, is at fault).

WHO MUST OBEY WHOM?
TEACHERS' VERSION

Solution (page 63)

The Athenians

Theseus
Marries Hippolyta to subjugate her; orders Hermia to obey her father and ordains that all lovers will be wedded with him.

Hippolyta
Does not complain of her role and seems to accept Theseus's dominance.

Egeus
Seeks Theseus's protection, carries out his orders and lets himself be overruled.

Lysander
Accepts the common nuptials but is not prepared to accept his ruling concerning Hermia.

Demetrius
Accepts all of Theseus's rulings and is prepared to carry out his work.

Hermia
At beginning owes obedience to father, which she refuses, as it goes against her feelings. After marriage, owes obedience to Lysander.

The Fairies

Oberon
Orders Puck around and makes Titania pay for disobeying him.

Puck
Jests for Oberon and also carries out his will concerning the lovers.

Titania
Refuses to obey Oberon to give him the changeling; when punished, accepts her role as his queen.

I SPY WITH MY LITTLE EYE
TEACHERS' VERSION

Solution (page 65)

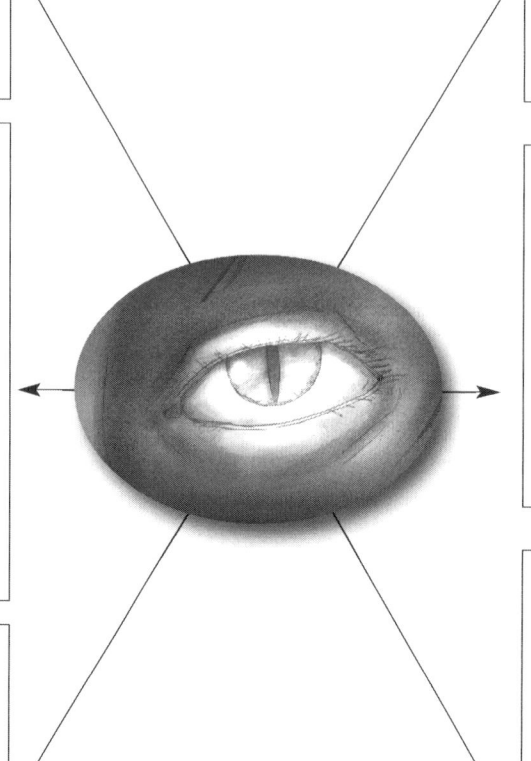

Hermia
Theseus asks her to look with her father's eyes and see Demetrius as a worthy husband. The fact that she refuses leads all the lovers into the woods.

Demetrius
a) Helena wishes he could see her with the eyes of all of Athens, who deem her fair (I.1).
b) Due to the love potion, he sees Helena with the eyes of doting, which leads to the two marrying. This paves the way for Hermia and Lysander to marry.

The Athenian Court
The Mechanicals ask them to believe the wall is a real wall, the lion not a lion, and that a man is the man in the moon. The irony is that they do not trust the audience's imagination.

Lysander
Due to the love potion, he looks with the eyes of doting on Helena. This leads to chaos and confusion (and comedy) in the woods. This change is reversed.

Titania
Due to the love potion, she looks with the eyes of doting on the ass-headed Bottom. This makes her give up the changeling boy and reconciles Oberon to her.

Egeus
Hermia asks him to look with her eyes to see that Lysander is as worthy a husband as Demetrius. His refusal leads to Hermia's flight and to Theseus overruling him at the end, ultimately allowing Hermia to marry Lysander.

WHO IS DREAMING WHAT?
TEACHERS' VERSION

Solution (page 66)

Who does the dream apply to?	Evidence from the text & content of the dream	Relevance of the dream
Theseus (I.1)	"Four nights will quickly dream away the time" The content of the dream is unknown – the purpose is that the four long nights that Theseus is bemoaning until his wedding will pass quickly, as he will dream – shortening the time.	As the play covers the time until the wedding and is titled "Dream", it seems that in a certain way a dream does shorten the time until the wedding. Also, to shorten the time until the wedding night, Theseus watches a play – "shadows" – which is reminiscent of a dream.
Hermia (II.2)	"What a dream was here! … Methought a serpent ate my heart away, / And you sat smiling at his cruel prey" Hermia, left alone by Lysander, dreams a snake slithered onto her breast to eat her heart, and Lysander, her love, did nothing to stop it.	This is the only real dream in the play. The dream seems to warn Hermia that Lysander has gone. The snake is an image of cunning that hurts her heart; it is cunning (Helena's art – so she believes) that lures Lysander away from her, leaving her heart wounded. As such the dream is not accurate, but possibly it is due to this dream that Hermia later blames Helena for having stolen Lysander from her.
Lovers (IV.1)	"May all to Athens back again repair, / And think no more of this night's accidents / But as the fierce vexation of a dream" (Oberon) "and by the way let us recount our dreams" (Demetrius) On waking the morning after the goings-on in the woods, the lovers all have the feeling they have been dreaming.	Oberon foretells that the lovers will believe all that happened to them was a dream (does he enchant them?). Indeed, this is what happens, probably because seeing it all as a dream is the easiest way to deal with it. If it was all a dream, Lysander can avoid searching questions from Hermia about his crush on Helena, and Helena and Hermia's friendship can remain intact. In this sense it is a *deus ex machina* solution (like at the end of a lot of pupils' stories: "Then I woke up: it was all a dream").

WHO IS DREAMING WHAT?
TEACHERS' VERSION

Solution (page 67)

Who does the dream apply to?	Evidence from the text & content of the dream	Relevance of the dream
Bottom (IV.1)	"I have had a most rare vision" Bottom thinks his experience with Titania has all been a dream. To what extent he ever realised he had an ass's head on is open to debate.	The dream quality here has more to do with the absolute unreality of what he has been through: being transformed and also the lover of the fairy queen. This puts encounters with fairies safely in the realm of dreams – meaning one doesn't have to deal with them. The experience does not seem to have changed him.
Titania (IV.1)	"My Oberon! what visions have I seen!" When woken from her trance induced by the love potion, she thinks that her loving a donkey was nothing but a dream.	Oberon shows Titania Bottom with the donkey's head, and she realises she has not been dreaming (she is the only affected character to realise that the happenings have not been a dream). This probably shocks her as it means there is no easy way to deal with what has happened. Titania realises how far Oberon is prepared to go to get his own way and is reconciled to him.
Audience (epilogue)	"And this weak and idle theme, / No more yielding but a dream" The whole play should be seen as having no more importance than a dream, if the audience is not pleased with it.	This is a somewhat puzzling request, as it calls into question the whole play and what Shakespeare is trying to tell us. On the other hand, the play is called "A Dream". Saying it should be seen as no more important than a dream makes us wonder what kind of dream – dreams can be taken very seriously as a reflection of the dreamer's psyche (or, in a more Elizabethan vein, as a prophetic vision). Also, if the play was all a dream, perhaps Shakespeare is suggesting our whole lives are but dreams – a thought elaborated in the film *The Matrix*.

CHASTE DIANA
TEACHERS' VERSION

Solution (page 69)

Extract	What does the extract mean?
Theseus, bewailing the fact that time passes too slowly until his wedding day (I.1) but, O, methinks, how slow This old moon wanes! She lingers my desires, Like to a step-dame, or a dowager, Long withering out a young man's revenue.	He suggests the moon (representing chastity, possibly) does not want him to marry quickly. The moon is like an old woman preventing a young man achieving his desire (i.e. marrying) by drawing out the moment he will receive his inheritance (enabling him to marry).
Theseus, describing to Hermia what fate awaits her, should she disobey her father (I.1) For aye to be in shady cloister mew'd, To live a barren sister all your life, Chanting faint hymns to the cold fruitless moon.	The adjectives used here have a strong negative connotation: it is obvious that for Theseus, living life as a nun is but a pale reflection of what a woman should do in life – marry. "Faint hymns" suggest that the songs are ineffective; a sentiment repeated by the "fruitless moon". Basically, Theseus is saying that as a nun, Hermia would fulfil no purpose and be wasted.
Oberon, describing how the flower "love-in-idleness" gained its power from Cupid's arrow (II.1) And loos'd his love-shaft smartly from his bow, As it should pierce a hundred thousand hearts. But I might see young Cupid's fiery shaft Quench'd in the chaste beams of the wat'ry moon	Oberon is describing how the flower received its power: Cupid was aiming at a fair virgin (often thought to be a reference to Elizabeth I), but the arrow was ineffectual, the chaste moon having put out its fire and thus its power to make the virgin fall in love. Here the moon is being called chaste, reinforcing the imagery of chastity. The fiery shaft quenched is like the dousing of ardent love in cold indifference, the quenching being reinforced by the "watery" moon – the cold shower that extinguishes strong desire.
Titania, enamoured, before she retires with Bottom (III.1) The moon, methinks, looks with a watery eye; And when she weeps, weeps every little flower, Lamenting some enforced chastity.	Here the chaste moon spreads dew on the land, which is seen as it crying. Titania, her lover in her arm, says the moon is crying because it is forced to remain chaste, when obviously all else is attuned to love. The phrase is ambiguous, though, and could also mean that the moon is weeping because its chastity has been violated. This double-meaning would fit in the sense that Titania's loyal love to Oberon (marital chastity) has been violated by her being forced to fall in love with Bottom.
Oberon, applying the cure for the love potion into Titania's eyes (IV.1) Be, as thou wast wont to be; See, as thou wast wont to see: Dian's bud o'er Cupid's flower Hath such force and blessed power.	Oberon seems to pronounce that chastity (Dian's bud) is stronger than the folly of love (Cupid's flower). Chastity is here seen as a positive trait that carries with it the power to resist love (as in II.1, above). For Titania it suggests a return to "chastity" (marital fidelity) from her night of mad doting on a monster, suggesting a connection to the moon goddess.

THESEUS'S SPEECH ON LOVERS, POETS AND MADMEN
TEACHERS' VERSION

Solution (page 70)

Why would a madman see devils? What connotation does this give to the madman?
This makes madmen seem more evil and apart from God – it makes them outcasts of society (which may reflect on lovers and poets, too).

Note the many references to eyes and seeing – how does this relate to the rest of the play?
Theseus suggests that the three groups see with their own eyes and do not see what "normal" people see, but only what they imagine.

Does "cool reason" sound positive or negative? Explain.
Cool reason is devoid of emotion, but it sounds quite detached and not desirable. We prefer warmth to cold or cool. So, in a way, Theseus is possibly not entirely convinced of his argument.

Who is the Helen being referred to here? The one from the play, or another? Why Egypt?
Although Helena is called Helen by both Lysander and Demetrius, Theseus is referring to Helen of Troy, renowned for her beauty. Here, he is comparing her against one of dark-skinned complexion, thought in Shakespeare's day to be unattractive.

What does the poet do with his pen?
He makes up imaginary places, people and creatures, and makes them seem like they really exist.

Is the poet more like the lover or the madman?
As the poet creates and sees things others don't, whereas the lover only changes how they see others, it seems the poet is more like a madman – seeing things that aren't there.

Do these last lines refer to poets only or to all three? Explain.
This is unclear. Could refer only to the poet, but could also refer to all three, making the bond between them closer. The two lines ending in "joy" could easily apply to lovers, too. The last two lines could be a reference to the *Pyramus and Thisbe* story, where the lovers are interrupted by a wild beast.

What do the words "frantic" and "fine frenzy" suggest?
That the three are almost in a fever, in a heightened state of emotions and thought, that possibly produces the visions.

CHARACTERISTIC ONE-LINERS
TEACHERS' VERSION

Solution (page 77)

Theseus	But, O, methinks, how slow this old moon wanes
Hippolyta	I never heard so musical a discord, such sweet thunder
Egeus	I beg the ancient privilege of Athens
Oberon	Thou shalt not from this grove, till I torment thee for this injury
Titania	The fairyland buys not the child of me
Robin Goodfellow	I am that merry wanderer of the night
Bottom	If I do it, let the audience look to their eyes
Quince	But, masters, here are your parts
Flute	Nay, faith, let me not play a woman; I have a beard coming
Starveling	All that I have to say, is, to tell you that the lantern is the moon; I, the man i' the moon
Snout	You can never bring in a wall
Snug	Have you the lion's part written? pray you, if it be, give it me, for I am slow of study
Helena	I will fawn on you: use me but as your spaniel
Hermia	I know not by what power I am made bold
Lysander	I am, my lord, as well deriv'd as he
Demetrius	I love thee not, therefore pursue me not

WORD JUMBLE
TEACHERS' VERSION

Solution (page 81)

Slay nerd	Lysander
Tiered Sum	Demetrius
She Suet	Theseus
Happy Toil	Hippolyta
He I Mar	Hermia
An Heel	Helena
She Tan	Athens
Hotplate Sir	Philostrate
Ron Beo	Oberon
I At A Nit	Titania
Wool Go Fled	Goodfellow
To Tomb	Bottom
Nic Que	Quince
Grist V Lane	Starveling
Guns	Snug
Not Us	Snout
Clang Hinge	Changeling
Seated Drums	Mustardseed
Lame Boss Pose	Peaseblossom
Ebb Cow	Cobweb
DI Puc	Cupid
Ms Mire Mud	Midsummer
Things	Nights
Armed	Dream
She Peaks Ear	Shakespeare

CROSSWORD
TEACHERS' VERSION

Solution (page 82)

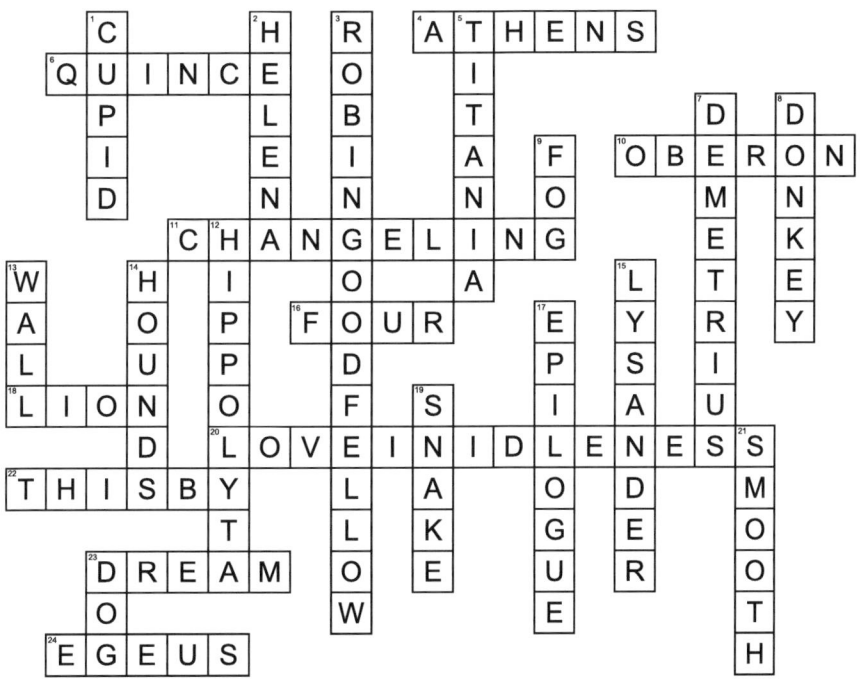

WORD SEARCH
TEACHERS' VERSION

Solution (page 83)

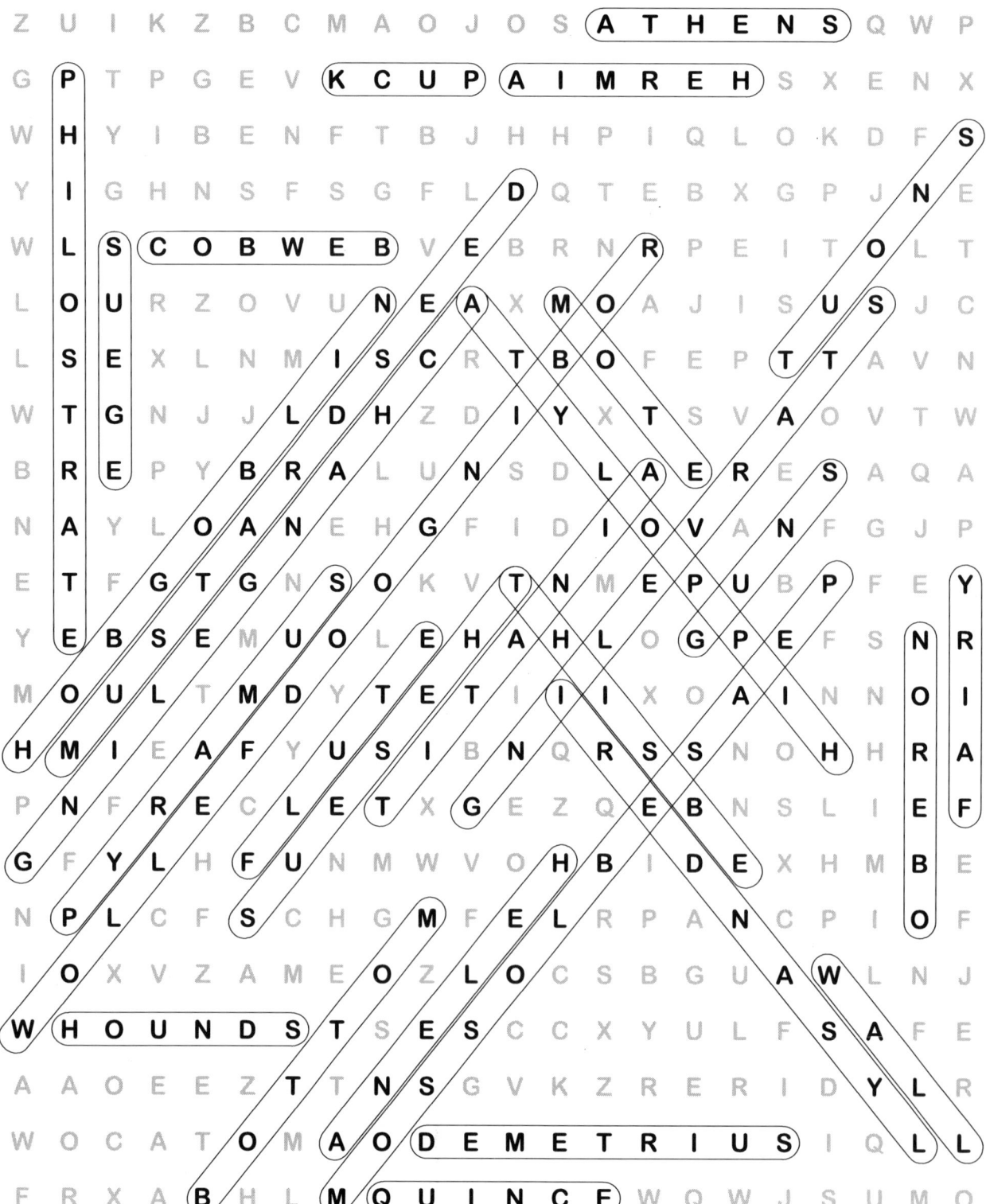

SECOND EDITION

AURALLY CODED ENGLISH

ACE SPELLING ACTIVITIES

DAVID MOSELEY AND GWYN SINGLETON

OVER 100 PHOTOCOPIABLE ACTIVITY SHEETS FOR USE WITH THE *ACE SPELLING DICTIONARY*

FIND WORDS **QUICKLY** AND **IMPROVE** YOUR SPELLING

ACE Spelling Activities (second edition)

ISBN: 978-1-85503-594-2

© David Moseley and Gwyn Singleton 2016
Illustrations by Yuliya Somina/Beehive Illustration

First edition published 1993
This edition published 2016
10 9 8 7 6 5 4

Printed in the UK by Page Bros (Norwich) Ltd
Cover design by Jason Roberts for View Creative Design Agency
Text design and typeset by Andy Wilson for Green Desert Ltd

LDA, 2 Gregory Street, Hyde, Cheshire, SK14 4HR

www.ldalearning.com

The right of David Moseley and Gwyn Singleton to be identified as the authors of this work has been asserted in accordance with Sections 77 and 78 of the Copyright, Designs and Patents Act 1988.

All rights reserved. This book contains materials which may be reproduced by photocopier or other means for use by the purchaser. The permission is granted on the understanding that these copies will be used within the educational establishment of the purchaser. The book and all its contents remain copyright. Copies may be made without reference to the publisher or the licensing scheme for the making of photocopies operated by the Publishers Licensing Society.

Contents

Preface v

Introducing ACE
Counting syllables 1
Learning how to use the *ACE Spelling Dictionary* in three easy lessons 2
More word-finding practice 13

Using ACE
Spellings for sounds 18
Spellings for sounds puzzles 50
Car registration games 61
Tricky word endings 64
Doubles or singles 68
Find the middle syllable 70
Find the two middle syllables 81
Words within words 83
Find the baseword or root 85
Introducing the parts of speech 87
Searching for patterns 93

Learning spellings
Words you need to know 94
Learn to spell these really useful words 97
Slippery Characters 109

Answers 121

All ACE Spelling Activities are suitable for individual work and for working under guidance in pairs or groups. As shown below, many can also be organised as class activities, provided that enough copies of the *ACE Spelling Dictionary* are available.

Activity	Pages	Starting age	Suitable for class work
Counting syllables	1	6	C
Learning how to use the *ACE Spelling Dictionary* in three easy lessons	2–12	6	C*
More word-finding practice	13–17	7	C*
Spellings for sounds	18–49	8	
Spellings for sounds puzzles	50–60	8	
Car registration games	61–63	8	C*
Tricky word endings	64–67	9	C*
Doubles or singles	68–69	9	C*
Find the middle syllable	70–80	9	C*
Find the two middle syllables	81–82	10	C*
Words within words	83–84	8	
Find the baseword or root	85–86	9	C
Introducing the parts of speech	87–92	9	C*
Searching for patterns	93	10	C
Words you need to know	94–96	8	C
Learn to spell these really useful words	97–108	7	
Slippery Characters	109–120	7	

*If these activities are to be done on a class basis, each person will need access to the *ACE Spelling Dictionary*.
All answers can be found on pages 121–143.

Preface

The *ACE Spelling Dictionary* was first published in 1986 and *ACE Spelling Activities* in 1993. Both consistently receive five-star reviews from home and school users who need to check spellings quickly. *ACE Spelling Activities* takes learners beyond looking up words to studying spellings and learning from personal lists. It is designed for users aged seven and above and provides a framework for all learners to get to grips with phonics and the English spelling system. Whilst especially valuable for dyslexic pupils, the ACE resources are designed to improve spelling and writing performance on a whole-school basis.

The 2015 edition of *ACE Spelling Activities* has been slightly adjusted to match the latest revisions of the *ACE Spelling Dictionary*, and a few rather dated references have been replaced. More importantly, the activities now fully cover the English statutory Spelling Lists for Years 3–6. There is a new six-page section, called Slippery Characters, which focuses on 240 frequently misspelt words between five and 13 letters in length. This provides practice in quickly finding words in a syllable column on a specified page of the *ACE Spelling Dictionary* and draws attention to the most tricky parts of word spellings. If words selected from this activity are studied and systematically learned, many misspellings which often persist for a lifetime can be avoided.

Counting syllables

Aim: The student should be able to say how many syllables there are in any spoken word (up to four syllables).

The teacher can work with a group or whole class, asking for individual or group responses. In one-to-one work a partner or teaching assistant can read out the words and say whether the responses are correct. The following three stages should be followed.

1 The teacher or tutor (**T**) says a word slowly and taps out the syllables at the same time. The student repeats the word and taps out the syllables. **T** asks 'How many taps?'. This should be done with the following words.

play-ground	win-dow	ba-na-na	mud	un-for-tu-nate
TAP-TAP	TAP-TAP	TAP-TAP-TAP	TAP	TAP-TAP-TAP-TAP

Repeat more slowly if necessary, with the words in a different order.

2 **T** says a word without tapping and asks the student to repeat the word and tap it out. Each time, **T** asks 'How many taps?'. This is done with words from the following list until ten words are tapped out correctly.

***	newspaper	**	picture	*	paint	****	television
**	spider	*	mice	**	monster	***	dinosaur
**	postman	**	burglar	***	acrobat	****	politician
**	pancake	***	margarine	****	supermarket	**	kitchen
*	crash	****	helicopter	**	rocket	***	motorbike

3 **T** says a word and simply asks 'How many syllables?'. This is done, taking words at random from the list below, until a success rate of 19/20 is obtained.

**	money	*	shop	**	birthday	**	present
**	bedroom	*	door	***	wallpaper	*	stairs
***	holidays	*	weeks	***	underground	****	underwater
***	crocodile	****	alligator	*	shark	**	danger
****	caterpillar	*	moth	***	butterfly	*	eggs
**	rabbit	****	invisible	*	hat	**	magic
*	win	***	manager	**	football	****	competition
****	everybody	**	children	**	mother	***	grandfather
*	clock	**	morning	***	afternoon	***	yesterday
****	mysterious	***	horrible	***	beautiful	***	exciting

Introducing ACE

Learning how to use the *ACE Spelling Dictionary* in three easy lessons

The *ACE Spelling Dictionary* improves spelling and enhances linguistic awareness at all levels of the National Curriculum.

Teachers who adopt the *ACE Spelling Dictionary* for class use are often surprised that their students find it so easy. As soon as students succeed in finding words, the advantages of the Dictionary become self-evident.

The 30-second guide to the *ACE Spelling Dictionary* found on the inside front cover of the Dictionary is an excellent introduction, especially when each student has a copy of the Dictionary. However, this initial demonstration does need to be followed up by practice with the Index page, covering the sounds in each section, and looking up words in the Dictionary itself.

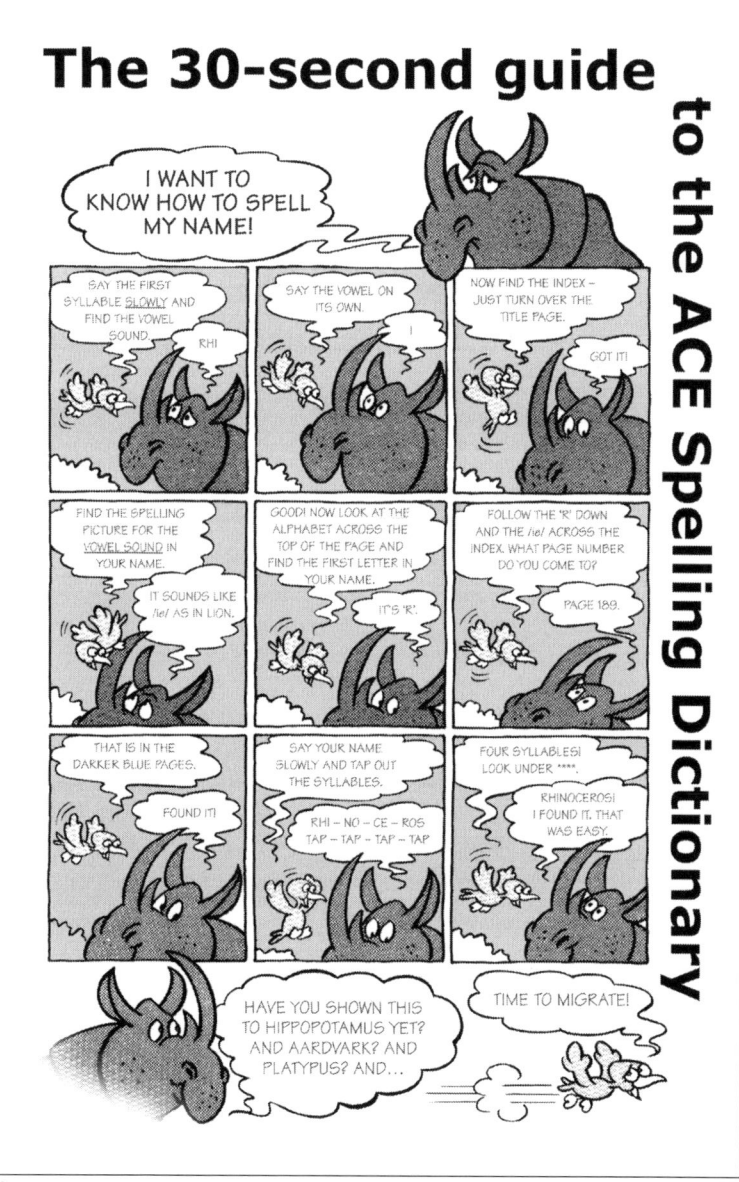

The following three lessons provide the necessary practice and are suitable for both small groups and whole classes. After following three lessons of direct instruction and practice, students should be able to find ten words in under five minutes and should then progress to an average speed of 20 seconds per word.

When introducing the Dictionary on a class basis, at least one copy per table is needed. Each of the lessons covers sounds from different sections of the Index – photocopy masters of these sections are provided so that each student can have their own copy to work with. Teachers may like to make digital copies of these to use in whole-class tuition.

Introducing ACE

Lesson 1

Aims: The student should be able to:
a) identify long vowel sounds in a selection of words
b) use the long vowel sounds part of the Index to find the page numbers for a selection of words
c) look up words in the darker blue part of the dictionary.

1 Begin with listening and speaking activities, starting with the long vowel animal names: **snail**, **eagle**, **lion**, **goat** and **newt**.

Ask the students if they can hear certain vowel sounds in each of these animal names. Use correct and incorrect vowel sounds, for example, 'Can you hear /**ae**/ in **snail**?', 'Can you hear /**ee**/ in **snail**?'

Make the vowel sounds longer and louder if you need to.

Continue until responses are confident and correct and then move on to identifying long vowel sounds in other words. For example, 'Can you hear /**ee**/ in **fine**?', 'Can you hear /**ae**/ in **baby**?'.

Again, continue until responses are confident and correct.

Selecting a long vowel sound, ask students if they can hear the sound in a variety of words. For example, 'Can you hear /**ae**/ in **pail**, **sail**, **tail**, **tile**?'.

Finally, ask students to give you the vowel sound they can hear in the long vowel animal names, giving a choice of three. For example, 'What is the vowel sound in **snail**: /**ae**/, /**ee**/ or /**ie**/?'. Continue with different animals and three vowel sound choices until the sounds in all the long vowel animal names are correctly identified.

2 Practise using the Index to find page numbers. Each student should have a copy of the long vowel part in the middle of the Index (see Index 1 on page 5). Teachers may also like to make a digital copy for class tuition.

Beginning with the animal picture words, ask students first to point to the snail picture next to the letters 'ae' which stand for the sound /**ae**/. Ask which letter **snail** begins with and have them find the letter 'S' in the alphabet across the top of the page. Then, show them how to move one finger along the line of page numbers from /**ae**/ and the other finger down from 'S', until they meet at a page number. **Snail** is on page 149!

Repeat this exercise with **eagle**, **lion**, **goat** and **newt**. You may need to prompt students with the vowel sound initially, but continue the exercise until the page numbers can be found by the students themselves.

Once students can readily achieve this, ask them to find the page numbers for the following animal words: **ape**, **beaver**, **bison**, **mule**, **poodle**, **reindeer**, **sheep**, **snake**, **tiger**, **whale**.

This time they will need to identify the spelling picture for the vowel sound first. For example, what is the first vowel sound in **tiger**? It is /**ie**/, which is the same as in **lion**.

Introducing ACE

Use these topic lists until students have mastered using Index 1 to find page numbers.

bacon, cake, cereal, cheese, doughnut, mousse, pie, steak, trifle, tuna

beans, beetroot, coleslaw, cucumber, leeks, maize, peanuts, peas, seaweed, swede

apricot, coconut, dates, grapefruit, lime, peach, pineapple, prunes, raisins, rhubarb

basin, bowl, knife, ladle, microwave, plate, scales, soap, teapot, toast

3 Practise looking up words from the above lists or elsewhere in the darker blue part of the Dictionary. After turning to the page, say the word in distinct syllables and have the class say, tap and count the syllables. Make sure they look in the correct column and, if there is a homonym, that they check the meaning. Where the word is not given in plural form (e.g. prune), an 's' should be added. Note that in one case (swede) the target word is in a section which continues for three pages.

Index

		A	B	C	D	E	F	G	H	I	J	K	L	M	N	O	P	Q	R	S	T	U	V	W	X	Y	Z		
LONG VOWEL	ae	137	138	139	140	141	142	143	144	144	145	145	145	146	146	147	147	148	148	149	151	151	151	152	—	—	—	ae	BABY SNAIL
LONG VOWEL	ee	153	154	155	156	157	158	159	160	161	162	162	163	164	165	165	166	167	167	169	172	—	173	174	—	175	—	ee	BREEDING EAGLE
LONG VOWEL	ie	176	177	178	178	180	181	182	182	183	184	184	185	186	187	187	188	189	189	190	192	193	193	194	—	—	194	ie	LIVELY LION
LONG VOWEL	oe	195	195	196	197	197	198	199	200	200	201	201	201	202	202	203	204	206	206	207	208	208	208	209	—	209	209	oe	LONELY GOAT
LONG VOWELS	ue oo	210 211	211	212	213	213	214	214	215	215	216	216	216	217	218	218	219	219	220	221	222	223	223	223	—	224	224	ue oo	SMOOTH NEWT

Lesson 2

Introducing ACE

Aims: The student should be able to:

a) identify short vowel sounds in a selection of words

b) use the short vowel sound part of the Index to find the page numbers for a selection of words

c) look up words in the first two parts of the Dictionary.

1 Begin with listening and speaking activities, starting with the short vowel animal names: **cat**, **elephant**, **pig**, **dog**, **duck** and **woodpecker**.

Ask the students if they can hear certain vowel sounds in each of these animal names, for example, 'Can you hear /**a**/ in **cat**?', 'Can you hear /**e**/ in **pig**?'.

Make the vowel sounds longer and louder if you need to.

Continue until responses are confident and correct and then move on to identifying short vowel sounds in other words. For example, 'Can you hear /**a**/ in **active**?', 'Can you hear /**i**/ in **big**?'.

Again, continue until responses are confident and correct.

Selecting a short vowel sound, ask students if they can hear the sound in a variety of words. For example, 'Can you hear /**a**/ in **pat**, **fat**, **mat**, **pet**?'.

Finally, ask students to give you the vowel sound they can hear in the short vowel animal names, giving a choice of three. For example, 'What is the vowel sound in **cat**: /**ae**/, /**a**/ or /**e**/?'. Continue with the different animals and three vowel sound choices until the sounds in all the short vowel names are correctly identified.

2 Practise using the Index to find page numbers first for short and then for both short and long vowel words. Each student should have a copy of the first two parts of the Index (see Index 2 on page 8). Teachers may also like to make a digital copy for class tuition.

Beginning with the animal picture words, ask students first to point to the cat picture next to the letter 'a', which stands for the sound /**a**/. Ask which letter **cat** begins with and have them find the letter 'C' in the alphabet across the top of the page. Then, show them how to move one finger along the line of page numbers from /**a**/ and the other finger down from 'C', until they meet at a page number. **Cat** is on page 7!

Repeat this exercise with **duck**, **pig**, **watchful** and **woodpecker**. You may need to prompt students with the vowel sounds initially, but continue the exercise until the page numbers can be found by the students themselves.

Once students can readily achieve this, ask them to find the page numbers for the following animal words: **camel, donkey, frog, hedgehog, kangaroo, leopard, monkey, pigeon, rabbit, rook**.

This time they will need to identify the spelling picture for the vowel sound first. For example, what is the first vowel sound in **rabbit**? It is /**a**/, which is the same as in **cat**.

Introducing ACE

Use these topic lists until students have mastered using Index 2 to find page numbers.

biscuit, bread, butter, chicken, chocolate, crisps, eggs, haddock, jam, popcorn

broccoli, cabbage, cauliflower, celery, lettuce, mushroom, onion, pepper, pumpkin, spinach

apple, blackberry, cherry, damson, fig, lemon, melon, orange, plum, tangerine

bottle, brush, clock, fridge, matches, mirror, rack, scissors, sieve, whisk

After working with Index 2, ask students to find the page numbers for both short and long vowel words from the following lists. If there is any confusion between short and long vowels, ask, for example, 'Is it short /a/ as in **cat**, or long /ae/ as in **snail**?' as appropriate.

black, blue, buff, crimson, gold, green, indigo, red, ruby, white

apron, boots, collar, dress, jeans, nightdress, shoes, sweater, tie, vest

bicycle, boat, glider, helicopter, motorcycle, scooter, submarine, train, van, yacht

bus, coach, cycle, ferry, hovercraft, liner, lorry, rocket, tricycle, truck

chewing, cooking, drinking, eating, helping, listening, nodding, sleeping, watching, writing

baker, bricklayer, cook, miner, optician, sailor, scientist, secretary, soldier, teacher

3 Practise looking up words from the above lists or elsewhere in the Dictionary. After turning to the page, say the word in distinct syllables and have the class say, tap and count the syllables. Make sure they look in the correct column and, if there is a homonym, that they check the meaning. Note that in some cases (apple, biscuit, bus, butter, crimson, drinking, fridge, indigo, matches, optician, orange, spinach, sweater) the target word is in a section which continues for two or more pages.

Index 2

Introducing ACE

		SHORT VOWELS	SHORT VOWEL	SHORT VOWEL	SHORT VOWEL	SHORT VOWEL	LONG VOWEL	LONG VOWEL	LONG VOWEL	LONG VOWEL	LONG VOWELS
		oo	a	e	i	o	u	ae	ee	ie	oe	ue	oo
A	1	116	5	31	56	94	116	137	153	176	195	210
B	5	116	7	32	57	95	116	138	154	177	195	211
C	10	118	11	33	59	96	118	139	155	178	196	212
D	11	120	12	34	61	99	120	140	156	178	197	213
E	12	120	14	36	65	99	120	141	157	180	197	213
F	14	121	16	39	68	100	121	142	158	181	198	214
G	16	122	17	39	70	101	122	143	159	182	199	214
H	17	123	18	40	71	102	123	144	160	182	200	215
I	18	124	18	41	72	102	124	144	161	183	200	215
J	19	124	—	42	77	103	124	145	162	184	201	216
K	20	125	22	42	78	103	125	145	162	184	201	216
L	21	126	24	43	79	104	126	145	163	185	201	217
M	—	127	24	44	80	105	127	146	164	186	202	218
N	22	127	25	45	81	105	127	146	165	187	202	218
O	24	128	28	45	81	106	128	147	165	187	203	219
P	24	128	29	46	82	108	128	147	166	188	204	219
Q	25	129	29	47	83	109	129	148	167	189	206	220
R	28	130	30	48	84	110	130	148	167	189	206	221
S	29	133	—	50	87	111	133	149	169	190	207	222
T	29	134	30	52	90	113	134	151	172	192	208	223
U	30	136	—	53	91	113	136	151	—	—	208	223
V	30	136	55	53	91	114	136	151	173	193	208	223
W	—	—	54	54	92	114	—	152	174	193	209	—
X	—	—	—	—	—	—	—	—	—	194	—	—
Y	30	136	55	55	—	115	136	152	175	—	209	224
Z	30	—	55	—	93	115	—	—	175	194	209	224
		oo DUCK AND WOODPECKER	**a** ACTIVE CAT	**e** HEALTHY ELEPHANT	**i** BIG PIGLET	**o** WATCHFUL DOG	**u**	**ae** BABY SNAIL	**ee** BREEDING EAGLE	**ie** LIVELY LION	**oe** LONELY GOAT	**ue** SMOOTH NEWT

8

© David Moseley and Gwyn Singleton 2015 | *ACE Spelling Activities* | LDA | Permission to photocopy

Lesson 3

Introducing ACE

Aims: The student should be able to:

a) identify long vowel sounds, in the third part of the Dictionary, in a selection of words

b) use the Index to find the page numbers for a selection of words

c) look up words in all three parts of the Dictionary.

1 Begin with listening and speaking activities, starting with the animal names from the third part of the Dictionary: **shark**, **bear**, **bird**, **horse**, **oyster** and **owl**.

Ask the students if they can hear certain vowel sounds in each of these animal names, for example, 'Can you hear /**ar**/ in **shark**?', 'Can you hear /**or**/ in **owl**?'.

Make the vowel sounds longer and louder if you need to.

Continue until responses are confident and correct and then move on to identifying these long vowel sounds in other words. For example, 'Can you hear /**ar**/ in **harmless**?', 'Can you hear /**oi**/ in **early**?'.

Again, continue until the responses are confident and correct.

Selecting one of these long vowel sounds, ask students if they can hear the sound in a variety of words. For example, 'Can you hear /**ar**/ in **car**, **fir**, **jar**, **tar**?'.

Finally, ask students to give you the vowel sound they can hear in the third group of vowel animal names, giving a choice of three. For example, 'What is the vowel sound in **shark**: /**ar**/, /**ae**/ or /**or**/?'. Continue with the different animals and three vowel sound choices until the sounds in all the third group of vowel animal names are correctly identified.

2 Practise using the Index to find page numbers for words containing the sounds /**ar**/, /**air**/, /**er**/, /**or**/, /**oi**/ and /**ou**/. Each student should have a copy of the whole Index (see Index 3 on page 11). Teachers may also like to make a digital copy for class tuition.

Beginning with the animal picture words, ask students first to point to the shark picture next to the letters 'ar', which stand for the sound /**ar**/. Ask which letter **shark** begins with and ask them to point to the letter 'S' in the alphabet across the top of the page. Then, show them how to move one finger along the line of page numbers from /**ar**/ and the other finger down from 'S', until they meet at a page number. **Shark** is on page 234!

Repeat this exercise with **rare**, **worm**, **warlike**, **oyster** and **sound**.

You may need to prompt students with the vowel sound initially, but continue the exercise until the page numbers can be found by the students themselves.

Once students can readily achieve this, ask them to find the page numbers for the following animal words: **armadillo**, **cow**, **earthworm**, **gerbil**, **hound**, **mouse**, **partridge**, **sardine**, **starfish**, **tortoise**.

This time they will need to identify the spelling picture for the vowel sound first. For example, what is the first vowel sound in **partridge**? It is /**ar**/, which is the same as in **shark**.

Introducing ACE

Use these topic lists until students have mastered using Index 3 to find page numbers.

> burger, cornflakes, flour, lard, marmalade, oil, pork, prawn, sardine, trout
>
> garlic, herbs, parsley, parsnips, pear, soya, sprouts, strawberry, turnip, walnut
>
> boiler, carton, door, fork, jar, larder, margarine, starch, torch, towel

After working with Index 3, ask students to find the page numbers for words from any of the three parts, using the following lists. If there is any confusion between any pair of patterns, ask, for example, 'Is it /a/ or /ow/?', 'Is it /o/ or /ar/?' as appropriate.

> aquamarine, brown, cream, ginger, grey, lilac, orange, pink, purple, rose, scarlet, silver, turquoise, violet, yellow
>
> blouse, braces, coat, jacket, leggings, overalls, sandals, scarf, shorts, skirt, slippers, socks, tights, trainers, trousers
>
> brushing, counting, cutting, ironing, learning, marking, painting, reading, serving, sewing, shaving, shopping, sweeping, swimming, working
>
> actor, artist, dentist, diver, doctor, fisherman, hairdresser, joiner, journalist, musician, nurse, plumber, priest, tailor, warden

4 Practise looking up words from the above lists or elsewhere in the dictionary. Note that in some cases (actor, aquamarine, cutting, slippers, sweeping, swimming) the target word is in a section which continues for two or more pages.

Index 3

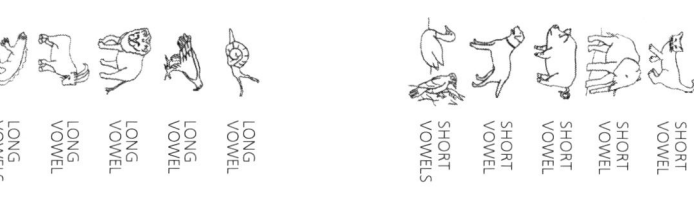

		A	B	C	D	E	F	G	H	I	J	K	L	M	N	O	P	Q	R	S	T	U	V	W	X	Y	Z		
SHORT VOWEL	a	1	5	7	10	11	12	14	16	17	18	19	20	21	—	22	24	24	25	28	29	29	30	—	30	30	a	ACTIVE CAT
SHORT VOWEL	e	31	32	33	34	36	39	39	40	41	42	42	43	44	45	45	46	47	48	50	52	53	53	54	54	55	55	e	HEALTHY ELEPHANT
SHORT VOWEL	i	56	57	59	61	65	68	70	71	72	77	78	79	80	81	81	82	83	84	87	90	91	91	92	—	93	—	i	BIG PIGLET
SHORT VOWEL	o	94	95	96	99	99	100	101	102	102	103	103	104	105	105	106	108	109	110	111	113	113	114	114	—	115	115	o	WATCHFUL DOG
SHORT VOWELS	u oo	116	116	118	120	120	121	122	123	123	124	124	125	126	127	127	128	128	129	130	133	134	136	136	—	136	—	u oo	DUCK AND WOODPECKER
		A	B	C	D	E	F	G	H	I	J	K	L	M	N	O	P	Q	R	S	T	U	V	W	X	Y	Z		
LONG VOWEL	ae	137	138	139	140	141	142	143	144	144	145	145	146	146	147	147	148	148	149	151	151	—	151	152	—	152	—	ae	BABY SNAIL
LONG VOWEL	ee	153	154	155	156	157	158	159	160	161	162	162	163	164	165	165	166	167	167	169	172	—	173	174	—	175	175	ee	BREEDING EAGLE
LONG VOWEL	ie	176	177	178	178	180	181	182	182	183	184	184	185	186	187	187	188	189	189	190	192	—	193	193	194	—	194	ie	LIVELY LION
LONG VOWEL	oe	195	195	196	197	197	198	199	200	200	201	201	201	202	202	203	204	206	206	207	208	208	208	209	—	209	209	oe	LONELY GOAT
LONG VOWELS	ue oo	210	211	212	213	213	214	214	215	215	216	216	216	217	218	218	219	219	220	221	222	223	223	223	—	224	224	ue oo	SMOOTH NEWT
		A	B	C	D	E	F	G	H	I	J	K	L	M	N	O	P	Q	R	S	T	U	V	W	X	Y	Z		
VOWEL SOUND	ar	225	226	227	228	228	229	229	230	230	230	231	231	232	232	—	233	233	233	234	235	—	235	—	—	235	235	ar	BASKING SHARK
VOWEL SOUND	air	236	236	236	237	238	238	238	239	—	—	239	239	—	—	239	—	240	240	241	—	241	241	—	—	—	—	air	RARE BEAR
VOWEL SOUND	er	242	243	244	245	246	246	247	247	248	248	248	249	249	250	251	251	252	253	254	254	255	255	—	255	—	er	EARLY BIRD WITH WORM
VOWEL SOUND	or	256	257	258	259	259	260	261	261	262	262	263	263	264	265	266	266	267	268	268	268	269	—	269	—	—	or	WARLIKE HORSE
VOWEL SOUND	oi	270	270	270	271	271	272	272	—	—	272	273	273	273	274	274	274	275	275	—	275	—	—	—	—	—	oi	JOYFUL OYSTER
VOWEL SOUND	ou	276	276	277	278	278	279	279	279	—	280	—	280	280	281	281	282	—	282	283	283	—	284	—	284	—	284	ou	AN OWL SOUND

© David Moseley and Gwyn Singleton 2015 | *ACE Spelling Activities* | LDA | Permission to photocopy

Further activities

Students will now be able to check and correct the spelling of any word they want to use. While most of the checking will be done after a draft has been produced, there should be no absolute ban on using the *ACE Spelling Dictionary* in the course of writing, especially in collaborative work.

As the students are able to look up words for themselves, the teacher should stop supplying spellings on demand. After completing a piece of writing or dictation the students should mark the words they wish to look up (perhaps to a maximum fixed by the teacher). This will not only encourage students' independence, but will also save the teacher time!

The more the Dictionary is used in different subject areas, the greater the benefits will be. Whenever the teacher wants to draw new vocabulary to the attention of the group or class, the students can look up the words in the *ACE Spelling Dictionary* and write them up for display. Homework assignments present further opportunities for Dictionary work.

Initially, it is a good idea to set speed targets for looking up words in the Dictionary. This may be done either as a class or as a homework activity. The words may be taken from prepared lists or may be chosen by the students. If small groups work together, perhaps in competition, they will soon discover good ways of cutting down word-search time and will reach and even exceed the target of 20 seconds per word. This is a realistic target for the words provided in Lessons 1–3, since these do not include words which begin with a neutral vowel sound.

After mastering the basic skill of word-finding by vowel sound and first letter, students will be ready to benefit from further instruction. The section on neutral vowels, on page x of the Dictionary, should form the basis of a separate lesson. Homonyms, plurals and tenses (pages 290–1 of the Dictionary) are also important topics to cover and to return to from time to time.

The *ACE Spelling Dictionary* provides a conceptual framework for understanding the complex relationships between sounds and spellings in English. Word study with the Dictionary, led by the need to communicate and to understand more about written language, is much more than a set of phonic exercises. We provide some starting points in these activity sheets and hope that many more ideas for actively exploring the *ACE Spelling Dictionary* will be developed by teachers and their students.

More word-finding practice
with the ACE Index and Dictionary

Aims: The student should be able to:

1) using the full ACE Index sheet, find and write down the page numbers for 20 specified words in five minutes

2) using the *ACE Spelling Dictionary*, find and write down 20 specified words in ten minutes.

These exercises provide extra practice with the ACE Index after Lessons 1–3 in 'Learning how to use the *ACE Spelling Dictionary*'. Alternatively, they can be used with the Dictionary itself to build up speed in finding words.

The teacher can work with a group or whole class using copies of the Index. The answers can be found at the back of the book.

For one-to-one or small group work, a partner or teaching assistant is needed to read out the words and to check the responses. Alternatively, the exercises can be recorded. If the topic lists are used for looking up words in the Dictionary, each student or small group will need access to a copy.

Introducing ACE

Practice with long vowel sounds
/ae/ /ee/ /ie/ /oe/ /ue/ / /oo/

List of topic words to be read out or played back.

FOOD

1. toast	6. pastry	11. sweet	16. cream
2. ice-cream	7. savoury	12. rice	17. loaf
3. roll	8. muesli	13. oats	18. fruit
4. flavour	9. gravy	14. soup	19. plaice
5. cake	10. meat	15. cheese	20. tasty

IN THE COUNTRY

1. lake	6. stream	11. pool	16. drainage
2. field	7. wheat	12. rye	17. hay
3. acorn	8. oak	13. tree	18. leaves
4. root	9. toadstool	14. flies	19. spider
5. stone	10. bluebells	15. nightingale	20. snake

SPORT

1. team	6. crew	11. race	16. skiing
2. skating	7. rowing	12. climbing	17. glider
3. height	8. diving	13. player	18. bowler
4. fielder	9. boot	14. try	19. goal
5. snooker	10. rival	15. losing	20. rules

OCCUPATIONS

1. playwright	6. director	11. agent	16. poet
2. waiter	7. cleaner	12. labourer	17. dealer
3. salesman	8. librarian	13. student	18. jeweller
4. miner	9. programmer	14. newsagent	19. painter
5. preacher	10. fireman	15. pirate	20. leader

TRAVEL

1. railway	6. road	11. pony	16. plane
2. scooter	7. bicycle	12. flight	17. cruise
3. breakdown	8. timetable	13. train	18. driver
4. motorist	9. wheels	14. pilot	19. vehicle
5. ocean	10. route	15. detour	20. scenery

The student EITHER fills in the page numbers on the sheet OR looks up the words in the *ACE Spelling Dictionary*.

Introducing ACE

Practice with short vowel sounds

/a/ /e/ /i/ /o/ /u/ / /oo/

List of topic words to be read out or played back.

WILDLIFE

1. butterfly	6. vixen	11. winkle	16. thrush
2. moth	7. cub	12. cockle	17. dove
3. squirrel	8. otter	13. mussel	18. swan
4. badger	9. jellyfish	14. lobster	19. kestrel
5. fox	10. crab	15. sparrow	20. slug

HOSPITAL

1. ambulance	6. splint	11. health	16. drug
2. bandage	7. temperature	12. lung	17. tablet
3. injury	8. blood	13. oxygen	18. pill
4. fracture	9. vaccine	14. scalpel	19. medication
5. limb	10. stethoscope	15. unconscious	20. stomach

WINTER

1. frost	6. gloves	11. decorate	16. mistletoe
2. shiver	7. anorak	12. presents	17. berries
3. wintry	8. robin	13. tinsel	18. sledge
4. blizzard	9. Christmas	14. glisten	19. pantomime
5. slush	10. carolling	15. holly	20. January

HOLIDAYS

1. sand	6. suntan	11. tent	16. visit
2. bucket	7. cottage	12. caravan	17. exhibition
3. paddle	8. fishing	13. disco	18. restaurant
4. swimming	9. camping	14. shopping	19. customs
5. deckchair	10. rucksack	15. trip	20. luggage

GAMES AND PASTIMES

1. cricket	6. badminton	11. snap	16. rugby
2. chess	7. squash	12. dominoes	17. boxing
3. golf	8. netball	13. lotto	18. sledging
4. hockey	9. putting	14. skipping	19. stilts
5. tennis	10. jigsaws	15. football	20. juggling

The student EITHER **fills in the page numbers on the sheet** OR **looks up the words in the *ACE Spelling Dictionary*.**

Introducing ACE

Practice with mixed long and short vowel sounds 1

List of topic words to be read out or played back.

SCHOOL

1. cloakroom	6. lesson	11. lunch	16. copy
2. desk	7. bell	12. monitor	17. science
3. seat	8. break	13. prefect	18. mathematics
4. teacher	9. snack	14. writing	19. games
5. subject	10. queue	15. notes	20. music

DRINKS

1. smoothie	6. chocolate	11. shandy	16. brandy
2. lemonade	7. grapefruit	12. beer	17. alcoholic
3. milk	8. juice	13. cider	18. fizzy
4. coffee	9. wine	14. scotch	19. tonic
5. tea	10. punch	15. whisky	20. soda

GUY FAWKES

1. evening	6. sticks	11. heat	16. banger
2. clothes	7. matches	12. bake	17. fuse
3. fire	8. light	13. sausages	18. taper
4. wood	9. flame	14. fireworks	19. glow
5. paper	10. crackle	15. colours	20. embers

MOUNTAINS

1. peak	6. huge	11. precipice	16. crag
2. massive	7. summit	12. sheer	17. crevice
3. rugged	8. ridge	13. edge	18. trail
4. boulders	9. slope	14. torrent	19. scramble
5. pinnacle	10. avalanche	15. rocky	20. gully

THE RAILWAY STATION

1. ticket	6. platform	11. diesel	16. sleeper
2. office	7. notice	12. carriage	17. signal
3. clock	8. timetable	13. train	18. buffers
4. case	9. kiosk	14. rails	19. bridge
5. trolley	10. engine	15. whistle	20. taxi

The student EITHER **fills in the page numbers on the sheet** OR **looks up the words in the *ACE Spelling Dictionary*.**

Practice with mixed long and short vowel sounds 2

List of topic words to be read out or played back.

FUN

1. smile	6. skipping	11. acting	16. chuckling
2. party	7. kissing	12. painting	17. giggling
3. happy	8. hugging	13. joke	18. merry
4. mirth	9. clown	14. tease	19. cartoon
5. joyful	10. tumbling	15. tickle	20. comic

ON THE FARM

1. tractor	6. yard	11. corn	16. cattle
2. plough	7. orchard	12. barley	17. bullock
3. furrow	8. hedgerow	13. crop	18. sheep
4. fertiliser	9. harvest	14. dairy	19. goose
5. slurry	10. grain	15. herd	20. turkey

WATER

1. waves	6. calm	11. whirlpool	16. trickle
2. splash	7. smooth	12. current	17. pour
3. spray	8. tranquil	13. squirt	18. still
4. choppy	9. river	14. jet	19. sparkling
5. rough	10. flow	15. fountain	20. pure

FLOWERS

1. snowdrop	6. tulip	11. lily	16. foxglove
2. cowslip	7. marigold	12. lavender	17. thistle
3. hyacinth	8. pansy	13. heather	18. poppy
4. crocus	9. carnation	14. gorse	19. buttercup
5. daffodil	10. orchid	15. broom	20. daisy

TREES

1. chestnut	6. birch	11. fir	16. oak
2. beech	7. ash	12. pine	17. olive
3. willow	8. palm	13. spruce	18. hazel
4. sycamore	9. holly	14. yew	19. mulberry
5. poplar	10. larch	15. bay	20. maple

The student EITHER **fills in the page numbers on the sheet** OR **looks up the words in the** ACE Spelling Dictionary.

Using ACE

Spellings for sounds

The short /a/ sound as in ACTIVE CAT

Spelt 'a'

Can you work out these words from the clues given? Each word contains the /a/ sound. The stars tell you how many syllables are in the word.

If you like, you can use the *ACE Spelling Dictionary* to help you find the answers.

Check all the spellings, unless you are absolutely sure. When you have filled in the missing letters, write the whole word on the line.

If you are working with a partner, one of you can find the answers while the other writes them down.

CLUES	SYLLABLES		WRITE
e.g. good-looking	**	h _ _ _ _ _ _ _	*handsome*
1. shaft to connect wheels	**	ax _ _	
2. forbidden	*	b _ _ _ _ _ _	
3. animal of the desert	**	c _ m _ _	
4. a root vegetable	**	c _ r _ _ _ _	
5. a section of a book	**	c _ _ _ t _ _	
6. to become bigger	**	e _ p _ _ _	
7. easily broken	**	f _ _ g _ _ _	
8. a damaging chance event	***	ac _ _ d _ _ _	
9. to take risks	**	g _ _ b _ _	
10. a suspended bed	**	h _ m _ _ _ _	
11. spoken in one or more countries	**	l _ _ g _ _ _ _	
12. method or way	**	m _ n _ _ _	
13. having a wife or husband	**	m _ r _ _ _ _	
14. a large Chinese animal	**	p _ _ d _	
15. a slight wound	*	s _ _ _	

18

Using ACE

Ⓗ beside a word means that it is a homonym. A homonym is a word which sounds the same as or very similar to another word, but which has a different meaning. Can you find all the homonyms (or sound-alike words) from the list you have been working on?

Use the *ACE Spelling Dictionary* to find the homonyms you need. Remember, homonyms are marked with a star in the Dictionary and members of a pair or small group are usually quite close to each other.

When you have found all the homonyms, make up a sentence using that word and at least one other homonym: e.g. 'When you buy tin **tacks** you have to pay **tax**'. Write out your sentences below and check the spelling of any hard words in the Dictionary.

Spellings for sounds

The short /e/ sound as in HEALTHY ELEPHANT

Spelt 'ai', 'e', 'ea', 'ei', 'eo', 'ie'

Can you work out these words from the clues given? Each word contains the /e/ sound. The stars tell you how many syllables are in the word.

If you like, you can use the *ACE Spelling Dictionary* to help you find the answers.

Check all the spellings, unless you are absolutely sure. When you have filled in the missing letters, write the whole word on the line.

If you are working with a partner, one of you can find the answers while the other writes them down.

CLUES	SYLLABLES		WRITE
e.g. an animal with spots	**	l _ _ p _ _ _	leopard
1. once more	**	ag _ _ _	
2. a long wooden seat	*	b _ _ _ _ _	
3. underground storage room	**	c _ l _ _ _	
4. stockist of medicines	**	c _ _ _ _ i _ _	
5. money owed	*	d _ _ _	
6. way out	**	e _ i _	
7. person known and liked	*	f _ _ _ _ _	
8. someone who accepts an invitation	*	g _ _ _ _	
9. free time	**	l _ _ s _ _ _	
10. what is learned	**	l _ s _ _ _	
11. grassy field	**	m _ _ _ d _ _	
12. foot lever	**	p _ d _ _ _	
13. a liquid fuel	**	p _ t _ _ _	
14. a safe haven	**	r _ f _ _ _ _	
15. very fine cord used for sewing	*	t _ _ _ _ _ _	

H beside a word means that it is a homonym. A homonym is a word which sounds the same as or very similar to another word, but which has a different meaning. Can you find all the homonyms (or sound-alike words) from the list you have been working on?

Use the *ACE Spelling Dictionary* to find the homonyms you need. Remember, homonyms are marked with a star in the Dictionary and members of a pair or small group are usually quite close to each other.

When you have found all the homonyms, make up a sentence using that word and at least one other homonym: e.g. 'The **weather** will change **whether** we like it or not'. Write out your sentences below and check the spelling of any hard words in the Dictionary.

Using ACE

Spellings for sounds

The short /i/ sound as in BIG PIGLET

Spelt 'i', 'u', 'ui', 'y'

Can you work out these words from the clues given? Each word contains the /i/ sound. The stars tell you how many syllables are in the word.

If you like, you can use the *ACE Spelling Dictionary* to help you find the answers.

Check all the spellings, unless you are absolutely sure. When you have filled in the missing letters, write the whole word on the line.

If you are working with a partner, one of you can find the answers while the other writes them down.

	CLUES	SYLLABLES		WRITE
	e.g. to whip with a circular movement	*	w _ _ _ _	*whisk*
	1. way over a river	*	b _ _ _ _ _	
ⓗ	2. to construct	*	b _ _ _ _	
	3. December 25th	**	C _ _ _ _ m _ _	
	4. like clear glass	**	c _ _ s _ _ _	
	5. very dirty	**	f _ _ t _ _	
ⓗ	6. a song sung in church	*	h _ _ _	
	7. a room in which food is cooked	**	k _ t _ _ _ _	
	8. neither solid nor gas	**	l _ q _ _ _	
	9. 60 seconds	**	m _ n _ _ _	
	10. small handgun	**	p _ _ t _ _	
	11. active and hardworking	**	b _ _ _	
ⓗ	12. jewellery worn on a finger	*	r _ _ _	
ⓗ	13. signs which have meaning	**	s _ _ b _ _ _	
ⓗ	14. a wicked person	**	v _ l _ _ _ _	
ⓗ	15. a woman thought to use magic	*	w _ _ _ _	

22

Using ACE

H beside a word means that it is a homonym. A homonym is a word which sounds the same as or very similar to another word, but which has a different meaning. Can you find all the homonyms (or sound-alike words) from the list you have been working on?

Use the *ACE Spelling Dictionary* to find the homonyms you need. Remember, homonyms are marked with a star in the Dictionary and members of a pair or small group are usually quite close to each other.

When you have found all the homonyms, make up a sentence using that word and at least one other homonym: e.g. 'The **prince** has a large collection of old **prints**'. Write out your sentences below and check the spelling of any hard words in the Dictionary.

Using ACE

Spellings for sounds

The short /o/ sound as in WATCHFUL DOG

Spelt 'a', 'o'

Can you work out these words from the clues given?
Each word contains the /o/ sound. The stars tell you how many syllables are in the word.

If you like, you can use the *ACE Spelling Dictionary* to help you find the answers.

Check all the spellings, unless you are absolutely sure. When you have filled in the missing letters, write the whole word on the line.

If you are working with a partner, one of you can find the answers while the other writes them down.

CLUES	SYLLABLES		WRITE
e.g. a citrus fruit	**	or _ _ _ _	*orange*
1. an explosive device	*	b _ _ _	
Ⓗ 2. to defeat in war	**	c _ _ q _ _ _ _	
3. an intelligent sea mammal	**	d _ _ p _ _ _	
4. shiny	**	g _ _ _ _ y	
5. banged	*	k _ _ _ _	
Ⓗ 6. a tied fastening	*	k _ _ _	
7. a shellfish with big claws	**	l _ _ s _ _ _	
8. a place of worship for Muslims	*	m _ _ _ _ _	
9. a book containing a long story	**	n _ v _ _	
10. a fruit which yields oil	**	ol _ _ _	
11. eggs beaten and fried	**	o _ _ l _ _ _ _	
Ⓗ 12. financial gain	**	p _ _ f _ _	
13. a place where rocks are blasted	**	q _ _ r _	
14. to squeeze tightly	*	s _ _ _ _ _	
Ⓗ 15. unit of electric power	*	w _ _ _	

24

Ⓗ beside a word means that it is a homonym. A homonym is a word which sounds the same as or very similar to another word, but which has a different meaning. Can you find all the homonyms (or sound-alike words) from the list you have been working on?

Use the *ACE Spelling Dictionary* to find the homonyms you need. Remember, homonyms are marked with a star in the Dictionary and members of a pair or small group are usually quite close to each other.

When you have found all the homonyms, make up a sentence using that word and at least one other homonym: e.g. 'The **cops** hid among the trees in the **copse**'. Write out your sentences below and check the spelling of any hard words in the Dictionary.

Using ACE

Spellings for sounds

The short /u/ or /oo/ sound as in DUCK AND WOODPECKER
Spelt 'o', 'o–e', 'ou', 'u'

Can you work out these words from the clues given? Each word contains the /u/ or /oo/ sound. The stars tell you how many syllables are in the word.

If you like, you can use the *ACE Spelling Dictionary* to help you find the answers.

Check all the spellings, unless you are absolutely sure. When you have filled in the missing letters, write the whole word on the line.

If you are working with a partner, one of you can find the answers while the other writes them down.

	CLUES	SYLLABLES		WRITE
	e.g. very ripe and delicious	**	l _ s _ _ _ _	*luscious*
1.	in the middle of	**	am _ _ _	
2.	to go red with embarrassment	*	b _ _ _ _	
3.	steamed or cooked dish, often sweet	**	p _ dd _ _	
H 4.	dried fruit, used in cakes	**	c _ r _ _ _ _	
5.	sufficient	**	en _ _ _ _	
6.	worn on the hands	*	g _ _ _ _ _	
7.	a baby buggy	**	p _ _ _ ch _ _	
8.	wild animals that hunt in packs	*	w _ l _ _ s	
H 9.	a soft, purple fruit	*	p _ _ _	
H 10.	a woman living in a convent	*	n _ _	
11.	stuff to be thrown away	**	r _ b _ _ _ _	
H 12.	bones protecting the brain	*	s _ _ _ _	
H 13.	at least a small amount or number	*	s _ _ _	
14.	unwanted problems	**	t _ _ _ b _ _ _	
15.	to the floor above	**	u _ s _ _ _ _	

Using ACE

Ⓗ beside a word means that it is a homonym. A homonym is a word which sounds the same as or very similar to another word, but which has a different meaning. Can you find all the homonyms (or sound-alike words) from the list you have been working on?

Use the *ACE Spelling Dictionary* to find the homonyms you need. Remember, homonyms are marked with a star in the Dictionary and members of a pair or small group are usually quite close to each other.

When you have found all the homonyms, make up a sentence using that word and at least one other homonym: e.g. 'She was the **one** who **won** a holiday'. Write out your sentences below and check the spelling of any hard words in the Dictionary.

Using ACE

Spellings for sounds

The short /ae/ sound as in BABY SNAIL

Spelt 'a', 'a–e', 'ai', 'ay', 'ea', 'ei'

Can you work out these words from the clues given? Each word contains the /ae/ sound. The stars tell you how many syllables are in the word.

If you like, you can use the *ACE Spelling Dictionary* to help you find the answers.

Check all the spellings, unless you are absolutely sure. When you have filled in the missing letters, write the whole word on the line.

If you are working with a partner, one of you can find the answers while the other writes them down.

CLUES	SYLLABLES		WRITE
e.g. a flatfish	*	p _ _ _ _ _	*plaice*
1. a continuing pain	*	a _ _ _	
2. very old indeed	**	a _ c _ _ _ _	
⊕ 3. to smash into pieces	*	b _ _ _ _	
4. a baby's bed	**	c _ _ d _ _	
5. to breathe out	**	e _ h _ _ _	
6. well-known	**	f _ m _ _ _	
⊕ 7. a way of walking	*	g _ _ _	
⊕ 8. rub into small pieces	*	g _ _ _ _	
9. misty	**	h _ _ _	
10. prison	*	j _ _ _	
11. put down in one place	*	l _ _ _	
⊕ 12. letters and parcels	*	m _ _ _	
13. an error	**	m _ _ t _ _ _	
⊕ 14. a board for carrying things	*	t _ _ _	
⊕ 15. heaviness	*	w _ _ _ _ _	

Using ACE

Ⓗ beside a word means that it is a homonym. A homonym is a word which sounds the same as or very similar to another word, but which has a different meaning. Can you find all the homonyms (or sound-alike words) from the list you have been working on?

Use the *ACE Spelling Dictionary* to find the homonyms you need. Remember, homonyms are marked with a star in the Dictionary and members of a pair or small group are usually quite close to each other.

When you have found all the homonyms, make up a sentence using that word and at least one other homonym: e.g. 'Will **plaice** do in **place** of cod?'. Write out your sentences below and check the spelling of any hard words in the Dictionary.

Using ACE

Spellings for sounds

The sound /ee/ as in BREEDING EAGLE

Spelt 'e', 'ea', 'ee', 'ei', 'ey'

Can you work out these words from the clues given? Each word contains the /ee/ sound. The stars tell you how many syllables are in the word.

If you like, you can use the *ACE Spelling Dictionary* to help you find the answers.

Check all the spellings, unless you are absolutely sure. When you have filled in the missing letters, write the whole word on the line.

If you are working with a partner, one of you can find the answers while the other writes them down.

CLUES	SYLLABLES		WRITE
e.g. trousers made of denim	*	j _ _ _ _	*jeans*
1. to come into view	**	ap _ _ _ _	
2. hard-backed insect	**	b _ _ t _ _	
3. a squeaking noise	*	c _ _ _ _	
4. an animal found in forests	*	d _ _ _	
5. to mislead with lies	**	d _ c _ _ _ _	
6. keen and enthusiastic	**	e _ g _ _	
7. having the same value	**	eq _ _ _ _	
8. occurring often	**	f _ _ q _ _ _ _	
9. opening in a lock	**	k _ _ h _ _ _	
10. rented	*	l _ _ _ _	
11. measuring machine	**	m _ t _ _	
12. small tool used for sewing	**	n _ _ d _ _	
13. period without war	*	p _ _ _ _	
14. feeling sick	**	q _ _ _ _ s _	
15. grab hold of	*	s _ _ _ _	

Using ACE

Ⓗ beside a word means that it is a homonym. A homonym is a word which sounds the same as or very similar to another word, but which has a different meaning. Can you find all the homonyms (or sound-alike words) from the list you have been working on?

Use the *ACE Spelling Dictionary* to find the homonyms you need. Remember, homonyms are marked with a star in the Dictionary and members of a pair or small group are usually quite close to each other.

When you have found all the homonyms, make up a sentence using that word and at least one other homonym: e.g. 'It is not easy to **steal** a safe made of **steel**'. Write out your sentences below and check the spelling of any hard words in the Dictionary.

Using ACE

Spellings for sounds

The sound /ie/ as in LIVELY LION

Spelt 'i', 'i–e', 'igh', 'uy', 'y', 'ye'

Can you work out these words from the clues given? Each word contains the /ie/ sound. The stars tell you how many syllables are in the word.

If you like, you can use the *ACE Spelling Dictionary* to help you find the answers.

Check all the spellings, unless you are absolutely sure. When you have filled in the missing letters, write the whole word on the line.

If you are working with a partner, one of you can find the answers while the other writes them down.

CLUES	SYLLABLES		WRITE
e.g. an absence of sound	**	s _ l _ _ _ _	*silence*
1. muscles in the arm	**	b _ c _ _ _	
2. gear for handling a horse	**	b _ _ d _ _	
3. someone who makes a purchase	**	b _ y _ _	
4. a person riding a bicycle	**	c _ c _ _ _ _	
5. to weaken a solution	**	d _ l _ _ _	
6. coloured liquid for staining	*	d _ _	
7. to ask	**	e _ q _ _ _ _	
8. good advice	**	g _ _ d _ _ _	
9. an image that is worshipped	**	id _ _	
10. an electric flash in the sky	**	l _ _ _ _ n _ _ _	
11. may, perhaps	*	m _ _ _ _	
12. tall metal support for cables	**	p _ l _ _	
13. rise and fall of the sea	*	t _ d _	
14. make weary	*	t _ _ _ _	
15. to shake rapidly	**	v _ b _ _ _ _	

Ⓗ beside a word means that it is a homonym. A homonym is a word which sounds the same as or very similar to another word, but which has a different meaning. Can you find all the homonyms (or sound-alike words) from the list you have been working on?

Use the *ACE Spelling Dictionary* to find the homonyms you need. Remember, homonyms are marked with a star in the Dictionary and members of a pair or small group are usually quite close to each other.

When you have found all the homonyms, make up a sentence using that word and at least one other homonym: e.g. 'If the cost is **higher** we won't **hire** it'. Write out your sentences below and check the spelling of any hard words in the Dictionary.

Using ACE

Spellings for sounds

The sound /oe/ as in LONELY GOAT

Spelt 'o', 'oa', 'o–e', 'ough', 'ow'

Can you work out these words from the clues given? Each word contains the /oe/ sound. The stars tell you how many syllables are in the word.

If you like, you can use the *ACE Spelling Dictionary* to help you find the answers.

Check all the spellings, unless you are absolutely sure. When you have filled in the missing letters, write the whole word on the line.

If you are working with a partner, one of you can find the answers while the other writes them down.

	CLUES	SYLLABLES		WRITE
	e.g. comfy and warm	**	c _ s _	cosy
H	1. brave and courageous	*	b _ _ _	
	2. a burglar may use this tool	**	c _ _ _ b _ _	
H	3. flour and water mixed together	*	d _ _ _ _	
	4. made solid by the cold	**	f _ _ z _ _	
	5. to shine in the dark	*	g _ _ _	
	6. an adult	**	g _ _ _ _ -u _	
H	7. something lent	*	l _ _ _	
	8. to complain or groan in pain	*	m _ _ _	
	9. an enormous area of sea	**	o _ _ _ _	
	10. to cook gently in water	*	p _ _ _ _	
H	11. lines of things	*	r _ _ _	
	12. a white winter flower	**	s _ _ _ d _ _ _	
H	13. under-part of the foot	*	s _ _ _	
	14. a monarch's chair	*	t _ _ _ _ _	
H	15. the yellow part of an egg	*	y _ _ _	

Ⓗ beside a word means that it is a homonym. A homonym is a word which sounds the same as or very similar to another word, but which has a different meaning. Can you find all the homonyms (or sound-alike words) from the list you have been working on?

Use the *ACE Spelling Dictionary* to find the homonyms you need. Remember, homonyms are marked with a star in the Dictionary and members of a pair or small group are usually quite close to each other.

When you have found all the homonyms, make up a sentence using that word and at least one other homonym: e.g. 'The **whole** class helped to dig the **hole**'. Write out your sentences below and check the spelling of any hard words in the Dictionary.

Using ACE

Spellings for sounds

The sound /**ue**/ or /**oo**/ as in SMOOTH NEWT

Spelt 'eau', 'eu', 'ew', 'oo', 'u', 'u–e', 'ui'

Can you work out these words from the clues given? Each word contains the /**oo**/ or /**ue**/ sound. The stars tell you how many syllables are in the word.

If you like, you can use the *ACE Spelling Dictionary* to help you find the answers.

Check all the spellings, unless you are absolutely sure. When you have filled in the missing letters, write the whole word on the line.

If you are working with a partner, one of you can find the answers while the other writes them down.

	CLUES	SYLLABLES		WRITE
	e.g. travel bag for clothes	**	s _ _ _ c _ _ _ _	*suitcase*
	1. to cause laughter or fun	**	am _ _ _ _	
	2. great attractiveness	**	b _ _ _ _ _ _	
(H)	3. a dark-coloured injury	*	b _ _ _ _ _	
(H)	4. to select	*	c _ _ _ _ _	
(H)	5. to holiday on a boat	*	c _ _ _ _ _	
(H)	6. morning wetness on the grass	*	d _ _	
	7. a continent	**	E _ _ _ _ _ _	
	8. depressed, cheerless	**	g _ _ _ _ _	
	9. the feet of horses or goats	*	h _ _ _ _ _	
	10. a liquid from fruit	*	j _ _ _ _ _	
(H)	11. recently made or obtained	*	n _ _	
	12. a pest, something annoying	**	n _ _ s _ _ _ _ _	
	13. to damage with unwanted material	**	p _ ll _ _ _	
	14. burial or cremation ceremony	**	f _ _ _ _ _ _	
(H)	15. to fire a gun	*	s _ _ _ _	

Using ACE

Ⓗ beside a word means that it is a homonym. A homonym is a word which sounds the same as or very similar to another word, but which has a different meaning. Can you find all the homonyms (or sound-alike words) from the list you have been working on?

Use the *ACE Spelling Dictionary* to find the homonyms you need. Remember, homonyms are marked with a star in the Dictionary and members of a pair or small group are usually quite close to each other.

When you have found all the homonyms, make up a sentence using that word and at least one other homonym: e.g. 'He joined the **queue** for a free snooker **cue**'. Write out your sentences below and check the spelling of any hard words in the Dictionary.

Using ACE

Spellings for sounds

*The sound /**ar**/ as in BASKING SHARK*

Spelt 'a', 'ar', 'arrh', 'ear', 'er'

Can you work out these words from the clues given? Each word contains the /**ar**/ sound. The stars tell you how many syllables are in the word.

If you like, you can use the *ACE Spelling Dictionary* to help you find the answers.

Check all the spellings, unless you are absolutely sure. When you have filled in the missing letters, write the whole word on the line.

If you are working with a partner, one of you can find the answers while the other writes them down.

	CLUES	SYLLABLES		WRITE
	e.g. a good buy	**	b _ _ g _ _ _	*bargain*
Ⓗ	1. part of a circle	*	a _ _	
	2. a grain crop	**	b _ _ l _ _	
	3. a floor covering	**	c _ _ p _ _	
	4. a cardboard container	**	c _ _ t _ _	
	5. mucus in the nose and throat	**	c _ t _ _ _	
Ⓗ	6. a greater distance	**	f _ _ t _ _ _	
	7. stringed musical instrument	**	g _ _ t _ _	
	8. spear for hunting fish	**	h _ _ p _ _ _	
	9. time to gather in crops	**	h _ _ v _ _ _	
Ⓗ	10. organ that pumps blood	*	h _ _ _ _	
	11. a light beer	**	l _ g _ _	
	12. a packet	**	p _ _ c _ _ _	
	13. worn round the neck	*	s _ _ _ _	
	14. rank in the army	**	s _ _ g _ _ _ _	
	15. a clear paint	**	v _ _ n _ _ _	

38

ⓗ beside a word means that it is a homonym. A homonym is a word which sounds the same as or very similar to another word, but which has a different meaning. Can you find all the homonyms (or sound-alike words) from the list you have been working on?

Use the *ACE Spelling Dictionary* to find the homonyms you need. Remember, homonyms are marked with a star in the Dictionary and members of a pair or small group are usually quite close to each other.

When you have found all the homonyms, make up a sentence using that word and at least one other homonym: e.g. 'We **aren't** going to stay with our **aunt**'. Write out your sentences below and check the spelling of any hard words in the Dictionary.

Using ACE

Spellings for sounds

*The sound /**air**/ as in RARE BEAR*

Spelt 'a', 'air', 'are', 'ere'

Can you work out these words from the clues given? Each word contains the /**air**/ sound. The stars tell you how many syllables are in the word.

If you like, you can use the *ACE Spelling Dictionary* to help you find the answers.

Check all the spellings, unless you are absolutely sure. When you have filled in the missing letters, write the whole word on the line.

If you are working with a partner, one of you can find the answers while the other writes them down.

	CLUES	SYLLABLES		WRITE
	e.g. make-believe little folk	**	f _ _ _ _ _ _	*fairies*
	1. conscious	**	aw _ _ _	
Ⓗ	2. uncovered	*	b _ _ _	
	3. hardly	**	b _ _ _ l _	
	4. lacking attention, not thorough	**	c _ _ _ l _ _ _	
	5. bravely taking risks	**	d _ r _ _ _	
Ⓗ	6. charge for a ride	*	f _ _ _	
	7. goodbye	**	f _ _ _ w _ _ _	
Ⓗ	8. animal like a rabbit	*	h _ _ _	
	9. mother or father	**	p _ r _ _ _	
	10. get ready	**	p _ _ p _ _ _	
	11. mend	**	r _ p _ _ _	
	12. frightening	**	s _ _ r _	
Ⓗ	13. look with a fixed gaze	*	s _ _ _	
Ⓗ	14. to or in that place	*	t _ _ _ _	
Ⓗ	15. to or in what place	*	w _ _ _ _	

Using ACE

H beside a word means that it is a homonym. A homonym is a word which sounds the same as or very similar to another word, but which has a different meaning. Can you find all the homonyms (or sound-alike words) from the list you have been working on?

Use the *ACE Spelling Dictionary* to find the homonyms you need. Remember, homonyms are marked with a star in the Dictionary and members of a pair or small group are usually quite close to each other.

When you have found all the homonyms, make up a sentence using that word and at least one other homonym: e.g. 'The **mayor** rode on a grey **mare**'. Write out your sentences below and check the spelling of any hard words in the Dictionary.

Using ACE

Spellings for sounds

The sound /er/ as in EARLY BIRD WITH WORM

Spelt 'ear', 'er', 'ir', 'ol', 'or', 'our', 'ur'

Can you work out these words from the clues given? Each word contains the **/er/** sound. The stars tell you how many syllables are in the word.

If you like, you can use the *ACE Spelling Dictionary* to help you find the answers.

Check all the spellings, unless you are absolutely sure. When you have filled in the missing letters, write the whole word on the line.

If you are working with a partner, one of you can find the answers while the other writes them down.

	CLUES	SYLLABLES		WRITE
	e.g. easily frightened	**	n _ _ v _ _ _	*nervous*
1.	ridiculous	**	a _ s _ _ _ _	
2.	on the look-out	**	al _ _ _ _	
3.	delivery of a baby	*	b _ _ _ _	
4.	thief who breaks in	**	b _ _ g _ _ _ _	
5.	army officer	**	c _ _ _ n _ _	
6.	not clean	**	d _ _ t _	
7.	to obtain money from working	*	e _ _ _	
8.	coat of an animal	*	f _ _	
9.	to make a bubbling sound	**	g _ _ g _ _	
10.	a daily record or paper	**	j _ _ _ n _ _	
11.	kill	**	m _ _ d _ _	
12.	speak in a low voice	**	m _ _ m _ _	
13.	scent	**	p _ _ f _ _ _	
14.	to buy	**	p _ _ c _ _ _ _ _	
15.	the earth	*	w _ _ _	

Ⓗ beside a word means that it is a homonym. A homonym is a word which sounds the same as or very similar to another word, but which has a different meaning. Can you find all the homonyms (or sound-alike words) from the list you have been working on?

Use the *ACE Spelling Dictionary* to find the homonyms you need. Remember, homonyms are marked with a star in the Dictionary and members of a pair or small group are usually quite close to each other.

When you have found all the homonyms, make up a sentence using that word and at least one other homonym: e.g. 'We took **turns** to look through the binoculars at the **terns**'. Write out your sentences below and check the spelling of any hard words in the Dictionary.

Spellings for sounds

The sound /or/ as in WARLIKE HORSE

Spelt 'al', 'ar', 'au', 'augh', 'aw', 'oar', 'or', 'ore', 'our'

Can you work out these words from the clues given? Each word contains the /**or**/ sound. The stars tell you how many syllables are in the word.

If you like, you can use the *ACE Spelling Dictionary* to help you find the answers.

Check all the spellings, unless you are absolutely sure. When you have filled in the missing letters, write the whole word on the line.

If you are working with a partner, one of you can find the answers while the other writes them down.

CLUES	SYLLABLES		WRITE
e.g. an animal you ride	*	h _ _ _ _	*horse*
1. dreadful	**	a _ f _ _	
2. a plank	*	b _ _ _ _	
3. a girl child	**	d _ _ _ _ t _ _	
4. strength or power	*	f _ _ _ _	
5. wealth, good luck	**	f _ _ t _ _ _	
6. splendid and attractive	**	g _ _ g _ _ _	
7. to visit as a ghost	*	h _ _ _ _	
8. a bird of prey	*	h _ _ _ _	
9. a period of grief after loss	**	m _ _ _ _ i _ _	
10. mischievous and disobedient	**	n _ _ _ _ _ t _	
11. cup and —	**	s _ _ c _ _	
12. beach	*	s _ _ _ _	
13. stem	*	s _ _ _ _	
14. to go somewhere on foot	*	w _ _ _	
15. prolonged fighting	*	w _ _	

Ⓗ beside a word means that it is a homonym. A homonym is a word which sounds the same as or very similar to another word, but which has a different meaning. Can you find all the homonyms (or sound-alike words) from the list you have been working on?

Use the *ACE Spelling Dictionary* to find the homonyms you need. Remember, homonyms are marked with a star in the Dictionary and members of a pair or small group are usually quite close to each other.

When you have found all the homonyms, make up a sentence using that word and at least one other homonym: e.g. 'They **fought** hard to capture the **fort**'. Write out your sentences below and check the spelling of any hard words in the Dictionary.

Using ACE

Spellings for sounds

*The sound /**oi**/ as in JOYFUL OYSTER*

Spelt 'oi', 'oy', 'uoy'

Can you work out these words from the clues given? Each word contains the /oi/ sound. The stars tell you how many syllables are in the word.

If you like, you can use the *ACE Spelling Dictionary* to help you find the answers.

Check all the spellings, unless you are absolutely sure. When you have filled in the missing letters, write the whole word on the line.

If you are working with a partner, one of you can find the answers while the other writes them down.

CLUES	SYLLABLES		WRITE
e.g. unpleasant loud sound	*	n _ _ _ _	*noise*
1. keep away from	**	a _ _ _ _	
2. bubbling hot	**	b _ _ l _ _ _	
3. floating marker	*	b _ _ _	
4. what you choose	*	c _ _ _ _ _	
5. money	*	c _ _ _	
6. take on for work	**	e _ p _ _ _	
7. a large entrance hall	**	f _ _ e _	
8. to heave up	*	h _ _ _ _	
9. full of happiness	**	j _ _ f _ _	
10. soothing cream	**	o _ _ _ m _ _ _	
11. shellfish in which pearls grow	**	o _ s _ _ _	
12. kill with a deadly substance	**	p _ _ s _ _	
13. show great happiness	**	r _ j _ _ _ _	
14. made dirty	*	s _ _ _ _ _	
15. hard work	*	t _ _ _	

46

Using ACE

Ⓗ beside a word means that it is a homonym. A homonym is a word which sounds the same as or very similar to another word, but which has a different meaning. Can you find all the homonyms (or sound-alike words) from the list you have been working on?

Use the *ACE Spelling Dictionary* to find the homonyms you need. Remember, homonyms are marked with a star in the Dictionary and members of a pair or small group are usually quite close to each other.

When you have found all the homonyms, make up a sentence using that word and at least one other homonym: e.g. 'I hurt my **groin** when I tried to leap over the **groyne**'. Write out your sentences below and check the spelling of any hard words in the Dictionary.

Using ACE

Spellings for sounds

The sound /**ou**/ as in AN OWL SOUND

Spelt 'ou', 'ough', 'ow'

Can you work out these words from the clues given? Each word contains the /**ou**/ sound. The stars tell you how many syllables are in the word.

If you like, you can use the *ACE Spelling Dictionary* to help you find the answers.

Check all the spellings, unless you are absolutely sure. When you have filled in the missing letters, write the whole word on the line.

If you are working with a partner, one of you can find the answers while the other writes them down.

	CLUES	SYLLABLES		WRITE
	e.g. a small animal with a long tail	*	m _ _ _ _	*mouse*
ⓗ	1. permitted	**	all _ _ _ _	
ⓗ	2. a branch	*	b _ _ _ _	
ⓗ	3. a person who lacks courage	**	c _ _ a _ _	
	4. a large group of people	*	c _ _ _ _	
	5. almost falling asleep	**	d _ _ _ s _	
ⓗ	6. blossom	**	f _ _ _ _ _	
ⓗ	7. disgusting	*	f _ _ _	
ⓗ	8. period of time	*	h _ _ _	
	9. part of the face	*	m _ _ _ _	
	10. dig up into furrows	*	p _ _ _ _	
	11. a game with bat and ball	**	r _ _ d _ _ _	
	12. noisy and badly behaved	**	r _ _ d _	
	13. start to grow	*	s _ _ _ _ _	
	14. 10 × 100	**	t _ _ _ s _ _ _	
	15. a garden tool	**	t _ _ _ _ _	

Using ACE

Ⓗ beside a word means that it is a homonym. A homonym is a word which sounds the same as or very similar to another word, but which has a different meaning. Can you find all the homonyms (or sound-alike words) from the list you have been working on?

Use the *ACE Spelling Dictionary* to find the homonyms you need. Remember, homonyms are marked with a star in the Dictionary and members of a pair or small group are usually quite close to each other.

When you have found all the homonyms, make up a sentence using that word and at least one other homonym: e.g. 'I advise and **counsel** you to stand for the **council**'. Write out your sentences below and check the spelling of any hard words in the Dictionary.

Spellings for sounds puzzles

The sound /ae/ as in BABY SNAIL

Can you follow the lines below to join the beginnings and endings of the words to the middle sound /ae/?

Remember that the sound /ae/ will be spelt in different ways, so check the words in the *ACE Spelling Dictionary* before you write them down.

When you have found all seven words, you can use them to fill in the crossword puzzle.

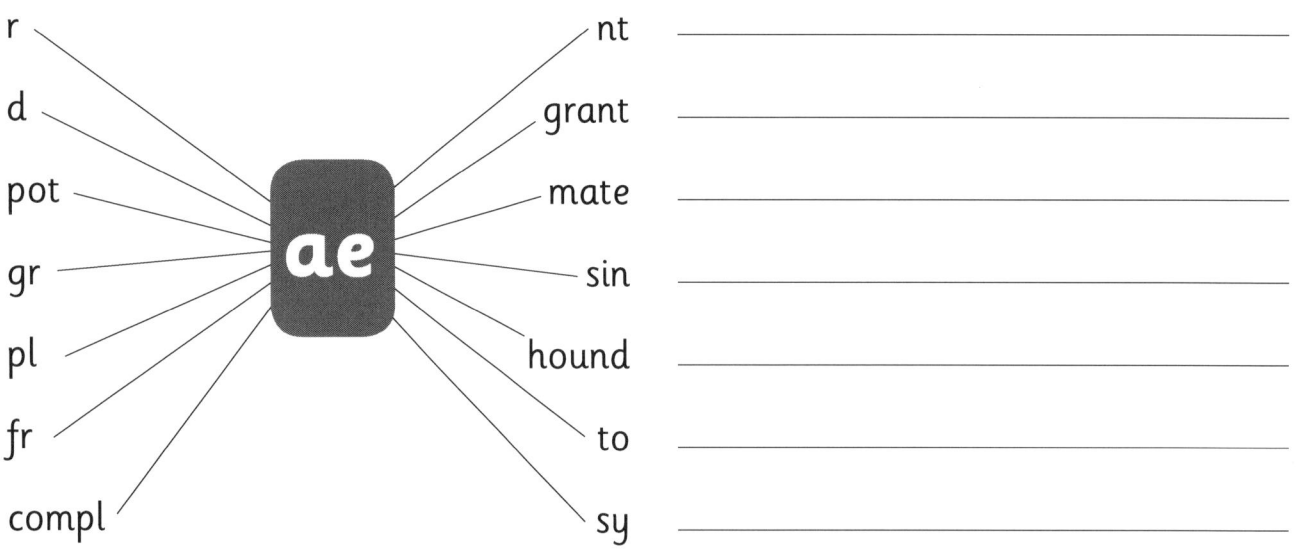

CLUES

1. a vegetable grown in the ground
2. a criticism
3. sweet-smelling
4. a racing dog
5. a common flower
6. a dried grape
7. a friend to have fun with

Using ACE

Spellings for sounds puzzles

The sound /ee/ as in BREEDING EAGLE

Can you follow the lines below to join the beginnings and endings of the words to the middle sound /**ee**/?

Remember that the sound /**ee**/ will be spelt in different ways, so check the words in the *ACE Spelling Dictionary* before you write them down.

When you have found all seven words, you can use them to fill in the crossword puzzle.

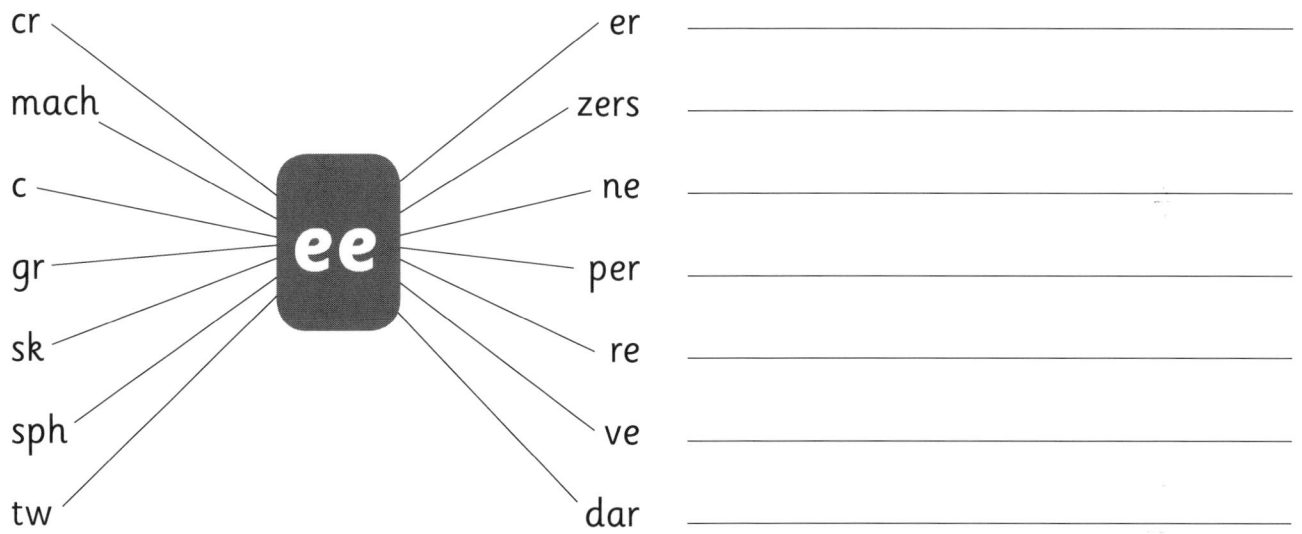

CLUES

1. a person gliding on snow
2. a climbing plant
3. show deep sadness
4. a solid circular shape
5. an evergreen tree
6. an instrument for plucking hairs
7. a mechanical device

Using ACE

Spellings for sounds puzzles

*The sound /**ie**/ as in LIVELY LION*

Can you follow the lines below to join the beginnings and endings of the words to the middle sound /**ie**/?

Remember that the sound /**ie**/ will be spelt in different ways, so check the words in the *ACE Spelling Dictionary* before you write them down.

When you have found all seven words, you can use them to fill in the crossword puzzle.

Beginnings: fr, pr, str, m, r, n, obl

Endings: ve, ge, vate, lon, grate, tened, ot

CLUES

1. to work hard to reach an aim
2. a revolt
3. not public
4. afraid
5. a fabric used for making thin tights
6. go to live in another country
7. to do a favour for someone

Spellings for sounds puzzles

The sound /oe/ as in LONELY GOAT

Can you follow the lines below to join the beginnings and endings of the words to the middle sound /**oe**/?

Remember that the sound /**oe**/ will be spelt in different ways, so check the words in the *ACE Spelling Dictionary* before you write them down.

When you have found all seven words, you can use them to fill in the crossword puzzle.

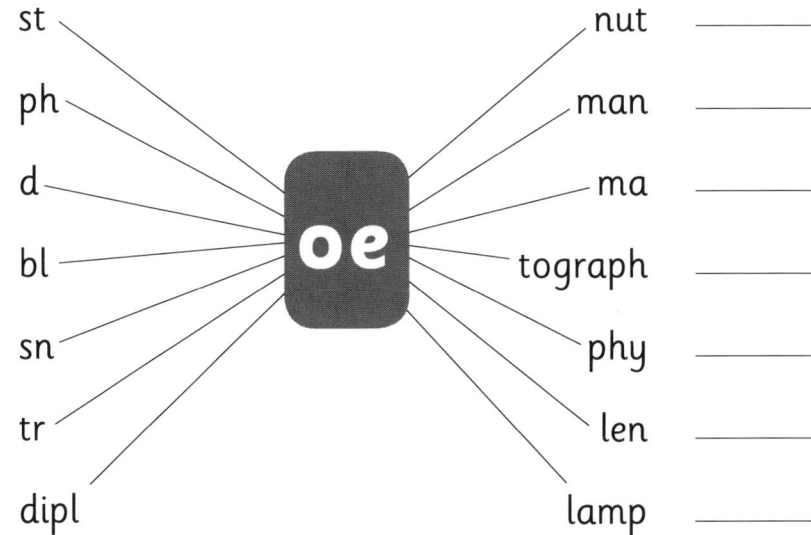

st, ph, d, bl, sn, tr, dipl — **oe** — nut, man, ma, tograph, phy, len, lamp

CLUES

1. burner making a hot flame
2. image captured on a camera
3. round cake with a hole
4. prize
5. taken dishonestly
6. figure who melts
7. certificate

Using ACE

Spellings for sounds puzzles

The sounds /oo/ or /ue/ as in SMOOTH NEWT

Can you follow the lines below to join the beginnings and endings of the words to the middle sounds /oo/ or /ue/?

Remember that the sound /oo/ and /ue/ will be spelt in different ways, so check the words in the *ACE Spelling Dictionary* before you write them down.

When you have found all seven words, you can use them to fill in the crossword puzzle.

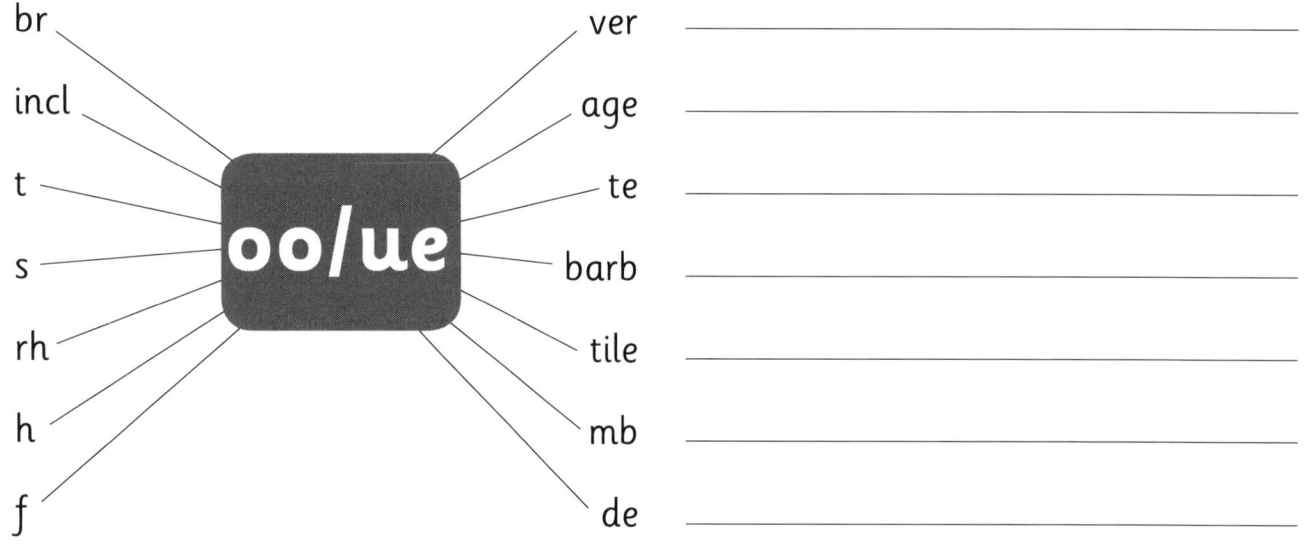

CLUES

1. plant with pink stems, used for pies
2. human waste
3. cleaning machine
4. useless
5. put in a group
6. burial chamber
7. a cruel person

Spellings for sounds puzzles

*The sound /**ar**/ as in BASKING SHARK*

Can you follow the lines below to join the beginnings and endings of the words to the middle sound /**ar**/?

Remember that the sound /**ar**/ will be spelt in different ways, so check the words in the *ACE Spelling Dictionary* before you write them down.

When you have found all seven words, you can use them to fill in the crossword puzzle.

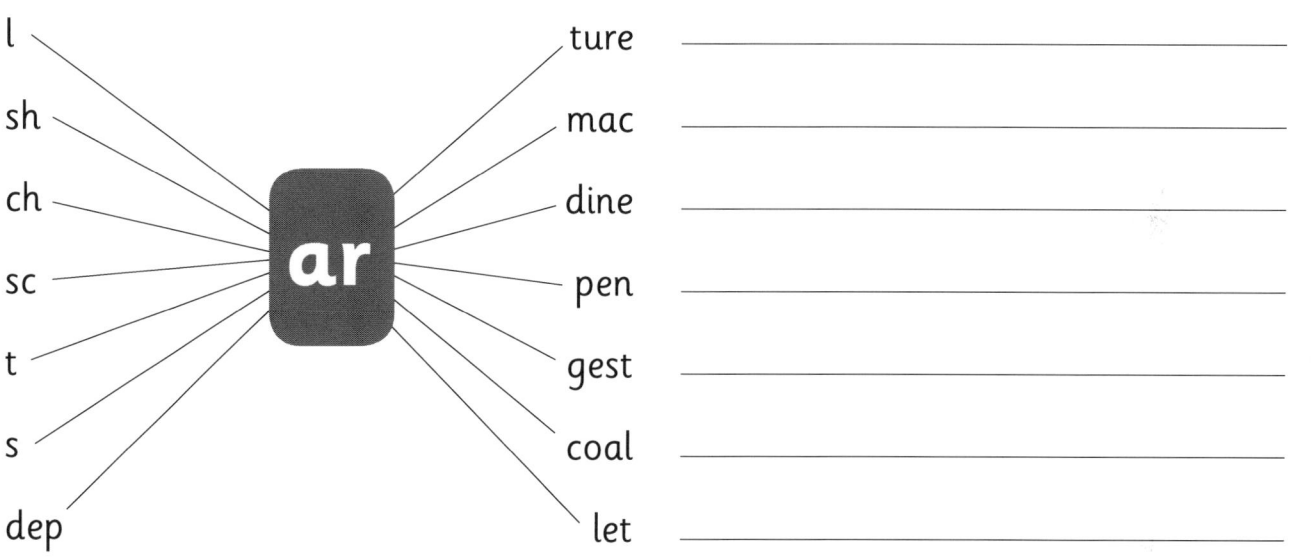

CLUES

1. a tinned fish
2. setting off on a journey
3. used for road surfaces
4. bright red
5. make into a point
6. charred wood
7. biggest

Using ACE

Spellings for sounds puzzles

*The sound /**air**/ as in RARE BEAR*

Can you follow the lines below to join the beginnings and endings of the words to the middle sound /**air**/?

Remember that the sound /**air**/ will be spelt in different ways, so check the words in the *ACE Spelling Dictionary* before you write them down.

When you have found all seven words, you can use them to fill in the crossword puzzle.

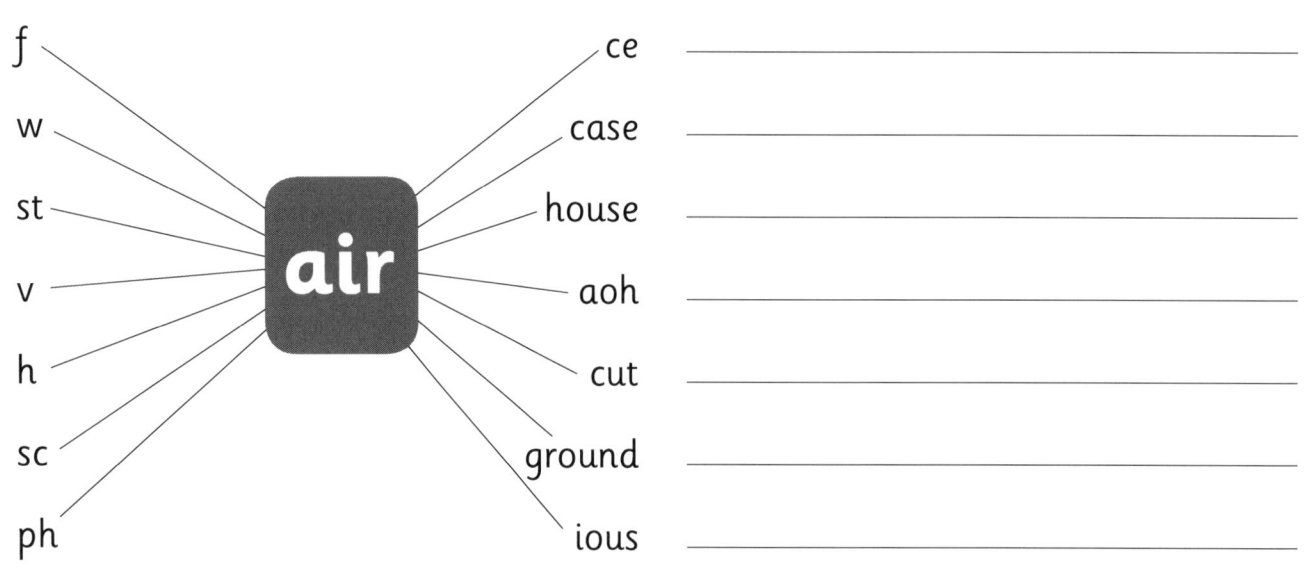

CLUES

1. in short supply

2. building for storing goods

3. ruler of ancient Egypt

4. a barber's handiwork

5. steps from floor to floor

6. of different kinds

7. amusement park

Using ACE

Spellings for sounds puzzles

The sound /er/ as in EARLY BIRD WITH WORM

Can you follow the lines below to join the beginnings and endings of the words to the middle sound /**er**/?

Remember that the sound /**er**/ will be spelt in different ways, so check the words in the *ACE Spelling Dictionary* before you write them down.

When you have found all seven words, you can use them to fill in the crossword puzzle.

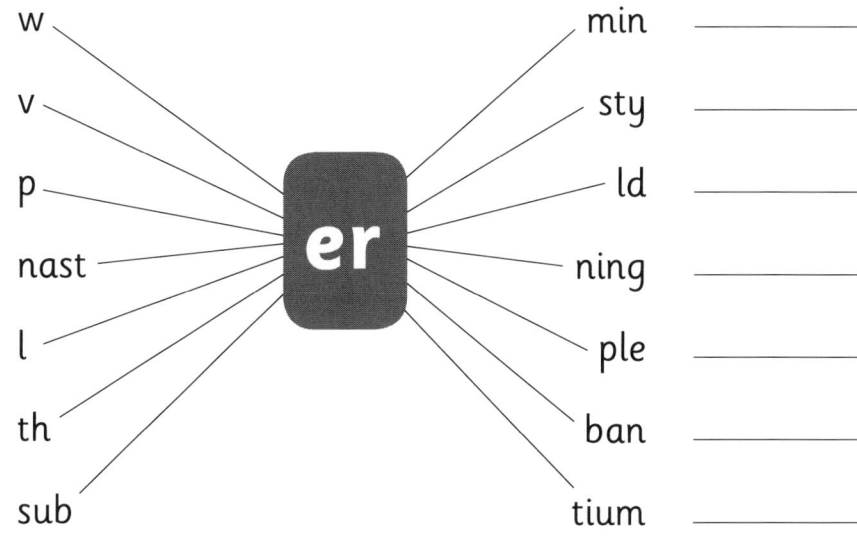

CLUES

1. needing a drink
2. gaining knowledge or skill
3. rats, mice and other pests
4. an orange trumpet-shaped flower
5. of the outer city
6. planet Earth and everything on it
7. a royal colour

Spellings for sounds puzzles

The sound /or/ as in WARLIKE HORSE

Can you follow the lines below to join the beginnings and endings of the words to the middle sound /or/?

Remember that the sound /or/ will be spelt in different ways, so check the words in the *ACE Spelling Dictionary* before you write them down.

When you have found all seven words, you can use them to fill in the crossword puzzle.

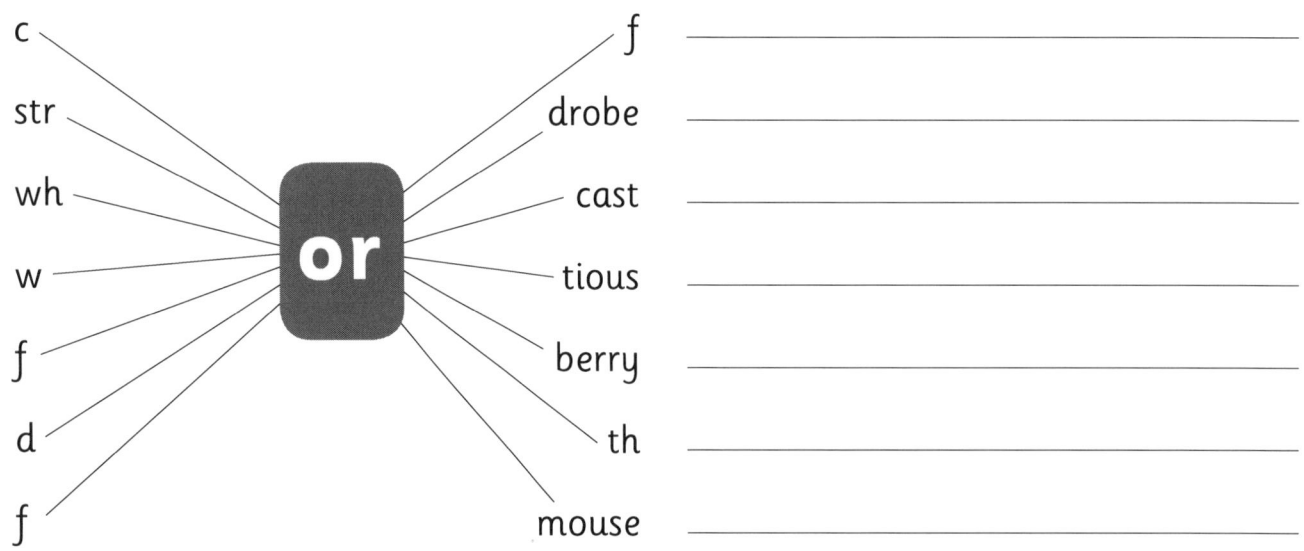

CLUES

1. a small, sleepy country creature

2. nervous and careful

3. a prediction

4. a place where ships unload

5. after third and before fifth

6. a soft red fruit

7. a cupboard for clothes

Spellings for sounds puzzles

The sound /oi/ as in JOYFUL OYSTER

Can you follow the lines below to join the beginnings and endings of the words to the middle sound /**oi**/?

Remember that the sound /**oi**/ will be spelt in different ways, so check the words in the *ACE Spelling Dictionary* before you write them down.

When you have found all seven words, you can use them to fill in the crossword puzzle.

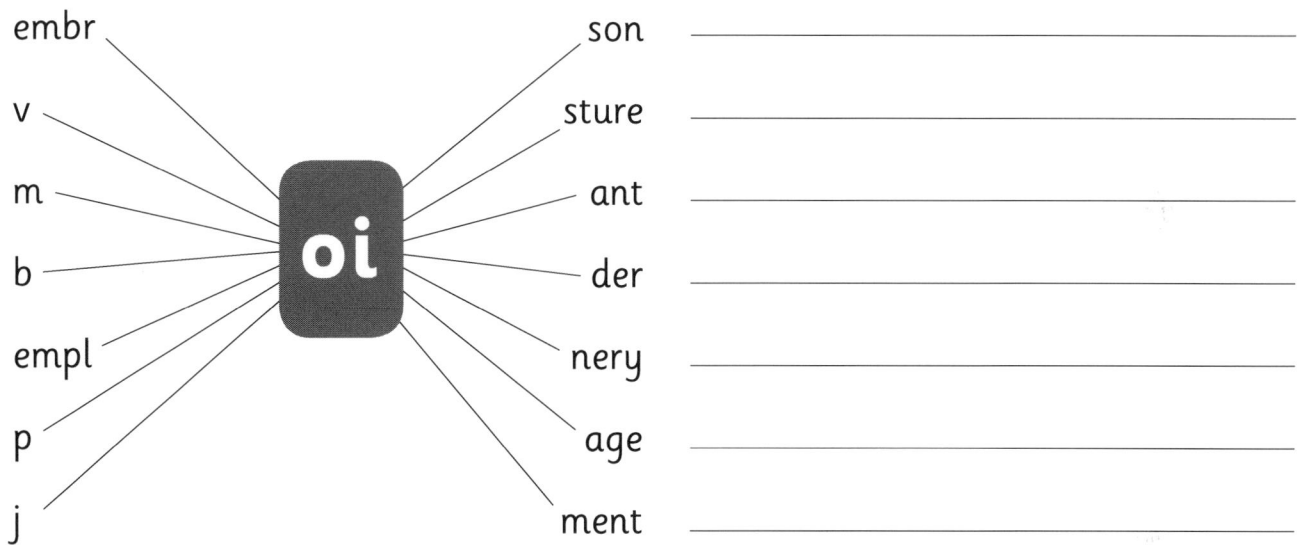

CLUES

1. dampness
2. carpentry on a small scale
3. decorate with stitches
4. able to float easily
5. deadly substance
6. sea journey
7. situation with pay

Using ACE

Spellings for sounds puzzles

*The sound /**ou**/ as in AN OWL SOUND*

Can you follow the lines below to join the beginnings and endings of the words to the middle sound /**ou**/?

Remember that the sound /**ou**/ will be spelt in different ways, so check the words in the *ACE Spelling Dictionary* before you write them down.

When you have found all seven words, you can use them to fill in the crossword puzzle.

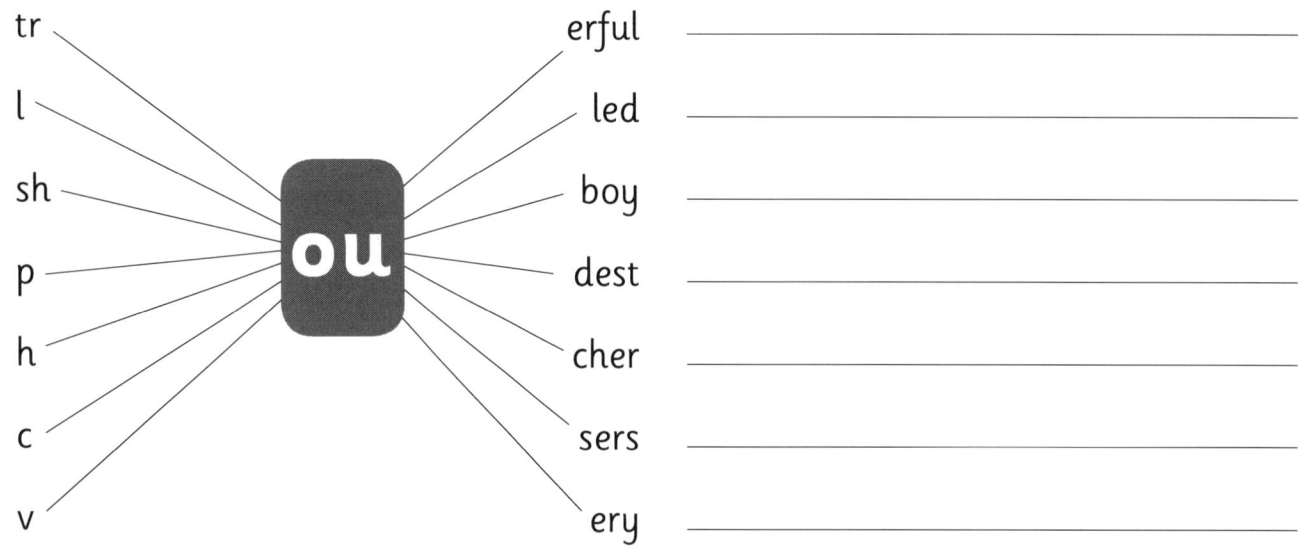

CLUES

1. cried like a wolf
2. noisiest
3. herder of cattle
4. a ticket worth money
5. full of strength
6. garment worn on legs
7. rainy

60 © David Moseley and Gwyn Singleton 2015 | *ACE Spelling Activities* | LDA | Permission to photocopy

Car registration games 1

Find words which include these car registration letters. The first letter must be the first letter in the word and the last letter the last letter of the word. You are also given an ACE vowel sound which is included in the word, but you are not told how that sound is spelt.

You will be able to find all the answers in the *ACE Spelling Dictionary* if you turn to the right page. All the words have two syllables (**).

CLUES

e.g.	JKY	🐕	o	page 103	*jockey*
1.	HVY	🐘	e	page 40	_ _ _ _ _
2.	BCN	🐌	ae	page 138	_ _ _ _ _
3.	BDY	🐕	o	page 95	_ _ _ _
4.	RWD	🐎	or	page 266	_ _ _ _ _ _
5.	WMN	🌿	oo	page 136	_ _ _ _ _ _
6.	BLT	🐌	ae	page 138	_ _ _ _ _ _ _
7.	RPN	🦁	ie	page 189	_ _ _ _ _ _
8.	SCT	🦅	ee	page 169	_ _ _ _ _ _

Now complete the square, using the eight words you have made.

CLUES

1. a breakfast food
2. a female person
3. a prize
4. a piece of jewellery worn around the wrist
5. you have one, dead or alive
6. hard to lift
7. something hidden or unrevealed
8. to grow towards perfection, as fruit does

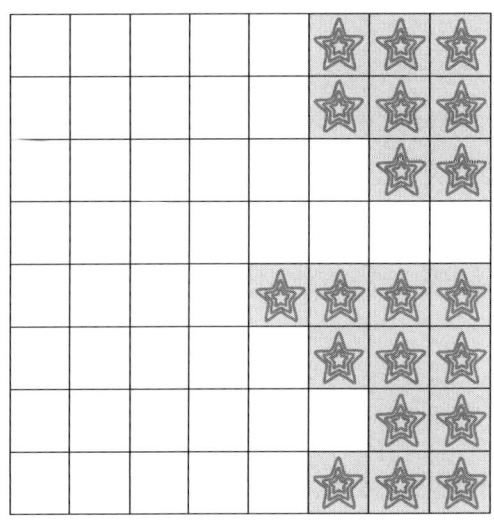

Using ACE

Car registration games 2

Find words which include these car registration letters. The first letter must be the first letter in the word and the last letter the last letter of the word. You are also given an ACE vowel sound which is included in the word, but you are not told how that sound is spelt.

You will be able to find all the answers in the *ACE Spelling Dictionary* if you turn to the right page. All the words have two syllables (**).

CLUES

e.g.	CBY	ou	page 227	*cowboy*
1.	KTP	e	page 42	_____
2.	NHL	ie	page 187	_____
3.	OTH	o	page 107	_____
4.	EHT	or	page 259	_____
5.	FSN	a	page 12	_____
6.	WPL	er	page 255	_____
7.	RSN	ee	page 167	_____
8.	WKT	i	page 92	_____

Now complete the square, using the eight words you have made.

CLUES

1. swirling water
2. fumes from a car
3. a long-legged bird
4. dusk followed by darkness
5. sauce
6. a popular style
7. an explanation for something
8. a target you bowl at in cricket

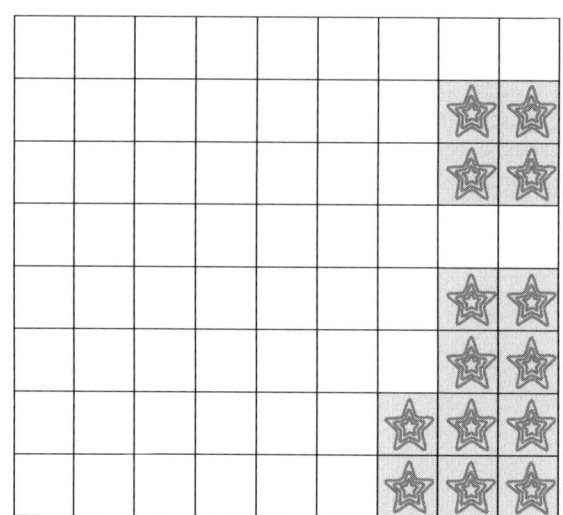

Car registration games 3

Find words which include these car registration letters. The first letter must be the first letter in the word and the last letter the last letter of the word. You are also given an ACE vowel sound which is included in the word, but you are not told how that sound is spelt.

You will be able to find all the answers in the *ACE Spelling Dictionary* if you turn to the right page. All the words have two syllables (**).

CLUES

e.g.	RHG	(eagle)	ee	page 167	*reaching*
1.	LPD	(elephant)	e	page 43	_____
2.	DNF	(cat)	a	page 10	_____
3.	OCN	(goat)	oe	page 203	_____
4.	GGS	(horse)	or	page 261	_____
5.	JFY	(pig)	i	page 77	_____
6.	RBY	(fish)	ue	page 220	_____
7.	RNR	(snail)	ae	page 148	_____
8.	DGN	(swan)	u	page 120	_____

Now complete the square, using the eight words you have made.

CLUES

1. an animal with antlers
2. a precious red stone
3. an underground prison
4. lovely
5. a great expanse of water
6. a moment
7. dead skin among hair
8. a wild animal with spots

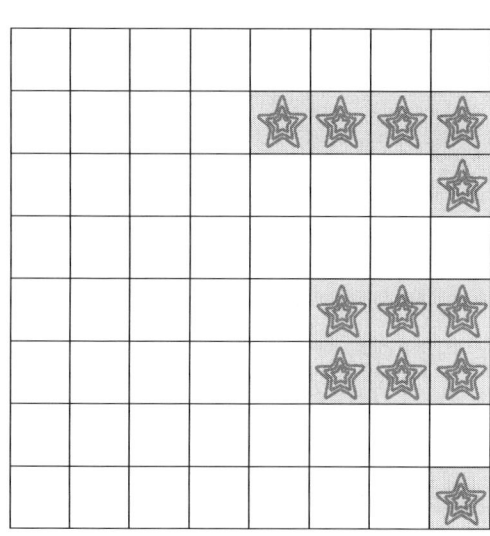

Using ACE

Tricky word endings 1

The vowel spellings are missing in these words, but each word ends with a neutral vowel sound, spelt 'ar', 'er' or 'or'. You must work out the answers from the clues and check them (especially the endings) in the *ACE Spelling Dictionary* or in the wordsearch below. Write in the missing vowel spellings.

CLUES

1.	the person who keeps an eye on prisoners	j __ __ l __ __
2.	a machine that sets something in motion	m __ t __ __
3.	a tool or handle to start a machine or raise something	l __ v __ __
4.	a person who does not tell the truth	l __ __ __
5.	someone who gives something (e.g. blood)	d __ n __ __
6.	a tall support	p __ ll __ __

Find the above six words in the wordsearch and circle them. Can you find and circle another four words with neutral vowel endings? The words go in the following directions: → ↓ ↘

```
p e f l a r i q s o
d t e f a r m e r t
l g p i r s o n a e
e d o u v o t e r n
s p o d o n o r a j
l c i i n u r o z a
e a t l b k l e o i
v s u n l c a i r l
e c k f y a i l a e
r l m o w e r s t r
```

Now write out six of the words you have found and think of a word which rhymes with each. The rhyming words do not have to end with the same spelling, but the endings must sound the same, e.g. 'peculiar' with 'Julia'. Check the spellings in the *ACE Spelling Dictionary* before you write the words down.

1. _____ rhymes with _____
2. _____ rhymes with _____
3. _____ rhymes with _____
4. _____ rhymes with _____
5. _____ rhymes with _____
6. _____ rhymes with _____

Tricky word endings 2

The vowel spellings are missing in these words, but each word ends with a neutral vowel sound, spelt 'an', 'en', 'in' or 'on'. You must work out the answers from the clues and check them (especially the endings) in the *ACE Spelling Dictionary* or in the wordsearch below. Write in the missing vowel spellings.

CLUES

1. to become firm and solid	h _ _ d _ _
2. to become stronger	t _ _ gh _ _
3. a relative	c _ _ s _ _
4. salted pork	b _ c _ _
5. to cover with the darkest colour	bl _ ck _ _
6. claw of a bird of prey	t _ l _ _

Find the above six words in the wordsearch and circle them. Can you find and circle another four words with neutral vowel endings? The words go in the following directions: → ↓ ↘

```
e  b  l  a  c  k  e  n  d  o
s  r  i  p  w  r  s  t  o  s
d  y  s  t  o  r  u  n  s  e
c  e  b  i  m  e  t  r  i  a
w  o  e  h  a  r  d  e  n  s
a  b  u  p  n  s  i  s  i  o
y  a  s  s  e  t  a  l  o  n
o  c  c  a  i  n  t  l  e  d
r  o  t  t  e  n  r  e  f  i
s  n  u  t  o  u  g  h  e  n
```

Now write out six of the words you have found and think of a word which rhymes with each. The rhyming words do not have to end with the same spelling, but the endings must sound the same, e.g. 'dozen' with 'cousin'. Check the spellings in the *ACE Spelling Dictionary* before you write the words down.

1. _____	rhymes with	_____
2. _____	rhymes with	_____
3. _____	rhymes with	_____
4. _____	rhymes with	_____
5. _____	rhymes with	_____
6. _____	rhymes with	_____

Using ACE

Tricky word endings 3

The vowel spellings are missing in these words, but each word ends with 'cian', 'sion' or 'tion'. You must work out the answers from the clues and check them (especially the endings) in the *ACE Spelling Dictionary* or in the wordsearch below. Write in the missing vowel spellings.

CLUES

1. country — n _ _ _ _ n
2. job — _ cc _ p _ _ _ _ n
3. crash — c _ l _ _ _ _ _ n
4. meeting of court — s _ s _ _ _ n
5. movement — m _ _ _ _ n
6. strong feeling — p _ s _ _ _ n
7. person who does clever tricks — m _ g _ _ _ _ n
8. a shortened word — _ bbr _ v _ _ _ _ n
9. answer to a problem — s _ l _ _ _ _ n
10. a person who makes and sells glasses — _ pt _ _ _ _ n

Find and circle in the wordsearch the ten words listed above. Can you find and circle another three words with 'tion' endings? The words go in the following directions: → ↓ ↘

m	o	t	i	o	n	l	f	a	v	o	t
a	b	b	r	e	v	i	a	t	i	o	n
g	p	c	r	e	a	t	s	i	o	c	o
i	a	o	p	t	i	f	v	a	p	c	p
c	s	l	t	s	a	u	e	l	t	u	s
i	s	l	b	i	n	t	x	o	i	p	e
a	i	i	w	f	o	r	a	t	c	a	s
n	o	s	u	r	e	n	t	i	i	t	s
i	n	i	l	t	o	d	i	o	a	i	i
o	s	o	l	u	t	i	o	n	n	o	o
n	i	n	a	t	i	o	n	t	o	n	n
s	f	c	r	e	t	h	n	s	i	d	e

66 © David Moseley and Gwyn Singleton 2015 | *ACE Spelling Activities* | LDA | Permission to photocopy

Using ACE

Tricky word endings 4

The vowel spellings are missing in these words, but each word ends with 'ary', 'ery' or 'ory'. You must work out the answers from the clues and check them (especially the endings) in the *ACE Spelling Dictionary* or in the wordsearch below. Write in the missing vowel spellings.

CLUES

1.	finding something new	d __ sc __ v __ r __
2.	a place where young children are cared for	n __ __ s __ r __
3.	good enough	s __ t __ sf __ ct __ r __
4.	highly unusual	__ xtr __ __ __ d __ n __ r __
5.	getting something back	r __ c __ v __ r __
6.	expressing praise	c __ mpl __ m __ nt __ r __
7.	great skill	m __ st __ r __
8.	a written account of the past	h __ st __ r __
9.	raining from time to time	sh __ __ __ r __
10.	defeat of an enemy	v __ ct __ r __

Find and circle in the wordsearch the ten words listed above. Can you find and circle another five words with 'ary', 'ery' or 'ory' endings? The words go in the following directions: → ↓

w	d	i	s	c	o	v	**e**	**r**	**y**	e	r	y
e	m	b	r	o	i	d	**e**	**r**	**y**	a	h	e
v	n	a	v	m	e	m	o	r	h	g	s	s
e	u	x	i	p	m	i	l	t	i	r	d	t
r	r	n	c	l	a	e	n	v	s	a	i	m
y	s	a	t	i	s	f	a	c	t	**o**	**r**	**y**
s	**e**	l	**o**	m	t	e	r	y	**o**	r	e	s
h	**r**	o	**r**	e	**e**	n	t	s	**r**	d	c	t
o	**y**	i	**y**	n	r	v	o	r	**y**	i	t	**e**
w	a	n	n	t	**y**	t	a	r	y	n	o	**r**
e	x	t	r	**a**	o	r	d	i	n	**a**	**r**	**y**
r	u	r	e	**r**	e	c	o	v	**e**	**r**	**y**	o
y	e	y	a	**y**	i	n	e	t	r	y	p	t

© David Moseley and Gwyn Singleton 2015 | *ACE Spelling Activities* | LDA | Permission to photocopy

Using ACE

Doubles or singles 1

Can you complete the words below? You are given the first two sounds, including the vowel.

Try both short and long sounds and see if you can think of an answer that fits the meaning. When you complete the words you will need to decide between single and double consonants: 'l' or 'll', 'm' or 'mm', 'n' or 'nn', 'p' or 'pp', 't' or 'tt'. Use the *ACE Spelling Dictionary* to check your answers, or to search for an answer if you are stuck.

MEANING	BEGINNING	WRITE
1. way, method of behaviour	ma	
2. hot seasoning	pe	
3. person in charge of an aeroplane	pi	
4. a toy you ride by pushing with one foot	scoo	
5. metal object shot from a gun	bu	
6. has been put down on paper	wri	
7. a tool for hitting nails	ha	
8. the front fold of a jacket or blazer	la	
9. a yellow spread for bread	bu	
10. a carved American Indian pole	to	

Do the double consonants follow a particular type of vowel sound?

Are there any exceptions to the rule?

Doubles or singles 2

Can you complete the words below? You are given the first two sounds, including the vowel.

Try both short and long sounds and see if you can think of an answer that fits the meaning. When you complete the words you will need to decide between single and double consonants: 'l' or 'll', 'm' or 'mm', 'n' or 'nn', 'p' or 'pp', 't' or 'tt'. Use the *ACE Spelling Dictionary* to check your answers, or to search for an answer if you are stuck.

MEANING	BEGINNING	WRITE
1. a green salad vegetable	le	
2. a person's rank in a group	sta	
3. to tease or vex	a	
4. lavatory	toi	
5. a large passenger boat	li	
6. a person who plays the drums	dru	
7. excellent	su	
8. a citrus fruit	le	
9. sickness	il	
10. a glowing light around a saint's head	ha	

Do the double consonants follow a particular type of vowel sound?

Are there any exceptions to the rule?

Using ACE

Find the middle syllable

The short /a/ sound as in ACTIVE CAT

Sometimes the middle of a long word is the hardest part to spell.

This exercise will help you to spell difficult longer words. Say the words slowly and clearly to yourself and fill in the missing letters.

You can check all your answers by looking in the *** (three-syllable) columns of the *ACE Spelling Dictionary*.

CLUES		WRITE
e.g. a hard-fired paint	e _ _ _ el	*enamel*
1. a device to help you float safely to earth	par _ chute	
2. twisted and caught up	en _ _ gled	
3. an unmarried man	bach _ lor	
4. eye makeup	mas _ ra	
5. brave, courageous	val _ ant	
6. picture made by sewing on canvas	tap _ try	
7. a spear thrown at a sports event	jav _ lin	
8. a large warship	bat _ _ ship	
9. taking numbers away	sub _ _ _ tion	
10. to make a product well-known	ad _ _ tise	
11. to desert, to leave	a _ _ don	
12. a cloth or tissue for wiping the nose	hand _ _ chief	
13. in a furious manner	an _ _ ly	
14. living creatures	an _ mals	
15. well-known	fa _ _ iar	

Find the middle syllable

The short /e/ sound as in HEALTHY ELEPHANT

Sometimes the middle of a long word is the hardest part to spell.

This exercise will help you to spell difficult longer words. Say the words slowly and clearly to yourself and fill in the missing letters.

You can check all your answers by looking in the *** (three-syllable) columns of the *ACE Spelling Dictionary*.

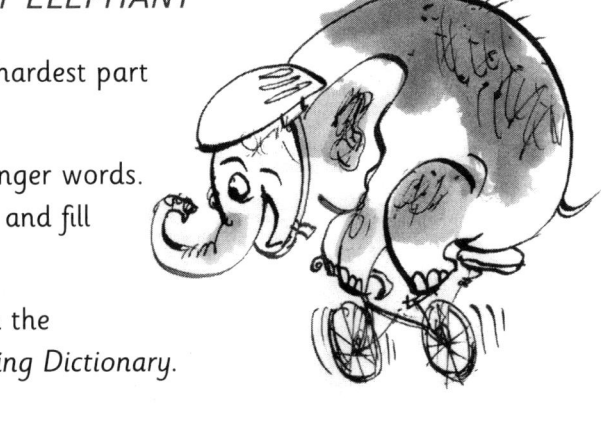

CLUES		WRITE
e.g. recall of events and experiences	mem __ ry	*memory*
1. one who examines a thing carefully	ins __ __ __ tor	
2. skin colour and appearance	com __ __ __ ion	
3. framework of bones	skel __ ton	
4. rubber boot	wel __ __ __ ton	
5. severely frighten	ter __ fy	
6. easily hurt or broken	del __ cate	
7. fun and laughter	mer __ __ ment	
8. instructions for preparing food	rec __ pe	
9. a punishment	pen __ __ ty	
10. deer meat	ven __ son	
11. a place to eat	res __ __ rant	
12. able to bend easily	flex __ ble	
13. unpleasant, attack	of __ __ sive	
14. someone who expects the worst	pes __ __ mist	
15. scale of temperature	Cel __ __ us	

Using ACE

Find the middle syllable

The short /i/ sound as in BIG PIGLET

Sometimes the middle of a long word is the hardest part to spell.

This exercise will help you to spell difficult longer words. Say the words slowly and clearly to yourself and fill in the missing letters.

You can check all your answers by looking in the *** (three-syllable) columns of the *ACE Spelling Dictionary*.

CLUES		WRITE
e.g. person who performs tricks	ma __ cian	*magician*
1. high-ranking soldier	brig __ dier	
2. long-legged pink bird	fla __ go	
3. delicately beautiful	ex __ ite	
4. not taking proper care	ne __ ful	
5. dangerous or evil-looking	sin __ ter	
6. weakly joined and easily broken	rick __ y	
7. small river flowing into a larger one	trib __ tary	
8. an ice-cream flavour	va __ la	
9. purpose or plan	in __ tion	
10. handgun	re __ ver	
11. go on happening	con __ ue	
12. a choice or judgment	de __ sion	
13. opposite of multiplication	di __ sion	
14. talking something over with someone	dis __ sion	
15. very hard	dif __ cult	

Find the middle syllable

The short /o/ sound as in WATCHFUL DOG

Sometimes the middle of a long word is the hardest part to spell.

This exercise will help you to spell difficult longer words. Say the words slowly and clearly to yourself and fill in the missing letters.

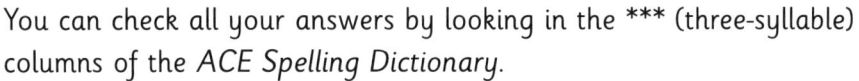

You can check all your answers by looking in the *** (three-syllable) columns of the *ACE Spelling Dictionary*.

CLUES		WRITE
e.g. eight-sided shape	oc _ _ gon	*octagon*
1. a chesty illness	bron _ _ _ tis	
2. a long passage	cor _ _ dor	
3. being alone	sol _ tude	
4. a person who offers unpaid help	vol _ _ teer	
5. an American Indian axe	tom _ hawk	
6. a building for people who are ill	hos _ tal	
7. making idle talk about other people	gos _ _ _ ing	
8. a biting insect that spreads malaria	mos _ _ _ to	
9. greatly surprised	as _ _ ished	
10. deny the statement of another person	con _ _ dict	
11. something put up as a memorial	mon _ ment	
12. more likely than not	prob _ _ ly	
13. suitably, correctly	prop _ ly	
14. in a determined way	dog _ _ ly	
15. huge	co _ _ sal	

Using ACE

Find the middle syllable

The short /u/ or /oo/ sound as in DUCK AND WOODPECKER

Sometimes the middle of a long word is the hardest part to spell.

This exercise will help you to spell difficult longer words. Say the words slowly and clearly to yourself and fill in the missing letters.

You can check all your answers by looking in the *** (three-syllable) columns of the *ACE Spelling Dictionary*.

CLUES		WRITE
e.g. unwilling to do something	re __ __ ctant	*reluctant*
1. a large cow-like animal	buf __ __ lo	
2. a soccer player	foot __ __ er	
3. the art of preparing hot food	cook __ __ y	
4. marvellous	won __ __ ful	
5. a large honey-making insect	bum __ __ bee	
6. person who buys something	cus __ __ er	
7. news report	bull __ in	
8. increase in number	mul __ ply	
9. lacking awareness through the senses	un __ __ scious	
10. guessing about what is happening	won __ __ ing	
11. one-storey house	bun __ low	
12. one more of the same kind	an __ er	
13. try to stop by showing disapproval	dis __ age	
14. a dried seedless grape	sul __ na	
15. quickly and unexpectedly	sud __ ly	

Find the middle syllable

The long /ae/ sound as in BABY SNAIL

Sometimes the middle of a long word is the hardest part to spell.

This exercise will help you to spell difficult longer words. Say the words slowly and clearly to yourself and fill in the missing letters.

You can check all your answers by looking in the *** (three-syllable) columns of the *ACE Spelling Dictionary*.

CLUES		WRITE
e.g. small peach-like fruit	a ____ cot	*apricot*
1. calmly and without complaining	pa _____ ly	
2. stone parts of a building	ma ____ ry	
3. envelopes and writing material	sta _____ ery	
4. great surprise or wonder	a _____ ment	
5. storyteller	nar ___ tor	
6. fixing a name to	la ____ ling	
7. in error	mis ___ ken	
8. local area	neigh _____ hood	
9. likely to cause harm	dan ____ ous	
10. large serving spoon	ta ____ spoon	
11. in a trembling manner	sha ___ ly	
12. unable to wait	im ___ tient	
13. a holiday period	va ___ tion	
14. annoyed diappointment	frus ____ tion	
15. large sports area for spectators	sta ___ um	

Using ACE

Find the middle syllable

The long /ee/ sound as in BREEDING EAGLE

Sometimes the middle of a long word is the hardest part to spell.

This exercise will help you to spell difficult longer words. Say the words slowly and clearly to yourself and fill in the missing letters.

You can check all your answers by looking in the *** (three-syllable) columns of the *ACE Spelling Dictionary*.

CLUES		WRITE
e.g. programme written in parts	se __ al	*serial*
1. came before	pre __ ded	
2. successful outcome	a __ ment	
3. strong and passionate	ve __ ment	
4. tiredness	wea __ ness	
5. a means of land transport	ve __ cle	
6. boring and tiring	te __ ous	
7. coming earlier in time or order	pre __ ous	
8. food in the form of grain	ce __ al	
9. restore confidence	re __ sure	
10. even-handedly, to the same degree	eq __ ly	
11. too proud, puffed up	con __ ed	
12. landscape features	scen __ ry	
13. gentle, merciful	le __ ent	
14. with genuine feeling	sin __ ly	
15. newspapers, television and radio	me __ a	

Find the middle syllable

The long /ie/ sound as in LIVELY LION

Sometimes the middle of a long word is the hardest part to spell.

This exercise will help you to spell difficult longer words. Say the words slowly and clearly to yourself and fill in the missing letters.

You can check all your answers by looking in the *** (three-syllable) columns of the *ACE Spelling Dictionary*.

CLUES		WRITE
e.g. a very hard precious stone	di __ mond	*diamond*
1. causing lively feelings	ex _____ ing	
2. moving home each season	mi _____ ting	
3. a three-sided shape	tri __ gle	
4. a musical instrument with flat bars	xy __ phone	
5. a collection of books	li _____ ry	
6. task	as _____ ment	
7. amazingly huge	gi _____ tic	
8. the line where sky and earth meet	ho __ zon	
9. way of earning a living	live __ hood	
10. joyfully successful	tri __ phant	
11. the material of elephant tusks	i __ ry	
12. offering something to influence judgment	bri __ ry	
13. to do with money	fi _____ cial	
14. a person who prepares a plan	de _____ er	
15. someone who remains alive after danger	sur __ vor	

Find the middle syllable

The short /oe/ sound as in LONELY GOAT

Sometimes the middle of a long word is the hardest part to spell.

This exercise will help you to spell difficult longer words. Say the words slowly and clearly to yourself and fill in the missing letters.

You can check all your answers by looking in the *** (three-syllable) columns of the *ACE Spelling Dictionary*.

CLUES		WRITE
e.g. left out	o _ _ ted	*omitted*
1. a strong (usually pleasant) smell	a _ _ ma	
2. unable to move	im _ _ bile	
3. lawful possession	ow _ _ ship	
4. steady affection, strong commitment	de _ _ tion	
5. food and household supplies	gro _ _ ries	
6. leaves	fo _ _ age	
7. very bad, shocking	a _ _ cious	
8. friendly, liking company	so _ _ ble	
9. lacking and wanting human contact	lone _ _ ness	
10. a strong feeling	e _ _ tion	
11. hateful, repulsive, very unpleasant	o _ _ ous	
12. a large, fibre-covered nut	co _ _ nut	
13. fierce	fe _ _ cious	
14. cheerily good-natured, jolly	jo _ _ al	
15. an orchestral stringed instrument	vi _ la	

Using ACE

Find the middle syllable

The /oo/ and /ue/ sounds as in SMOOTH NEWT

Sometimes the middle of a long word is the hardest part to spell.

This exercise will help you to spell difficult longer words. Say the words slowly and clearly to yourself and fill in the missing letters.

You can check all your answers by looking in the *** (three-syllable) columns of the *ACE Spelling Dictionary*.

CLUES		WRITE
e.g. eager to find out, unusual	cu __ ous	*curious*
1. where old things may be displayed	mu __ __ um	
2. a rude, noisy troublemaker	hoo __ __ gan	
3. an exact copy	du __ __ cate	
4. shaped like a hollow pipe	tu __ __ lar	
5. a pleasant pastime	a __ __ __ ment	
6. a time of celebration to mark an event	ju __ __ lee	
7. a person who goes by car or train to work	com __ __ ter	
8. apply oil	lu __ __ __ cate	
9. causing destruction, decayed	ru __ __ ous	
10. containing or worked by air	pneu __ __ __ ic	
11. lovely	beau __ __ ful	
12. someone who enters without permission	in __ __ __ der	
13. very quiet and private	se __ __ ded	
14. a person escaping from capture	fu __ __ tive	
15. shining in the dark	lu __ __ nous	

© David Moseley and Gwyn Singleton 2015 | *ACE Spelling Activities* | LDA | Permission to photocopy

Using ACE

Find the middle syllable

using all sections of the Dictionary

Sometimes the middle of a long word is the hardest part to spell.

This exercise will help you to spell difficult longer words. Say the words slowly and clearly to yourself and fill in the missing letters.

You can check all your answers by looking in the *** (three-syllable) columns of the *ACE Spelling Dictionary*.

CLUES		ANIMAL PICTURE CLUE	WRITE
e.g. a food not unlike butter	mar ___ rine		*margarine*
1. a pair of glasses	spec ___ cles		
2. tired out, completely used up	ex ___ ed		
3. full of energy	vig ___ ous		
4. a person who designs buildings	ar ___ tect		
5. a clear, fizzy drink	lem ___ ade		
6. a two-wheeled machine	bi ___ cle		
7. wonderful	mar ___ lous		
8. a large ape	go ___ la		
9. breaking in and stealing	bur ___ ry		
10. a person from another country	fo ___ er		
11. musicians under a conductor	or ___ tra		
12. a picture made with small tiles	mo ___ ic		
13. definitely	cer ___ ly		
14. full of very high hills	moun ___ ous		
15. an arrangement to meet	ap ___ ment		

Find the two middle syllables

using all sections of the Dictionary

Sometimes the middle of a long word is the hardest part to spell.

This exercise will help you to spell difficult longer words. Say the words slowly and clearly to yourself and fill in the missing letters.

You can check all your answers by looking in the **** (four-syllable) columns of the *ACE Spelling Dictionary*.

CLUES		ANIMAL PICTURE CLUE	WRITE
e.g. not natural, man-made	ar _ _ _ _ cial		*artificial*
1. triumphant in battle	vic _ _ _ ous		
2. not achievable	im _ _ _ _ ble		
3. the total of inhabitants	pop _ _ _ tion		
4. surroundings	en _ _ _ _ _ ment		
5. process of growing or changing	de _ _ _ _ _ ment		
6. a belief based on ignorant fear	su _ _ _ _ _ _ tion		
7. capturing images on camera	pho _ _ _ _ _ phy		
8. exactly the same	i _ _ _ _ _ cal		
9. absurd	ri _ _ _ _ lous		
10. looking or sounding good	fa _ _ _ _ _ ble		
11. a measurement of distance	kil _ _ _ tre		
12. the smallest part of a group	mi _ _ _ _ ty		
13. making a person feel awkward	em _ _ _ _ _ _ ing		
14. public commemoration	me _ _ _ al		
15. unplanned, done on impulse	spon _ _ _ _ ous		

Using ACE

Find the two middle syllables

using all sections of the Dictionary ②

Sometimes the middle of a long word is the hardest part to spell.

This exercise will help you to spell difficult longer words. Say the words slowly and clearly to yourself and fill in the missing letters.

You can check all your answers by looking in the **** (four-syllable) columns of the *ACE Spelling Dictionary*.

CLUES		ANIMAL PICTURE CLUE	WRITE
e.g. clever	in _____ gent	🐖	*intelligent*
1. well-known for something bad	no _____ ous		
2. a ceremony of crowning	co _____ tion		
3. to build up or collect	ac _____ late		
4. not lasting	tem _____ ry		
5. owner of a business or building	pro _____ tor		
6. savings in outgoing costs	e _____ mies		
7. make known	com _____ cate		
8. plant growth	veg _____ tion		
9. causing much laughter	hi _____ ous		
10. study of the heavenly bodies	as _____ my		
11. large self-service store	su _____ ket		
12. meat-eating	car _____ rous		
13. a severe throat infection	ton _____ tis		
14. strange, special	pe _____ ar		
15. at right angles to vertical	hor _____ tal		

Words within words 1

Find the baseword or simplest form of each word and write it in the box. To do this remove the word ending.

Then, using the *ACE Spelling Dictionary*, find another word which starts with the baseword and write it on the line. The longer word must have at least three more letters than the baseword.

Take care with double consonants and with basewords which end with a 'magic e'.

CLUES	BASEWORD	WRITE
e.g. sunny	*sun*	*sunburnt*
1. safety		
2. careless		
3. fitted		
4. funniest		
5. rocky		
6. thundered		
7. netting		
8. raindrop		
9. downwards		
10. earthed		
11. shopper		
12. slipped		
13. footstep		
14. brightly		
15. sometimes		

Using ACE

Words within words 2

Find the baseword or simplest form of each word and write it in the box. To do this remove the word ending.

Then, using the *ACE Spelling Dictionary*, find another word which starts with the baseword and write it on the line. The longer word must have at least three more letters than the baseword.

Take care with double consonants and with basewords which end with a 'magic e'.

CLUES	BASEWORD	WRITE
e.g. thirsty	*thirst*	*thirstiness*
1. centimetre		
2. dirty		
3. cheerfully		
4. signing		
5. wholemeal		
6. dreaded		
7. infectious		
8. personal		
9. favourite		
10. governor		
11. schooling		
12. greedy		
13. timer		
14. pointer		
15. agreeable		

Using ACE

Find the baseword or root   1

Basewords are simple words from which others derive their meaning. You can often find them on the same page of the *ACE Spelling Dictionary* as the words based on them.

Underline the correct meaning of each numbered word. Write the root or baseword in the box.

CLUES

e.g. the baseword for **personality** is **person**

e.g. the baseword for **leadership** is **lead**

1. politely
   a) in a well-mannered way
   b) in a clever way

2. explosion
   a) unprotected from the weather
   b) a loud noise when something is blown up

3. miner
   a) less important
   b) a mineworker

4. plantation
   a) a large group of trees grown by people
   b) a garden centre

5. cheater
   a) a person who breaks rules for profit
   b) a fast-running animal

6. scornfully
   a) walking painfully on sore feet
   b) mockingly

7. globally
   a) circular in shape
   b) worldwide

8. reliable
   a) able to relay a message
   b) dependable

9. simplicity
   a) an uncomplicated state
   b) stupidity

10. fictitious
    a) fierce
    b) invented, untrue

Using ACE

Find the baseword or root 2

Basewords are simple words from which others derive their meaning. You can often find them on the same page of the *ACE Spelling Dictionary* as the words based on them.

Underline the correct meaning of each numbered word. Write the root or baseword in the box.

CLUES

e.g. the baseword for **numerous** is **number**

e.g. the baseword for **migration** is **migrate**

1. mortally	a) made with bricks and mortar b) fatally	
2. liberation	a) the experience of being set free b) a group of librarians	
3. joyfully	a) showing pleasure and excitement b) joining two things	
4. optician	a) someone who looks on the bright side b) someone who tests eyesight	
5. navigator	a) an explorer b) someone who chooses the correct direction	
6. review	a) a survey or critical account b) a second chance	
7. streamer	a) a little stream b) a paper decoration	
8. employee	a) someone who offers work b) someone who gets paid for work	
9. lessen	a) reduce b) a period of instruction	
10. accepted	a) not included b) received	

Introducing the parts of speech

NOUNS 1

Words which can have 'a' or 'the' in front of them are used to name things. They are nouns. In this exercise all the words which fill the gaps are nouns. The *ACE Spelling Dictionary* page number is given to help you find them, together with the number of syllables.

PAGE 138

**	**1.** The fire _____ was called out after the explosion.
*	**2.** At last the fierce _____ was extinguished.
*	**3.** Each pony has a _____ of hay in its stable.
**	**4.** He gave his wife a silver necklace and _____.

PAGE 200

**	**1.** The air _____ demonstrated the safety drill.
**	**2.** We stayed in a _____ near the beach.
*	**3.** Grandma did not want to live in a retirement _____.
**	**4.** We use a _____ to wash the car.

PAGE 120

*	**1.** My little brother likes to bang his toy _____.
**	**2.** The baby cries if she loses her _____.
***	**3.** It doesn't matter if I get dirt on my _____.
*	**4.** The white _____ cooed on the window-sill.

PAGE 246

***	**1.** Dad bought new _____ for my bedroom.
*	**2.** I gave Mum a pretty green _____ in a pot.
**	**3.** Metals are heated in a _____.
****	**4.** Horse manure is an organic _____.

© David Moseley and Gwyn Singleton 2015 | *ACE Spelling Activities* | LDA | Permission to photocopy

Using ACE

Introducing the parts of speech

NOUNS 2

Words which can have 'a' or 'the' in front of them are used to name things. They are nouns. In this exercise all the words which fill the gaps are nouns. The *ACE Spelling Dictionary* page number is given to help you find them, together with the number of syllables.

PAGE 164

* **1.** Mum brought some _____ for Sunday lunch.
** **2.** The weighing _____ did not speak the truth.
** **3.** The doctor said my spots were the _____.
* **4.** We went to a restaurant for a _____.

PAGE 240

* **1.** The bus went round the _____.
** **2.** I stuffed an old suit to make a _____.
* **3.** My brother made me do my _____ of the washing-up.
** **4.** We carried the bed up the _____.

PAGE 212

*** **1.** The boy carried the _____ into the church.
*** **2.** I bought some new games for my _____.
*** **3.** We had ham and _____ sandwiches.
* **4.** The detective looked for a _____ to the murder.

PAGE 277

* **1.** There was not a _____ in the sky.
*** **2.** The town _____ made a long speech.
* **3.** The Queen wears a _____ when she opens Parliament.
* **4.** I lay on the _____ to watch my favourite TV programme.

Introducing the parts of speech

VERBS

A verb often follows a noun (or a pronoun such as 'we') to express an action (actual or possible), thought or feeling. In this exercise all the words which fill the gaps are verbs. The *ACE Spelling Dictionary* page number is given to help you find them, together with the number of syllables.

PAGE 142

** 1. We _____ the cake with chocolate.

* 2. I think that photograph should be enlarged and _____.

** 3. I knew the TV was broken when the picture _____ away.

** 4. Dad _____ us for borrowing his camera without permission.

PAGE 46

* 1. The hen began to _____ at the food.

** 2. He _____ his parents for a new phone.

*** 3. She was on her bike, _____ very fast.

* 4. We _____ on, trying to make up lost time.

PAGE 277

** 1. I was _____ my sweets when the baby grabbed one.

** 2. The injured man _____ as the soldier raised his rifle.

* 3. It is time to _____ the carnival queen.

** 4. We _____ into the lift instead of using the stairs.

PAGE 133

** 1. It was hard going, _____ up the steep hill.

* 2. My dog _____ its tail when I opened a tin of its favourite food.

*** 3. The moles in the garden are always _____ away.

* 4. Don't _____ that cake until teatime.

Using ACE

Introducing the parts of speech

VERBS 2

A verb often follows a noun (or a pronoun such as 'we') to express an action (actual or possible), thought or feeling. In this exercise all the words which fill the gaps are verbs. The *ACE Spelling Dictionary* page number is given to help you find them, together with the number of syllables.

PAGE 252

** 1. I was _____ all over town for some new trainers.

* 2. I _____ the pancake mixture thoroughly.

** 3. The _____ sea heaved the small boat against the rocks.

* 4. He had to _____ to avoid hitting the traffic island.

PAGE 192

* 1. I could _____ simple knots when I was five.

*** 2. The teacher _____ French lessons for Friday mornings.

* 3. She _____ to phone her mum, but the phone was out of signal.

* 4. I shall _____ the race with my stopwatch.

PAGE 154

** 1. The invading army _____ the town.

* 2. She will buy a stud farm and _____ racehorses.

* 3. We could hardly _____ in the crowded room.

* 4. We hoped that we would _____ the record.

PAGE 96

** 1. We spent all morning _____ wood.

* 2. Make sure there's no traffic before you _____ the road.

** 3. He did not _____ on her appearance.

*** 4. Please don't _____ my plans by trying to change them.

Using ACE

Introducing the parts of speech

ADJECTIVES

Adjectives are words which add to the meaning of names like persons, places, ideas or things. They often answer a question such as 'What is it like?'. In this exercise all the words which fill the gaps are adjectives. The *ACE Spelling Dictionary* page number is given to help you find them, together with the number of syllables.

PAGE 188

** 1. She rudely turned down my _____ request.

** 2. I would love my own _____ helicopter.

** 3. Do hypnotists really have _____ powers?

*** 4. Five-year-olds go to _____ school.

PAGE 24

*** 1. That big lion looks _____.

*** 2. The _____ shed was blown down in a gale.

** 3. My clothes were torn and _____.

** 4. _____ numbers are called out in a bingo session.

PAGE 113

** 1. Some chemical waste is highly _____.

*** 2. The _____ rainforests are being destroyed.

** 3. Ben won a _____ apple at the fair.

** 4. I have got a _____ headache.

PAGE 263

** 1. Brian was put on the _____ step as a punishment.

** 2. A body temperature of 37° Celsius is completely _____.

*** 3. Sailors used to rely on _____ charts.

** 4. The Tyne is a river in _____ England.

Using ACE

Introducing the parts of speech

ADVERBS

Adverbs are words which add to the meaning of verbs or adjectives. Many of them end in 'ly'. They answer questions such as 'How?', 'How much?', 'Where?' and 'When?'. In this exercise all the words which fill the gaps are adverbs. The *ACE Spelling Dictionary* page number is given to help you find them, together with the number of syllables.

PAGE 134

***** 1. _____, my teacher was worried about my nosebleed.

****** 2. Julie was always dressed _____.

**** 3. Bouncer was _____ the best dog in the show.

*** 4. The ground was rough and stony _____.

PAGE 190

** 1. Sharon came forward _____ to receive her prize.

****** 2. The experimental results must be analysed _____.

*** 3. The small boy nodded _____.

**** 4. _____, they won all three matches.

PAGE 52

***** 1. The traffic lights were _____ out of action.

**** 2. The violin solo was _____ very difficult.

**** 3. It rained _____ for three hours.

*** 4. After the party we were _____ late to bed.

PAGE 28

*** 1. I replied very _____, so as not to give offence.

*** 2. They died _____ in a car crash.

***** 3. The dictator ruled _____ for 25 years.

*** 4. She _____ accepted the seat he gave up for her.

Searching for patterns

Here are some further ideas for your students, to help them recognise some of the many spelling patterns and the exceptions!

1. When you add **ing** to words ending with **e**, you knock off the **e**. This does not apply if the ending is **ee** or **oe**. See how many words you can find in two minutes that fit this pattern.

2. See how many three-syllable words you can find where a final **y** changes to an **ie**. Group these under the headings: **ies**, **ied** and **ier/iest**.

3. With words like **wit** (with a one-letter vowel and a single final consonant) you double the final consonant when you add endings such as **ed**, **ing**, **er**, **est**, **y**, **ier** and **iest**. So you get: slow-**witted**, out**witting**, **witty**, **wittier**, **wittiest**.

   See how many one-syllable words you can find in ten minutes that fit this pattern. Are there any exceptions?

4. Find ten words like **itch** (one syllable, with a single letter short vowel and the /**tch**/ sound right after the vowel).

   Find ten more one-syllable words with a letter between the short vowel and the /**ch**/ sound, such as **belch**, **inch**, **lunch**.

   Find 20 words ending in **ch** from any of the long vowel sections.

   What pattern do you notice? Are there any exceptions, apart from **rich**, **much** and **such**? Can you explain in a simple way when to use **tch**?

   Carry out similar searches in order to establish when to use **dge** rather than **ge** and when to use **ck** rather than **k**.

5. Think about this spelling rule: **i** before **e** except after **c**. What is the ratio of hits to misses if this rule is applied to words in the long vowel /**ee**/ section?

6. How many words of four or more syllables in which the last syllable contains a neutral vowel sound can you find in five minutes?

7. Make a list of homonym pairs from the /**or**/ section where spelling confusion is likely.

8. truthful – truthfully
   helpful – helpfully
   grateful – gratefully

   Full of …? Find five more words listed in the *ACE Spelling Dictionary* that fit this pattern.

Learning spellings

Words you need to know

Some of the words you meet every day are not easy to write. 'Friend' is one of those unfriendly words. Words which break the law should be treated with suspicion. You need to use an IDENTIKIT card to check the special features of these suspect words. The master list of suspects is on page 95.

What to do

1. Put a tick next to each word on the list which you know very well. These words are innocent and may even be friendly. The others will make up your list of suspects. You will find that some of the suspects have split personalities and may seem to be two separate words, although they are really only one.

2. Get a piece of card which will fit into your *ACE Spelling Dictionary* or into your notebook if folded down the middle.

3. Copy your list of suspects, with further particulars if provided, in two columns. You can add some words of your own if you want to. Then use a highlighter pen to mark any special features of the suspect words which will help you to remember them.

4. Make a second copy of your list of suspects on the back of your card, but this time do not add the further particulars. Leave a space or draw a box beside each word so that you can tally marks to show how many times you have recognised a suspect.

5. Ask a friendly word-inspector to check your IDENTIKIT card when it is ready for use.

6. Get to know your suspects better. Take four words at a time and make up some sentences using these words. Write out your sentences and when you get to a suspect word, find it on your card so you can copy it. Try to copy it after looking at it only once and as you write it notice any special features. When you have finished, ask your friendly word-inspector to double-check what you have written, using your card and the *ACE Spelling Dictionary* if necessary.

How to use your IDENTIKIT card

Get out your card every time you do some writing. Whenever a suspect word comes along, check it on your card before you write it down. Every time you do this, turn your card over and put a tally mark next to the word. You can cross off suspect words when you no longer need to check them on your card, but you should not do this until you have at least ten tally marks against a word.

IDENTIKIT master list of suspect words

again		right	(✓ or →)
always	(al‌l ___ ___ ___ ___)	running	
an	(a .. e .. i .. o .. u ..)	sometimes	
another		still	
bought		stopped	
caught	(did catch)	suddenly	
decided		their	(ownership)
friend		there	(there is …
heard	(___ ear ___)		there are …
hour	(60 minutes)		there was …
inside			there were …
into			there will be …
it's	(it is)		there would be …
kept			there could be … etc.
knew	(silent k)	⟶	to or in that place)
know	(silent k)	thought	
lot	(a lot)	through	(by way of)
might	(?igh?)	too	(too much/as well)
myself		tried	
off	(not on)	turned	
opened		until	(___ ___ till)
outside		want	
police		were	(in the past)
		where	(place)

It is a good idea to make a new IDENTIKIT card once a term until you have narrowed down your list of suspects to one or two dangerous individuals. If you succeed in doing this you will have reduced the crime rate by up to 20%.

Learning spellings

How to remember the special features of the most dangerous suspects

always	This is **always** one word with one **l**, all the time.
an	An egg, **an** anything beginning with **a e i o u**.
caught	Her naughty daughter **caught** a cold.
heard	Did hear, by **ear**.
hour	60 minutes.
it's	**It's** short for 'it is' and the ' stands for the letter **i**.
knew	(silent **k**) – understood.
know	(silent **k**) – understand?
lot	'**A lot**' is NOT one word.
might	I **might** get it right!
off	On and off, '**off**' is confused with '**of**'.
right	Did you write it on the **right** and get it **right**?
their	Our dog is ours, not yours – **their** dog is theirs.
there	Here and **there there** are some rare bears.
through	Although it was rough, he thought we would get **through**.
too	Not TOO many **o**'s to count in twos!
until	One **l** as in **1-nil**: unlike fill, hill, kill, pill, till, will.
were	Why **were** we waiting when the light was green?
where	**Where** were you when the fire broke out in that place?

Learn to spell these really useful words

and get them right when you write!

Three lists of 220 useful words each have been prepared from samples of children's speech and writing. The lists do not include the 40 most commonly misspelt high-frequency words. These can be found on page 95 and are best learned by using the IDENTIKIT card in the course of writing. Simple words which present no spelling problems have been left out. Taken together, the three lists plus the 40 IDENTIKIT words account for between 40% and 60% of the words found in children's writing at ages 9–11.

Each list can be covered in one term, at the rate of 20 words a week. This allows for some repeated learning of words misspelt in weekly tests. Students who need an accelerated spelling programme can work on the lists for a whole year.

It is recommended that useful hard-to-spell words as well as chosen interesting words should be entered into the *ACE Spelling Word Bank*. There is room for up to 1500 words to be added into the Word Bank.

Using the three lists

It is not intended that the same list should be given to all members of a class. All three lists are needed in order to provide for a typical range of ability and teachers may want to add others which are more or less demanding. The following tests can be used to decide which list should be used by which students.

Learning spellings

Spelling test

Say each word, repeat it in a phrase or sentence, pause briefly and then say the word again.

1.	SHIP	...	The passengers boarded the SHIP	...	SHIP
2.	FOOTBALL	...	My FOOTBALL strip	...	FOOTBALL
3.	READING	...	What are you READING?	...	READING
4.	TELL	...	TELL me a story	...	TELL
5.	SEVEN	...	SEVEN puppies in a basket	...	SEVEN
6.	SPOKE	...	I SPOKE to Gran on the phone	...	SPOKE
7.	SLOWLY	...	We walked very SLOWLY	...	SLOWLY
8.	NEAR	...	We live NEAR the park	...	NEAR
9.	PERSON	...	Who is that PERSON crossing the road?	...	PERSON
10.	ANYTHING	...	Have you ANYTHING to report?	...	ANYTHING
11.	PRETTY	...	The garden was looking very PRETTY	...	PRETTY
12.	BEFORE	...	Tidy your room BEFORE you go out	...	BEFORE
13.	OWNER	...	Who is the OWNER of this car?	...	OWNER
14.	MUSIC	...	I listen to MUSIC on my phone	...	MUSIC
15.	HAPPENED	...	What HAPPENED in the playground?	...	HAPPENED
16.	FOLLOWED	...	The stray dog FOLLOWED me	...	FOLLOWED
17.	SUGAR	...	SUGAR in your tea	...	SUGAR
18.	MOUNTAIN	...	The top of the MOUNTAIN	...	MOUNTAIN
19.	USUAL	...	I woke up at seven, as USUAL	...	USUAL
20.	INTERESTING	...	An INTERESTING story	...	INTERESTING

Students scoring:

0–4 should work with List 1

5–14 should work with List 2

15–20 should work with List 3

The 220 words in each list have been grouped into sets of four words, on the basis of a topic or language pattern. There are five word sets across the page; five sets are enough for a week's work. Nouns, verbs, adjectives and adverbs have been grouped together, with some miscellaneous sets at the end. This makes it easier to think of meaningful links between words and to use the words in sentences.

Note that words with an asterisk (*) against them may need special attention, as it is hard or impossible to find a rhyming word with the same spelling pattern. You may be able to think of a non-rhyming word with the same letter string (e.g. watch/match) or find some other way of remembering the letters.

The word sets are not arranged in order of difficulty.

Individual lists

Students can follow individual paths, so that they do not study words they can already spell. The alphabetical lists can be used in this way, preferably in conjunction with the *ACE Spelling Word Bank*.

Every fortnight, students choose 20, 40 or 60 words to learn from one of the lists. These are words which the student would like to be able to spell. The words are underlined and then written down in sets of four. If possible, there should be some meaningful link between the words in a set, as this makes the words and their spellings easier to remember. Students can choose words that will fit into a sentence, that are linked by topic or that have the same spelling pattern. Searching in the *ACE Spelling Dictionary* or the *ACE Spelling Word Bank* will make it easy to put together groups of four words with the same spelling pattern.

Regular testing of small groups of words learned in a daily routine is essential. This can be organised in pairs, with students testing each other. It is not advisable to give the same spelling test to a whole class.

After a test, selected words can be entered into a personal *ACE Spelling Word Bank*. These words may serve either as a celebration of successful learning or as prompts for further study.

Spelling patterns for vowels are the main source of difficulty in English spelling. Grouping words by their vowel sound or vowel spelling is an excellent way of making learning more effective.

Another kind of individual list, for use in correcting drafts, is described on pages 101–102.

How to learn

If you look at words in a list and have someone test you, you may not remember the spellings very well. A more active approach will lead to better results. You should **STUDY**, **COPY**, **CHECK**, **HIGHLIGHT** and then **LEARN**. Try the different methods of learning given below and decide which work best for you.

STUDY	look at the word and count the syllables
COPY	you are allowed only one glance per syllable
CHECK	letter by letter or in strings of up to four letters
HIGHLIGHT	mark the parts you need to remember
LEARN	by one or more of these methods:

a) pronounce the words in a different way, according to the spelling
b) trace over or write the word, saying the letter names before you write each letter string
c) shut your eyes and say or spell the word as you 'write' it in large letters with your finger
d) with eyes shut see the word in your mind, count the letters in groups and then check
e) study the word so well that you can spell it backwards

Learning spellings

f) study the word, say a tongue-twister or count to ten, then spell the word

g) think of a memory link or mnemonic for the whole word or just for the tricky part (e.g. On **Fri**day and at the week**end** I'll see my friends. **F**ind **R**eally **I**nteresting **FRI**ends.)

h) look for a common word ending, such as an **es** plural and **ed** tense ending, or **y** changing to **ies** or **ied**

i) use the *ACE Spelling Dictionary* to find a word which rhymes with the one you are learning and is spelt in the same way. Think of a rhyme and then check the spelling, or simply look through the one- and two-syllable columns in a single vowel section (**Note**: words marked * do not have suitable rhymes)

j) find another word you already know which has the same spelling pattern, (e.g. tongue, argue)

k) learn the tricky part (or parts) first, before trying the whole word.

REPEAT say, write and spell really rapidly, like a R-A-PP-E-R

TEST look, cover, write, check

At the end of a learning session, write down a sentence containing the words you have studied. This may help you to spell those words correctly later on when you are writing – which is the whole point!

The daily routine

Every day you will study two, four or six words from your list. It is helpful if the words are related in some way. Enter the date and the words to be learned in a notebook.

Steps to success

1st word	learn (using chosen method)
self-test	look, cover, write, check
2nd word	learn
self-test	look, cover, write, check
double-check	look at both words, cover, write, check
	Continue if both words are correct; otherwise, practise and try the test again
3rd word	learn
self-test	look, cover, write, check
4th word	learn
self-test	look, cover, write, check
double-check	look at both words, cover, write, check
	Continue if both words are correct; otherwise, practise and try the test again
final test	all four words should be written correctly when dictated in a random order

If you do not pass the final test, you must try to learn the words again, perhaps by a different method. On the other hand, it may be better to attempt two words instead of four.

When you succeed on the final test, a responsible person should initial the list in your notebook and record the learning method(s) from a) to k).

If you find four words easy to learn, you might like to work with groups of six instead.

Note that if you are trying to learn six words you can double-check with groups of two or three words.

The weekly test

Once a week, test sessions should be set up in pairs, so that each learner both gives and receives a test on the 8, 16 or 24 words chosen for that week. Words spelt correctly should be given a tick in the notebook and on the master list. Those not spelt correctly may be studied again the following week, but if so they should be spaced out over the week.

Spelling correctly and correcting mistakes

If you use the **STUDY**, **COPY**, **CHECK**, **HIGHLIGHT**, **LEARN** approach, you will probably make fewer mistakes with words you have recently studied. You can hardly expect that you will never have to think about those words again. Indeed, every time you realise that you have used a word that is on your list or seems to fit a familiar pattern, you score a success. All you then have to do is to check the spelling. If it is correct, that is EXCELLENT!

Good spellers are aware of common patterns between 'families' of words. The more often you look up words in the *ACE Spelling Dictionary* or enter new words in the *ACE Spelling Word Bank*, the more you will notice these patterns. Looking for word families based on Lists 1–3 can introduce you to thousands of words. Learning method i) (looking up rhyming words) is one of the best ways of getting to know more word families. This method also encourages you to use a wider vocabulary when you write.

Most people miss spelling mistakes when they read through a piece of work. You can improve at this if you make a personal alphabetical list of the words you want to learn from Lists 1, 2 and 3. It is sensible to include some interesting words from the same 'families' and any hard-to-spell words you have previously attempted. If you arrange the list in syllable columns, as in the *ACE Spelling Dictionary*, it will be easier to scan. Read through the list before you check your draft: this will make it much more likely that you will recognise the words in the piece you have written.

Learning spellings

Your list might look like this:

*	**	*** (+)
aren't	against	ambulance
board	allow	arrival
break	answer	beautiful
brought	answered	disappeared
clothes	believe	February
course	buried	hospital
guard	curtain	idea
it's	harbour	investigate
knocked	haunted	parliament
let's	later	remembered
passed	people	suitable
past	present	unfortunately
piece	quickly	vegetables
race	really	
spare	swimming	
they're	themselves	
threw	without	
you're		

It is a good idea to check your draft at least three times, each time concentrating on a limited range of words. First, look for any words of three or more syllables which need to be checked. Then go through the passage again, looking for two-syllable words which might present problems. Finally, concentrate on one-syllable words, taking care not to skim over words such as **it's**, **they** and **was** which do not 'leap off the page'.

The more often you correct your own spelling mistakes, the better your spelling will become. When you know how to put things right, you can really concentrate on what you are writing.

List 1

Number of words: 220

father	* baby	dog	bus	money
dad	babies	hair	car	gold
mother	boy	way	road	bank
mum	girl	park	street	shop
look	ask	come	be	* are
looked	asked	* coming	been	will
find	call	came	* being	could
found	called	went	stay	couldn't
one	some	bad	* front	* his
* two	left	good	ready	* her
three	all	better	nice	our
four	more	best	happy	your
garden	door	tea	book	king
farm	room	water	story	queen
wood	window	time	bed	lady
sea	fire	things	night	man
go	* was	woke	see	catch
goes	* wasn't	help	saw	make
* going	would	told	* put	made
gone	wouldn't	sleep	seen	eat
black	big	next	my	away
blue	little	last	* this	around
red	new	long	that	back
white	old	round	other	home
* children	* morning	* Christmas	* woman	* people
sister	* afternoon	tree	teacher	name
brother	week	day	school	hand
* aunt	year	dinner	work	* eyes
do	* has	give	dance	* watch
don't	* have	gave	walk	* watching
did	* having	take	walking	start
* didn't	had	took	walked	started
when	how	first	no	by
just	so	* once	yes	for
now	down	out	* very	with
then	here	over	well	without
giant	he	him	* who	please
* castle	she	himself	* someone	me
ghost	we	you	which	* that's
house	they	them	* something	much
play	named	like	upon	or
playing	think	married	about	but
played	say	live	* from	* because
fell	* said	* lived	after	while

Learning spellings

List 2

Number of words: 220

* aeroplane	animals	present	* clothes	prince
air	bird	balloon	* body	princess
plane	snake	* colour	* shoes	life
* world	* horse	* music	foot	love
tell	listen	read	point	hold
spoke	listened	reading	write	* build
shouted	* answer	mean	writing	built
hear	* answered	meant	written	* covered
* these	high	* every	wide	* usual
those	* higher	its	* straight	* different
any	smaller	sure	near	* interesting
many	short	true	real	* coloured
wife	* family	* sugar	boat	* football
* husband	table	* breakfast	ship	field
* person	chair	meat	shape	line
* group	* kitchen	* course	* owner	* corner
hope	pick	drop	try	* finish
hoped	picked	dropped	trying	* finished
hoping	pull	break	cry	leave
getting	* pulled	* breaking	cried	fly
* young	whole	tired	dead	* nearby
* beautiful	closed	* lonely	broken	* maybe
* pretty	past	dark	dry	quite
dear	seven	* careful	strange	alright
* machine	dragon	ears	* word	* radio
wheel	head	nose	* idea	station
hole	* heart	mouth	* notice	* minutes
light	blood	* voice	* language	* sentence
seemed	die	sitting	meet	should
* imagine	died	waiting	brought	* does
guess	jumped	* happen	passed	* doesn't
* understand	killed	* happened	followed	done
quickly	already	* even	nearly	onto
slowly	behind	* also	* usually	across
early	ever	* really	* finally	along
later	o'clock	enough	together	against
mountain	piece	* numbers	few	* no-one
side	* picture	* nothing	half	* everyone
ice	place	* thousands	* anyone	* everything
winter	* village	* difference	* anything	whose
buy	before	* I'd	* you'd	* what
wear	why	* I'll	* you'll	* what's
used	whether	* I'm	* you're	* let's
grown	* whenever	* I've	* you've	* themselves

List 3

Number of words: 220

mouse	* squirrel	creatures	fish	* chocolate
mice	goat	* butterfly	* rabbit	coffee
* puppy	* wolf	* dinosaur	* potato	flour
* puppies	* elephant	* monster	* potatoes	* apron
wash	* allow	swim	* arrived	threw
washing	* allowed	swimming	* offered	throw
washed	wished	rain	received	blew
dressed	* cannot	raining	grabbed	blow
* basket	lawn	shirt	* drawer	crash
* bowl	flowers	skirt	shelf	surprise
* board	patch	sheet	shelves	fright
brush	* vegetables	* curtain	stairs	* skeleton
fishing	believe	approach	lie	drag
float	* wondering	* recognised	lying	dragged
floated	* realised	remember	lay	* bury
drowned	* investigate	* remembered	laid	* buried
shock	* uncle	* February	* harbour	pony
* ambulance	* cousin	* months	beach	* ponies
* hospital	* grandfather	* holiday	* island	saddle
* oxygen	* neighbours	* Saturday	cave	stable
* climb	push	hopped	* whisper	* burst
tied	* pushed	hopping	* whispered	guard
falling	knocked	pretended	* whistle	* chase
slipped	smashed	hurt	screamed	* disappeared
pencil	* alphabet	* camera	* parliament	noise
* rubber	* calendar	* film	* palace	* policeman
* ruler	fractions	* submarine	* television	* uniform
* scissors	* graph	* magazine	* programme	* court
* dangerous	frightening	* favourite	* curious	lazy
* terrible	* poisonous	* orange	spare	dirty
massive	frightened	* purple	* quiet	* impossible
* enormous	scared	* visible	haunted	funny
* telephone	* visitor	* system	switch	flame
* message	* Germany	defence	* contact	volcano
rhyme	* London	* exhibition	* explosion	thunder
* tongue	* countries	* manager	bridge	* lightning
* motor	* excellent	* British	dining	* downstairs
racing	* wonderful	* Chinese	* hungry	* upstairs
tight	* fantastic	* Japanese	fried	* somewhere
* physical	* exciting	* Egyptian	* frozen	* everywhere
* bicycle	* hello	he'd	* aren't	* anyway
bike	* everybody	he'll	we'd	* somehow
race	* quietly	* he's	we'll	* anybody
track	* sixth	* they're	* we're	* somebody

Learning spellings

Alphabetical list 1

Number of words: 220

about	eyes	man	started
after	farm	married	stay
afternoon	father	me	story
all	fell	money	street
are	find	more	take
around	fire	morning	tea
ask	first	mother	teacher
asked	for	much	that
aunt	found	mum	that's
away	four	my	them
babies	from	name	then
baby	front	named	they
back	garden	new	things
bad	gave	next	think
bank	ghost	nice	this
be	giant	night	three
because	girl	no	time
bed	give	now	told
been	go	old	took
being	goes	once	tree
best	going	one	two
better	gold	or	upon
big	gone	other	very
black	good	our	walk
blue	had	out	walked
book	hair	over	walking
boy	hand	park	was
brother	happy	people	wasn't
bus	has	play	watch
but	have	played	watching
by	having	playing	water
call	he	please	way
called	help	put	we
came	her	queen	week
car	here	ready	well
castle	him	red	went
catch	himself	road	when
children	his	room	which
Christmas	home	round	while
come	house	said	white
coming	how	saw	who
could	just	say	will
couldn't	king	school	window
dad	lady	sea	with
dance	last	see	without
day	left	seen	woke
did	like	she	woman
didn't	little	shop	wood
dinner	live	sister	work
do	lived	sleep	would
dog	long	so	wouldn't
don't	look	some	year
door	looked	someone	yes
down	made	something	you
eat	make	start	your

Alphabetical list 2

Number of words: 220

across	early	line	shoes
aeroplane	ears	listen	shirt
against	enough	listened	should
air	even	lonely	shouted
along	ever	love	side
already	every	machine	sitting
alright	everyone	many	slowly
also	everything	maybe	smaller
animals	family	mean	snake
answer	few	meant	spoke
answered	field	meat	station
any	finally	meet	straight
anyone	finish	minutes	strange
anything	finished	mountain	sugar
balloon	fly	mouth	sure
beautiful	followed	music	table
before	foot	near	tell
behind	football	nearby	themselves
bird	getting	nearly	these
blood	group	no-one	those
boat	grown	nose	thousands
body	guess	nothing	tired
break	half	notice	together
breakfast	happen	numbers	true
breaking	happened	o'clock	try
broken	head	onto	trying
brought	hear	owner	understand
build	heart	passed	used
built	high	past	usual
buy	higher	person	usually
careful	hold	pick	village
chair	hole	picked	voice
closed	hope	picture	waiting
clothes	hoped	piece	wear
colour	hoping	place	what
coloured	horse	plane	what's
corner	husband	point	wheel
course	I'd	present	whenever
covered	I'll	pretty	whether
cried	I'm	prince	whole
cry	I've	princess	whose
dark	ice	pull	why
dead	idea	pulled	wide
dear	imagine	quickly	wife
die	interesting	quite	winter
died	its	radio	word
difference	jumped	read	world
different	killed	reading	write
does	kitchen	real	writing
doesn't	language	really	written
done	later	seemed	you'd
dragon	leave	sentence	you'll
drop	let's	seven	you're
dropped	life	shape	you've
dry	light	ship	young

Alphabetical list 3

Number of words: 220

allow	Egyptian	lie	screamed
allowed	elephant	lightning	sheet
alphabet	enormous	London	shelf
ambulance	everybody	lying	shelves
anybody	everywhere	magazine	shirt
anyway	excellent	manager	shock
approach	exciting	massive	sixth
apron	exhibition	message	skeleton
aren't	explosion	mice	skirt
arrived	falling	monster	slipped
basket	fantastic	months	smashed
beach	favourite	motor	somebody
believe	February	mouse	somehow
bicycle	film	neighbours	somewhere
bike	fish	noise	spare
blew	fishing	offered	squirrel
blow	flame	orange	stables
board	float	oxygen	stairs
bowl	floated	palace	submarine
bridge	flour	parliament	surprise
British	flowers	patch	swim
brush	fractions	pencil	swimming
buried	fried	physical	switch
burst	fright	poisonous	system
bury	frightened	policeman	telephone
butterfly	frightening	ponies	television
calendar	frozen	pony	terrible
camera	funny	potato	they're
cannot	Germany	potatoes	threw
cave	goat	pretended	throw
chase	grabbed	programme	thunder
Chinese	grandfather	puppies	tied
chocolate	graph	puppy	tight
climb	guard	purple	tongue
coffee	harbour	push	track
contact	haunted	pushed	uncle
countries	he'd	quiet	uniform
court	he'll	quietly	upstairs
cousin	he's	rabbit	vegetables
crash	hello	race	visible
creatures	holiday	racing	visitor
curious	hopped	rain	volcano
curtain	hopping	raining	wash
dangerous	hospital	realised	washed
defence	hungry	received	washing
dining	hurt	recognised	we'd
dinosaur	impossible	remember	we'll
dirty	investigate	remembered	we're
disappeared	island	rhyme	whisper
downstairs	Japanese	rubber	whispered
drag	knocked	ruler	whistle
dragged	laid	saddle	wished
drawer	lawn	Saturday	wolf
dressed	lay	scared	wonderful
drowned	lazy	scissors	wondering

Slippery Characters

Both short and long words often have tricky spellings, such as 'often'. Here are 240 words which are often misspelt, in groups of ten. You can find the missing letters by looking up the words in the *ACE Spelling Dictionary*. You have been given the ACE page number, number of syllables and word length to help you. Words 1–20 have only five letters.

	PAGE NUMBER	SYLLABLES	
1.	66	**	_ qu _ _
2.	93	**	w _ m _ n
3.	106	**	o _ _ _ n
4.	126	**	m _ n _ _
5.	141	*	_ _ _ _ t
6.	148	*	r _ _ _ n
7.	155	*	ch _ _ f
8.	174	*	w _ i _ d
9.	182	*	g _ _ d _
10.	185	**	l _ _ _ g
11.	189	*	r _ _ me
12.	214	*	g _ _ _ p
13.	240	**	s _ _ _ y
14.	245	**	_ _ _ ly
15.	245	*	_ _ _ th
16.	247	*	h _ _ rd
17.	248	*	l _ _ _ n
18.	249	**	o _ _ _ r
19.	256	**	_ fu _
20.	260	**	f _ _ ty

It's a good idea to copy words you want to learn into your personal spelling bank and use them for learning four at a time and/or checking as described on pages 99–102.

Learning spellings

	PAGE NUMBER	SYLLABLES	
21.	1	**	ac _ _ _ l
22.	16	**	_ _ ra _ _
23.	29	**	vac _ _ m
24.	32	*	b _ _ _ th
25.	33	**	_ _ nt _ _
26.	37	***	_ n _ _ g _
27.	37	**	e _ _ ept
28.	43	*	_ _ _ _ th
29.	82	**	pig _ _ n
30.	85	**	r _ _ thm
31.	89	**	sy _ _ _ l
32.	89	**	s _ _ _ _ m
33.	106	***	o _ _ up _
34.	125	***	l _ _ _ _ _ y
35.	126	**	m _ s _ l _
36.	141	*	_ _ _ _ th
37.	157	**	ex _ _ _ _
38.	159	***	_ _ n _ _ s
39.	167	**	r _ c _ _ t
40.	176	**	_ _ _ v _

It's a good idea to copy words you want to learn into your personal spelling bank and use them for learning four at a time and/or checking as described on pages 99–102.

	PAGE NUMBER	SYLLABLES	
41.	178	**	d _ _ _ _ _
42.	183	**	i _ l _ _ d
43.	208	*	_ _ ou _ _
44.	214	**	f _ _ ure
45.	219	**	p _ _ s _ _
46.	223	***	u _ _ b _ _
47.	225	**	_ ns _ _ _
48.	225	**	ar _ ti _
49.	244	**	c _ _ cl _
50.	260	*	f _ _ _ th

	PAGE NUMBER	SYLLABLES	
51.	1	**	ab _ _ n _ _
52.	2	***	am _ t _ _ _
53.	3	**	a _ _ _ _ ct
54.	3	**	av _ r _ _
55.	15	*	gram _ _ _
56.	17	***	_ ma _ _ _
57.	21	***	n _ _ _ _ _ l
58.	23	**	p _ _ _ aps
59.	28	***	tra _ _ _ y
60.	31	**	_ _ _ _ _ ss

It's a good idea to copy words you want to learn into your personal spelling bank and use them for learning four at a time and/or checking as described on pages 99–102.

Learning spellings

	PAGE NUMBER	SYLLABLES	
61.	33	***	cen _ _ _ _
62.	35	***	d _ v _ _ _
63.	44	**	men _ _ _ _
64.	46	**	p _ _ _ _ ss
65.	48	***	reg _ l _ _
66.	50	**	_ _ v _ _ _ l
67.	51	**	spe _ _ _ l
68.	51	**	s _ _ _ est
69.	52	*	twe _ _ _ _
70.	54	**	we _ th _ _

	PAGE NUMBER	SYLLABLES	
71.	88	***	sim _ l _ _
72.	91	**	vi _ _ _ _ s
73.	100	**	f _ _ _ _ _ n
74.	108	***	pop _ _ _ _
75.	108	**	prom _ _ _
76.	150	*	_ _ _ a _ _ _
77.	153	**	_ ch _ _ _ _
78.	156	**	_ _ _ _ ve
79.	156	**	d _ _ ea _ _
80.	157	**	ex _ _ _ m _

It's a good idea to copy words you want to learn into your personal spelling bank and use them for learning four at a time and/or checking as described on pages 99–102.

Learning spellings

PAGE	NUMBER	SYLLABLES	
81.	167	**	r __ __ e __ __ t
82.	170	**	s __ n __ __ __ __
83.	172	*	th __ __ v __ __
84.	182	**	h __ gi __ n __
85.	185	**	li __ __ nc __
86.	193	****	__ __ r __ __ __ y
87.	207	**	s __ __ __ ose
88.	222	*	th __ __ __ __
89.	225	***	__ __ ti __ l __
90.	226	**	b __ __ g __ __ n

PAGE	NUMBER	SYLLABLES	
91.	226	**	b __ z __ __ __ __ __
92.	239	**	__ __ __ __ __ __ h
93.	243	**	b __ __ gl __ __
94.	244	**	c __ __ __ __ n
95.	246	**	f __ __ th __ __
96.	250	**	p __ __ __ __ s __
97.	256	**	__ __ __ w __ __ d
98.	261	**	f __ __ w __ __ d
99.	266	**	q __ __ __ __ er
100.	268	*	th __ __ __ __ __

It's a good idea to copy words you want to learn into your personal spelling bank and use them for learning four at a time and/or checking as described on pages 99–102.

Learning spellings

	PAGE NUMBER	SYLLABLES	
101.	1	***	a _ _ _ d _ _ _
102.	1	****	ac _ u _ _ _ y
103.	3	***	_ _ _ ar _ nt
104.	3	**	a _ _ _ ch _ _
105.	7	****	cat _ g _ _ _
106.	20	**	ma _ _ _ _ ge
107.	25	**	san _ wi _ _ _
108.	33	***	cem _ t _ r _
109.	34	***	def _ n _ t _
110.	38	***	e _ e _ _ ise

	PAGE NUMBER	SYLLABLES	
111.	39	***	Fe _ _ _ _ ry
112.	44	***	med _ _ _ n _
113.	46	**	pl _ _ _ _ nt
114.	47	**	p _ _ ss _ r _
115.	47	**	q _ _ _ _ _ _ n
116.	48	***	rel _ v _ nt
117.	50	**	sent _ n _ _
118.	50	**	sep _ r _ _
119.	51	*	str _ _ _ th
120.	56	***	ad _ i _ _ _ n

It's a good idea to copy words you want to learn into your personal spelling bank and use them for learning four at a time and/or checking as described on pages 99–102.

	PAGE	NUMBER	SYLLABLES	
121.	58	**	b _ s _ n _ _ _
122.	59	***	c _ ns _ _ _
123.	66	**	_ qui _ _ _ _
124.	71	***	h _ _ if _ _
125.	72	**	in _ _ _ _ s _
126.	73	**	int _ _ _ st
127.	80	**	mis _ _ _ _ f
128.	80	**	mi _ spe _ _
129.	81	***	_ mi _ _ _ _ n
130.	82	***	_ _ _ _ ical

	PAGE	NUMBER	SYLLABLES	
131.	82	***	p _ si _ _ _ n
132.	95	***	bro _ _ _ l _
133.	107	***	o _ _ _ s _ t _
134.	108	***	po _ _ _ bl _
135.	133	**	th _ r _ _ _ _
136.	143	**	gr _ t _ f _ _
137.	147	***	o _ _ a _ _ _ _
138.	150	*	_ _ ai _ t
139.	155	***	c _ mpl _ t _ _ _
140.	164	****	m _ t _ _ _ _ l

It's a good idea to copy words you want to learn into your personal spelling bank and use them for learning four at a time and/or checking as described on pages 99–102.

Learning spellings

	PAGE NUMBER	SYLLABLES	
141.	179	**	de _ _ _ _ b _
142.	182	**	g _ _ d _ n _ _
143.	191	**	su _ pr _ _ _
144.	207	**	sh _ _ ld _ _
145.	256	**	_ _ th _ _ _ _
146.	215	***	h _ m _ r _ _ s
147.	226	***	b _ _ b _ c _ _
148.	234	**	s _ r _ _ _ nt
149.	235	***	t _ m _ t _ _ _
150.	261	**	f _ _ w _ _ _

	PAGE NUMBER	SYLLABLES	
151.	11	***	emba _ _ _ _ _
152.	14	***	g _ ar _ nt _ _
153.	25	***	_ _ c _ _ f _ _ _
154.	34	**	desp _ r _ _ _
155.	38	***	e _ c _ _ _ _ nt
156.	45	***	ne _ _ _ _ _ r _
157.	46	***	pr _ j _ _ _ _ _
158.	48	***	_ _ cog _ _ _ _
159.	48	***	rec _ _ _ end
160.	53	***	_ _ _ _ t _ b _ _

It's a good idea to copy words you want to learn into your personal spelling bank and use them for learning four at a time and/or checking as described on pages 99–102.

PAGE NUMBER	SYLLABLES		
161.	57	***	b _ gi _ _ ing
162.	59	***	c _ _ _ i _ tee
163.	60	***	crit _ _ _ _ _
164.	62	**	d _ _ _ _ rent
165.	63	***	disa _ _ _ _ r
166.	66	***	_ qu _ p _ _ _ t
167.	67	***	e _ ist _ _ _ _
168.	71	**	hin _ _ _ _
169.	75	***	in _ _ _ fe _ _
170.	75	***	int _ _ _ upt

PAGE NUMBER	SYLLABLES		
171.	80	***	mini _ _ _ _ _
172.	83	***	prin _ _ _ _ l
173.	83	***	priv _ l _ _ _
174.	85	***	r _ li _ _ _ _ s
175.	87	***	sig _ _ _ _ _
176.	97	**	cons _ _ _ _ s
177.	103	**	k _ _ _ l _ _ _ e
178.	116	****	_ _ _ _ _ p _ n _
179.	137	****	av _ _ l _ _ _ _
180.	138	***	b _ s _ c _ _ _ _

It's a good idea to copy words you want to learn into your personal spelling bank and use them for learning four at a time and/or checking as described on pages 99–102.

Learning spellings

	PAGE NUMBER	SYLLABLES	
181.	161	****	_ _ _ _ di _ t _
182.	167	***	re _ y _ _ _ ng
183.	205	**	pro _ _ a _ _ _
184.	211	***	b _ _ t _ _ _
185.	212	****	_ _ mm _ n _ t _
186.	212	*****	c _ r _ o _ it _
187.	233	**	r _ _ _ b _ _ _ _
188.	241	**	th _ _ _ f _ _ _ _
189.	256	***	a _ _ _ _ d _ _ _
190.	262	***	_ p _ _ t _ _ t

	PAGE NUMBER	SYLLABLES	
191.	11	****	_ xa _ _ _ ra _ e
192.	31	****	a _ _ el _ r _ t _
193.	31	****	a _ _ ept _ _ _ _
194.	31	***	a _ _ _ e _ _ iv _
195.	37	****	espe _ _ _ _ _ y
196.	38	****	ex _ _ _ i _ _ _ t
197.	43	***	l _ _ _ ten _ _ _
198.	46	***	_ o _ _ ess _ _ n
199.	47	***	pr _ fe _ _ _ _ n
200.	53	*****	veg _ t _ r _ _ n

It's a good idea to copy words you want to learn into your personal spelling bank and use them for learning four at a time and/or checking as described on pages 99–102.

Learning spellings

PAGE	NUMBER	SYLLABLES	
201.	62	***	dic __ __ n __ __ __
202.	63	***	disa __ __ __ nt
203.	63	***	dis __ __ pl __ __ __
204.	74	*****	__ __ d __ vid __ __ __
205.	82	****	p __ tic __ l __ __
206.	85	****	ridic __ l __ __ s
207.	88	***	su __ __ i __ __ __ __ t
208.	97	**	con __ __ __ __ __ ce
209.	97	***	co __ __ __ spond
210.	116	***	a __ __ __ mpl __ sh

PAGE	NUMBER	SYLLABLES	
211.	122	***	g __ v __ __ n __ __ __
212.	147	**	play __ __ __ __ t
213.	153	***	a __ __ ear __ __ __
214.	153	****	a __ __ __ e __ i __ t __
215.	157	****	exp __ r __ __ __ __
216.	158	***	__ __ __ qu __ __ t __ __
217.	210	****	a __ __ umu __ __ __
218.	228	***	d __ s __ st __ __ __
219.	245	***	d __ __ er __ __ __ d
220.	281	***	out __ __ __ __ __ s

It's a good idea to copy words you want to learn into your personal spelling bank and use them for learning four at a time and/or checking as described on pages 99–102.

Learning spellings

	PAGE NUMBER	SYLLABLES	
221.	1	*****	__ cc __ __ __ t __ __ y
222.	12	****	fas __ __ n __ __ ing
223.	23	****	pra __ t __ c __ l __ __
224.	38	****	expl __ n __ __ __ __
225.	46	****	prep __ r __ __ __ __ __
226.	48	***	r __ memb __ __ __ __
227.	73	****	ind __ p __ nd __ nt
228.	80	***	mis __ __ __ v __ __ __
229.	94	****	acc __ __ __ __ d __ t __
230.	96	****	comp __ ti __ __ __

	PAGE NUMBER	SYLLABLES	
231.	97	****	cont __ ov __ __ __ __
232.	107	*****	o __ __ __ t __ n __ ty
233.	128	*****	pr __ nun __ __ __ __ ion
234.	135	*****	u __ ne __ __ __ __ ry
235.	137	***	__ __ qu __ __ nt __ __ ce
236.	146	***	m __ __ nt __ __ __ ce
237.	147	*****	o __ __ a __ __ __ __ __ ly
238.	155	****	__ __ __ ve __ __ nce
239.	161	*****	imm __ __ __ __ __ ly
240.	265	***	p __ __ f __ __ __ __ nce

It's a good idea to copy words you want to learn into your personal spelling bank and use them for learning four at a time and/or checking as described on pages 99–102.

Answers

PRACTICE WITH LONG VOWEL SOUNDS

PAGE 14

FOOD

1. toast	208	6. pastry	147	11. sweet	171	16. cream	155
2. ice-cream	183	7. savoury	149	12. rice	189	17. loaf	201
3. roll	206	8. muesli	217	13. oats	203	18. fruit	214
4. flavour	142	9. gravy	143	14. soup	221	19. plaice	147
5. cake	139	10. meat	164	15. cheese	155	20. tasty	151

IN THE COUNTRY

1. lake	145	6. stream	171	11. pool	219	16. drainage	140
2. field	158	7. wheat	174	12. rye	189	17. hay	144
3. acorn	137	8. oak	203	13. trees	172	18. leaves	163
4. root	220	9. toadstool	208	14. flies	181	19. spider	191
5. stone	207	10. bluebells	211	15. nightingale	187	20. snake	149

SPORT

1. team	172	6. crew	212	11. race	148	16. skiing	170
2. skating	149	7. rowing	206	12. climbing	178	17. glider	182
3. height	182	8. diving	179	13. player	147	18. bowler	195
4. fielder	158	9. boot	211	14. try	192	19. goal	199
5. snooker	221	10. rival	189	15. losing	216	20. rules	220

OCCUPATIONS

1. playwright	147	6. director	179	11. agent	137	16. poet	205
2. waiter	152	7. cleaner	155	12. labourer	145	17. dealer	156
3. salesman	149	8. librarian	185	13. student	221	18. jeweller	216
4. miner	186	9. programmer	205	14. newsagent	218	19. painter	147
5. preacher	166	10. fireman	181	15. pirate	188	20. leader	163

TRAVEL

1. railway	148	6. road	206	11. pony	205	16. plane	147
2. scooter	221	7. bicycle	177	12. flight	181	17. cruise	212
3. breakdown	138	8. timetable	192	13. train	151	18. driver	179
4. motorist	202	9. wheels	174	14. pilot	188	19. vehicle	173
5. ocean	203	10. route	220	15. detour	156	20. scenery	169

Answers

PRACTICE WITH SHORT VOWEL SOUNDS

PAGE 15

WILDLIFE

1. butterfly	116	**6.** vixen	91	**11.** winkle	92	**16.** thrush	133
2. moth	105	**7.** cub	118	**12.** cockle	96	**17.** dove	120
3. squirrel	89	**8.** otter	107	**13.** mussel	126	**18.** swan	112
4. badger	5	**9.** jellyfish	42	**14.** lobster	104	**19.** kestrel	42
5. fox	100	**10.** crab	8	**15.** sparrow	27	**20.** slug	130

HOSPITAL

1. ambulance	2	**6.** splint	88	**11.** health	40	**16.** drug	120
2. bandage	5	**7.** temperature	52	**12.** lung	125	**17.** tablet	28
3. injury	74	**8.** blood	116	**13.** oxygen	107	**18.** pill	82
4. fracture	13	**9.** vaccine	29	**14.** scalpel	26	**19.** medication	44
5. limb	79	**10.** stethoscope	51	**15.** unconscious	134	**20.** stomach	131

WINTER

1. frost	100	**6.** gloves	122	**11.** decorate	34	**16.** mistletoe	80
2. shiver	87	**7.** anorak	2	**12.** presents	47	**17.** berries	32
3. wintry	92	**8.** robin	110	**13.** tinsel	90	**18.** sledge	50
4. blizzard	58	**9.** Christmas	59	**14.** glisten	70	**19.** pantomime	22
5. slush	130	**10.** carolling	7	**15.** holly	102	**20.** January	18

HOLIDAYS

1. sand	25	**6.** suntan	132	**11.** tent	52	**16.** visit	91
2. bucket	117	**7.** cottage	97	**12.** caravan	7	**17.** exhibition	38
3. paddle	22	**8.** fishing	69	**13.** disco	62	**18.** restaurant	49
4. swimming	89	**9.** camping	7	**14.** shopping	111	**19.** customs	119
5. deckchair	34	**10.** rucksack	129	**15.** trip	90	**20.** luggage	125

GAMES AND PASTIMES

1. cricket	59	**6.** badminton	5	**11.** snap	26	**16.** rugby	129
2. chess	33	**7.** squash	111	**12.** dominoes	99	**17.** boxing	95
3. golf	101	**8.** netball	45	**13.** lotto	104	**18.** sledging	51
4. hockey	102	**9.** putting	128	**14.** skipping	88	**19.** stilts	88
5. tennis	52	**10.** jigsaws	77	**15.** football	121	**20.** juggling	124

Answers

PRACTICE WITH MIXED LONG AND SHORT VOWEL SOUNDS

PAGE 16

SCHOOL

1. cloakroom	196	6. lesson	43	11. lunch	125	16. copy	97
2. desk	34	7. bell	32	12. monitor	105	17. science	190
3. seat	169	8. break	138	13. prefect	166	18. mathematics	20
4. teacher	172	9. snack	26	14. writing	193	19. games	143
5. subject	131	10. queue	219	15. notes	202	20. music	217

DRINKS

1. smoothie	221	6. chocolate	96	11. shandy	26	16. brandy	6
2. lemonade	43	7. grapefruit	143	12. beer	154	17. alcoholic	2
3. milk	80	8. juice	216	13. cider	178	18. fizzy	69
4. coffee	96	9. wine	193	14. scotch	111	19. tonic	113
5. tea	172	10. punch	128	15. whisky	92	20. soda	207

GUY FAWKES

1. evening	157	6. sticks	88	11. heat	160	16. banger	5
2. clothes	196	7. matches	21	12. bake	138	17. fuse	214
3. fire	181	8. light	185	13. sausages	111	18. taper	151
4. wood	136	9. flame	142	14. fireworks	181	19. glow	199
5. paper	147	10. crackle	9	15. colours	118	20. embers	36

MOUNTAINS

1. peak	166	6. huge	215	11. precipice	46	16. crag	8
2. massive	20	7. summit	132	12. sheer	170	17. crevice	33
3. rugged	129	8. ridge	84	13. edge	36	18. trail	151
4. boulders	195	9. slope	207	14. torrent	113	19. scramble	26
5. pinnacle	82	10. avalanche	3	15. rocky	110	20. gully	122

THE RAILWAY STATION

1. ticket	90	6. platform	23	11. diesel	156	16. sleeper	170
2. office	106	7. notice	202	12. carriage	8	17. signal	87
3. clock	96	8. timetable	192	13. train	151	18. buffers	117
4. case	139	9. kiosk	162	14. rails	148	19. bridge	57
5. trolley	113	10. engine	36	15. whistle	92	20. taxi	28

© David Moseley and Gwyn Singleton 2015 | *ACE Spelling Activities* | LDA | Permission to photocopy

Answers

PAGE 17

FUN

1. smile	190	6. skipping	88	11. acting	1	16. chuckling	118
2. party	233	7. kissing	78	12. painting	147	17. giggling	70
3. happy	16	8. hugging	123	13. joke	201	18. merry	44
4. mirth	249	9. clown	277	14. tease	172	19. cartoon	227
5. joyful	272	10. tumbling	133	15. tickle	90	20. comic	96

ON THE FARM

1. tractor	28	6. yard	235	11. corn	258	16. cattle	8
2. plough	282	7. orchard	264	12. barley	226	17. bullock	117
3. furrow	121	8. hedgerow	40	13. crop	96	18. sheep	170
4. fertiliser	246	9. harvest	230	14. dairy	237	19. goose	214
5. slurry	130	10. grain	143	15. herd	247	20. turkey	253

WATER

1. waves	152	6. calm	227	11. whirlpool	255	16. trickle	90
2. splash	26	7. smooth	221	12. current	119	17. pour	265
3. spray	149	8. tranquil	29	13. squirt	252	18. still	88
4. choppy	96	9. river	86	14. jet	42	19. sparkling	234
5. rough	129	10. flow	198	15. fountain	279	20. pure	219

FLOWERS

1. snowdrop	207	6. tulip	222	11. lily	79	16. foxglove	100
2. cowslip	277	7. marigold	20	12. lavender	19	17. thistle	90
3. hyacinth	182	8. pansy	22	13. heather	40	18. poppy	108
4. crocus	196	9. carnation	227	14. gorse	261	19. buttercup	116
5. daffodil	10	10. orchid	264	15. broom	211	20. daisy	140

TREES

1. chestnut	33	6. birch	243	11. fir	246	16. oak	203
2. beech	154	7. ash	1	12. pine	188	17. olive	106
3. willow	92	8. palm	233	13. spruce	221	18. hazel	144
4. sycamore	88	9. holly	102	14. yew	224	19. mulberry	126
5. poplar	108	10. larch	231	15. bay	138	20. maple	146

Answers

SPELLINGS FOR SOUNDS

PAGE 18	PAGE 20	PAGE 22	PAGE 24
1. axle	1. again	1. bridge	1. bomb
2. banned	2. bench	2. build	2. conquer
3. camel	3. cellar	3. Christmas	3. dolphin
4. carrot	4. chemist	4. crystal	4. glossy
5. chapter	5. debt	5. filthy	5. knocked
6. expand	6. exit	6. hymn	6. knot
7. fragile	7. friend	7. kitchen	7. lobster
8. accident	8. guest	8. liquid	8. mosque
9. gamble	9. leisure	9. minute	9. novel
10. hammock	10. lesson	10. pistol	10. olive
11. language	11. meadow	11. busy	11. omelette
12. manner	12. pedal	12. ring	12. profit
13. married	13. petrol	13. symbols	13. quarry
14. panda	14. refuge	14. villain	14. squash
15. scratch	15. thread	15. witch	15. watt

PAGE 26	PAGE 28	PAGE 30	PAGE 32
1. among	1. ache	1. appear	1. biceps
2. blush	2. ancient	2. beetle	2. bridle
3. pudding	3. break	3. creak	3. buyer
4. currant	4. cradle	4. deer	4. cyclist
5. enough	5. exhale	5. deceive	5. dilute
6. gloves	6. famous	6. eager	6. dye
7. pushchair	7. gait	7. equal	7. enquire
8. wolves	8. grate	8. frequent	8. guidance
9. plum	9. hazy	9. keyhole	9. idol
10. nun	10. jail	10. leased	10. lightning
11. rubbish	11. laid	11. meter	11. might
12. skull	12. mail	12. needle	12. pylon
13. some	13. mistake	13. peace	13. tide
14. troubles	14. tray	14. queasy	14. tire
15. upstairs	15. weight	15. seize	15. vibrate

Answers

PAGE 34	PAGE 36	PAGE 38	PAGE 40
1. bold	1. amuse	1. arc	1. aware
2. crowbar	2. beauty	2. barley	2. bare
3. dough	3. bruise	3. carpet	3. barely
4. frozen	4. choose	4. carton	4. careless
5. glow	5. cruise	5. catarrh	5. daring
6. grown-up	6. dew	6. farther	6. fare
7. loan	7. Europe	7. guitar	7. farewell
8. moan	8. gloomy	8. harpoon	8. hare
9. ocean	9. hooves	9. harvest	9. parent
10. poach	10. juice	10. heart	10. prepare
11. rows	11. new	11. lager	11. repair
12. snowdrop	12. nuisance	12. parcel	12. scary
13. sole	13. pollute	13. scarf	13. stare
14. throne	14. funeral	14. sergeant	14. there
15. yolk	15. shoot	15. varnish	15. where

PAGE 42	PAGE 44	PAGE 46	PAGE 48
1. absurd	1. awful	1. avoid	1. allowed
2. alert	2. board	2. boiling	2. bough
3. birth	3. daughter	3. buoy	3. coward
4. burglar	4. force	4. choice	4. crowd
5. colonel	5. fortune	5. coin	5. drowsy
6. dirty	6. gorgeous	6. employ	6. flower
7. earn	7. haunt	7. foyer	7. foul
8. fur	8. hawk	8. hoist	8. hour
9. gurgle	9. mourning	9. joyful	9. mouth
10. journal	10. naughty	10. ointment	10. plough
11. murder	11. saucer	11. oyster	11. rounders
12. murmur	12. shore	12. poison	12. rowdy
13. perfume	13. stalk	13. rejoice	13. sprout
14. purchase	14. walk	14. soiled	14. thousand
15. world	15. war	15. toil	15. trowel

Answers

SPELLINGS FOR SOUNDS PUZZLES

PAGE 50

1. potato
2. complaint
3. fragrant
4. greyhound
5. daisy
6. raisin
7. playmate

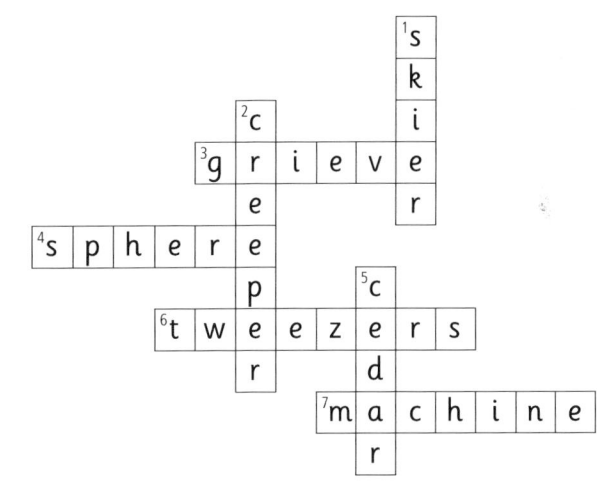

PAGE 51

1. skier
2. creeper
3. grieve
4. sphere
5. cedar
6. tweezers
7. machine

PAGE 52

1. strive
2. riot
3. private
4. frightened
5. nylon
6. migrate
7. oblige

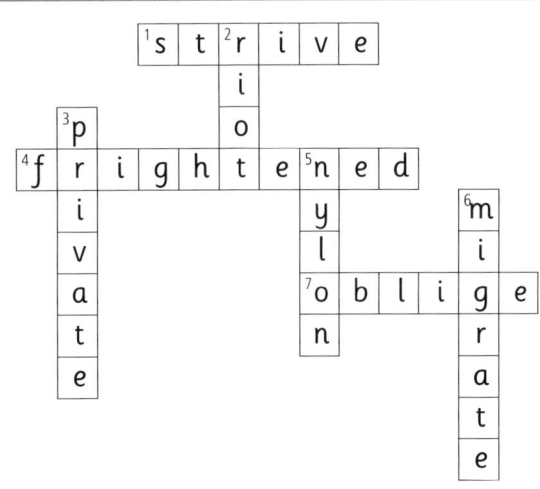

© David Moseley and Gwyn Singleton 2015 | *ACE Spelling Activities* | LDA | Permission to photocopy

Answers

PAGE 53

1. blowlamp
2. photograph
3. doughnut
4. trophy
5. stolen
6. snowman
7. diploma

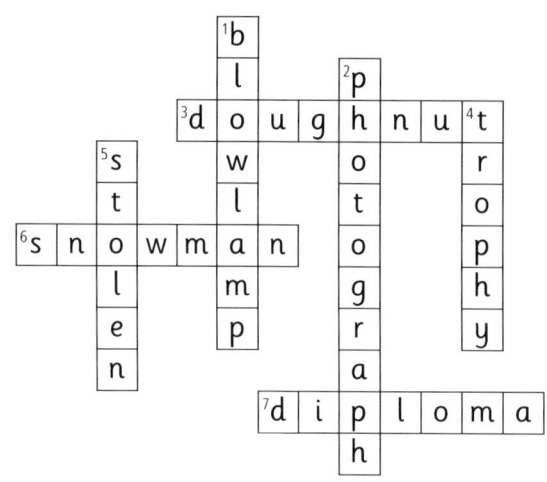

PAGE 54

1. rhubarb
2. sewage
3. hoover
4. futile
5. include
6. tomb
7. brute

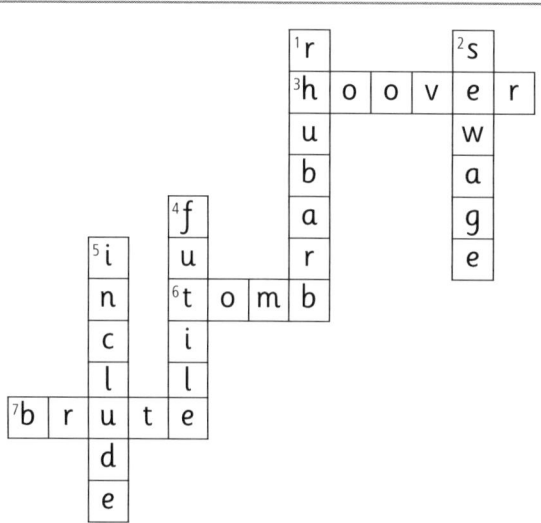

PAGE 55

1. sardine
2. departure
3. tarmac
4. scarlet
5. sharpen
6. charcoal
7. largest

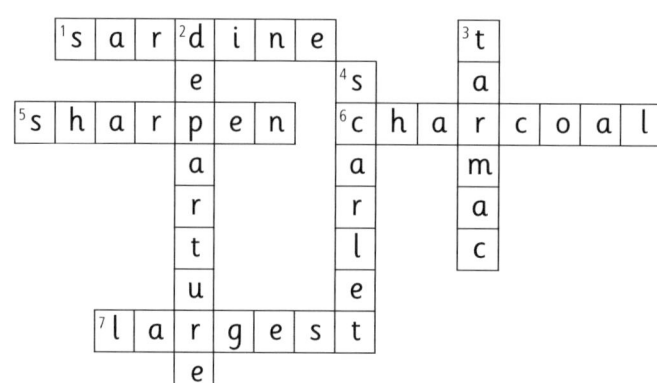

Answers

PAGE 56

1. scarce
2. warehouse
3. pharaoh
4. haircut
5. staircase
6. various
7. fairground

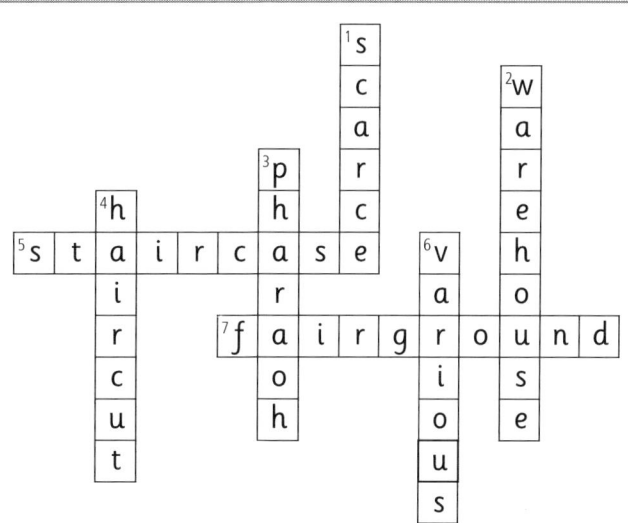

PAGE 57

1. thirsty
2. learning
3. vermin
4. nasturtium
5. suburban
6. world
7. purple

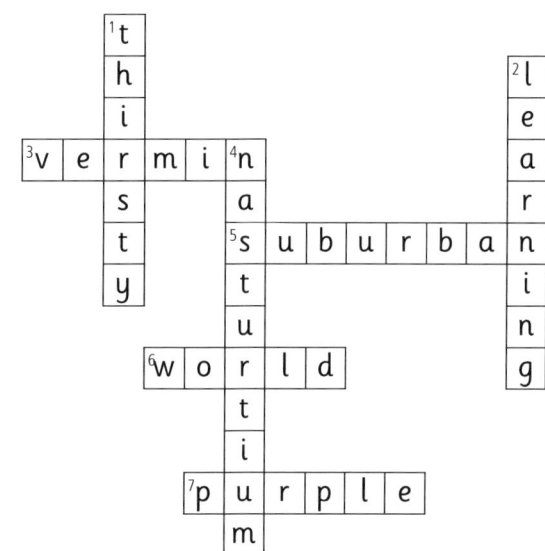

PAGE 58

1. dormouse
2. cautious
3. forecast
4. wharf
5. fourth
6. strawberry
7. wardrobe

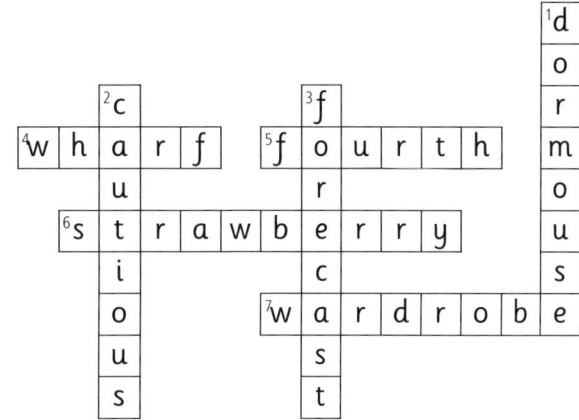

PAGE 59

1. moisture
2. joinery
3. embroider
4. buoyant
5. poison
6. voyage
7. employment

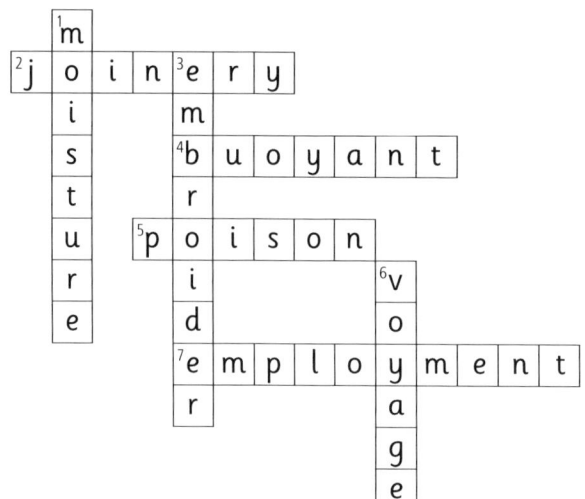

PAGE 60

1. howled
2. loudest
3. cowboy
4. voucher
5. powerful
6. trousers
7. showery

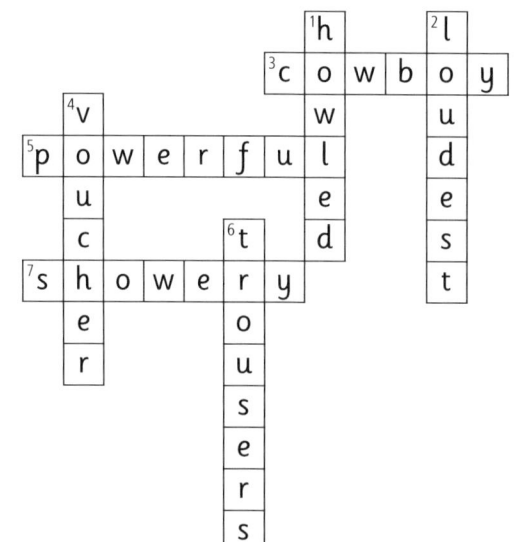

Answers

CAR REGISTRATION GAMES

PAGE 61

1. heavy
2. bacon
3. body
4. reward
5. woman
6. bracelet
7. ripen
8. secret

b	a	c	o	n	☆	☆	☆
w	o	m	a	n	☆	☆	☆
r	e	w	a	r	d	☆	☆
b	r	a	c	e	l	e	t
b	o	d	y	☆	☆	☆	☆
h	e	a	v	y	☆	☆	☆
s	e	c	r	e	t	☆	☆
r	i	p	e	n	☆	☆	☆

PAGE 62

1. ketchup
2. nightfall
3. ostrich
4. exhaust
5. fashion
6. whirlpool
7. reason
8. wicket

w	h	i	r	l	p	o	o	l
e	x	h	a	u	s	t	☆	☆
o	s	t	r	i	c	h	☆	☆
n	i	g	h	t	f	a	l	l
k	e	t	c	h	u	p	☆	☆
f	a	s	h	i	o	n	☆	☆
r	e	a	s	o	n	☆	☆	☆
w	i	c	k	e	t	☆	☆	☆

PAGE 63

1. leopard
2. dandruff
3. ocean
4. gorgeous
5. jiffy
6. ruby
7. reindeer
8. dungeon

r	e	i	n	d	e	e	r
r	u	b	y	☆	☆	☆	☆
d	u	n	g	e	o	n	☆
g	o	r	g	e	o	u	s
o	c	e	a	n	☆	☆	☆
j	i	f	f	y	☆	☆	☆
d	a	n	d	r	u	f	f
l	e	o	p	a	r	d	☆

© David Moseley and Gwyn Singleton 2015 | *ACE Spelling Activities* | LDA | Permission to photocopy

TRICKY WORD ENDINGS

PAGE 64

1. jailer
2. motor
3. lever
4. liar
5. donor
6. pillar

Additional words:
    farmer
    voter
    razor
    mower

PAGE 65

1. harden
2. toughen
3. cousin
4. bacon
5. blacken
6. talon

Additional words:
    woman
    season
    deepen
    rotten

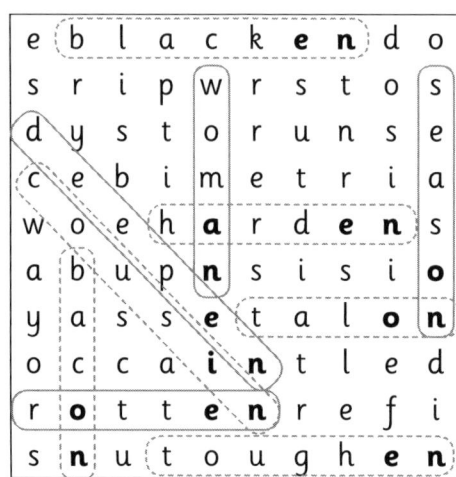

Answers

PAGE 66

1. nation
2. occupation
3. collision
4. session
5. motion
6. passion
7. magician
8. abbreviation
9. solution
10. optician

Additional words:
  potion
  vexation
  lotion

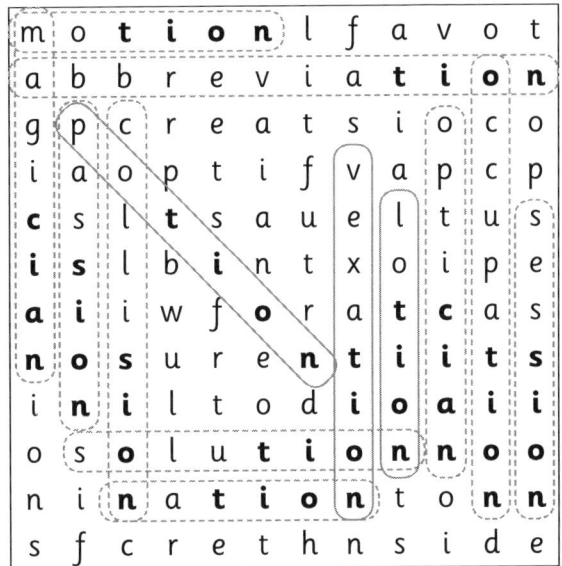

PAGE 67

1. discovery
2. nursery
3. satisfactory
4. extraordinary
5. recovery
6. complimentary
7. mastery
8. history
9. showery
10. victory

Additional words:
  embroidery
  every
  mystery
  ordinary
  rectory

Answers

DOUBLES OR SINGLES

PAGE 68	PAGE 69
1. manner	1. lettuce
2. pepper	2. status
3. pilot	3. annoy
4. scooter	4. toilet
5. bullet	5. liner
6. written	6. drummer
7. hammer	7. super
8. lapel	8. lemon
9. butter	9. illness
10. totem	10. halo

Answers

FIND THE MIDDLE SYLLABLE

PAGE 70	PAGE 71	PAGE 72	PAGE 73
1. parachute	1. inspector	1. brigadier	1. bronchitis
2. entangled	2. complexion	2. flamingo	2. corridor
3. bachelor	3. skeleton	3. exquisite	3. solitude
4. mascara	4. wellington	4. neglectful	4. volunteer
5. valiant	5. terrify	5. sinister	5. tomahawk
6. tapestry	6. delicate	6. rickety	6. hospital
7. javelin	7. merriment	7. tributary	7. gossiping
8. battleship	8. recipe	8. vanilla	8. mosquito
9. subtraction	9. penalty	9. intention	9. astonished
10. advertise	10. venison	10. revolver	10. contradict
11. abandon	11. restaurant	11. continue	11. monument
12. handkerchief	12. flexible	12. decision	12. probably
13. angrily	13. offensive	13. division	13. properly
14. animals	14. pessimist	14. discussion	14. doggedly
15. familiar	15. Celsius	15. difficult	15. colossal

PAGE 74	PAGE 75	PAGE 76	PAGE 77
1. buffalo	1. patiently	1. preceded	1. exciting
2. footballer	2. masonry	2. achievement	2. migrating
3. cookery	3. stationery	3. vehement	3. triangle
4. wonderful	4. amazement	4. weariness	4. xylophone
5. bumblebee	5. narrator	5. vehicle	5. library
6. customer	6. labelling	6. tedious	6. assignment
7. bulletin	7. mistaken	7. previous	7. gigantic
8. multiply	8. neighbourhood	8. cereal	8. horizon
9. unconscious	9. dangerous	9. reassure	9. livelihood
10. wondering	10. tablespoon	10. equally	10. triumphant
11. bungalow	11. shakily	11. conceited	11. ivory
12. another	12. impatient	12. scenery	12. bribery
13. discourage	13. vacation	13. lenient	13. financial
14. sultana	14. frustration	14. sincerely	14. designer
15. suddenly	15. stadium	15. media	15. survivor

Answers

PAGE 78	PAGE 79	PAGE 80
1. aroma	1. museum	1. spectacles
2. immobile	2. hooligan	2. exhausted
3. ownership	3. duplicate	3. vigorous
4. devotion	4. tubular	4. architect
5. groceries	5. amusement	5. lemonade
6. foliage	6. jubilee	6. bicycle
7. atrocious	7. commuter	7. marvellous
8. sociable	8. lubricate	8. gorilla
9. loneliness	9. ruinous	9. burglary
10. emotion	10. pneumatic	10. foreigner
11. odious	11. beautiful	11. orchestra
12. coconut	12. intruder	12. mosaic
13. ferocious	13. secluded	13. certainly
14. jovial	14. fugitive	14. mountainous
15. viola	15. luminous	15. appointment

Answers

FIND THE TWO MIDDLE SYLLABLES

PAGE 81	PAGE 82
1. victorious	1. notorious
2. impossible	2. coronation
3. population	3. accumulate
4. environment	4. temporary
5. development	5. proprietor
6. superstition	6. economies
7. photography	7. communicate
8. identical	8. vegetation
9. ridiculous	9. hilarious
10. favourable	10. astronomy
11. kilometre	11. supermarket
12. minority	12. carnivorous
13. embarrassing	13. tonsillitis
14. memorial	14. peculiar
15. spontaneous	15. horizontal

Answers

WORDS WITHIN WORDS

PAGE 83

The following answers are those which can be found in the *ACE Spelling Dictionary*. Other correct answers (e.g. thundershower) are, of course, acceptable.

1.	safe	safeguard
2.	care	carefree, careful, carefully, carelessly, caretaker
3.	fit	fitting, fitness
4.	fun	funfair, funnier, funnily
5.	rock	rockery, rockier, rockiest
6.	thunder	thunderbolt, thunderclap, thundercloud, thunderous, thunderstorm, thunderstruck
7.	net	netball, netted, netware, network, networking
8.	rain	rainbow, raincoat, rainfall, rainier, raining
9.	down	downcast, downfall, downhill, downland, download, downright, downstairs, downstream, downturn, downward
10.	earth	earthenware, earthquake, earthworm
11.	shop	shopkeeper, shoplift, shopping
12.	slip	slipper, slippered, slippery, slipping, slipstone
13.	foot	football, foothill, foothold, footpath
14.	bright	brightened, brightest, brightness
15.	some	somebody, somehow, someone, something, sometime, somewhat, somewhere

Answers

PAGE 84

The following answers are those which can be found in the *ACE Spelling Dictionary*. Other correct answers (e.g. personable) are, of course, acceptable.

1.	cent	centenary, centigrade, centipede, centrifugal, centrifugally, centurion, century
2.	dirt	dirtied, dirtier, dirties, dirtiest
3.	cheer	cheerful, cheering
4.	sign	signpost
5.	whole	wholegrain, wholehearted, wholeheartedly, wholesale, wholesome
6.	dread	dreadful, dreadfully
7.	infect	infection, infectious
8.	person	personality, personally, personnel
9.	favour	favourable, favourably, favouritism
10.	govern	government, governmental
11.	school	schoolboy, schoolgirl, schoolmaster, schoolmistress, schoolteacher
12.	greed	greedier, greediest, greedily
13.	time	timeless, timescale, timetable, timetabling
14.	point	pointedly, pointing, pointless
15.	agree	agreement

Answers

FIND THE BASEWORD OR ROOT

PAGE 85			**PAGE 86**		
1.	a	polite	1.	b	mortal
2.	b	explode	2.	a	liberate
3.	b	mine	3.	a	joy
4.	a	plant	4.	b	optic
5.	a	cheat	5.	b	navigate
6.	b	scorn	6.	a	view
7.	b	globe	7.	b	stream
8.	b	rely	8.	b	employ
9.	a	simple	9.	a	less
10.	b	fiction	10.	b	accept

Answers

INTRODUCING THE PARTS OF SPEECH

PAGE 87	**PAGE 88**	**PAGE 89**	**PAGE 90**
1. brigade 2. blaze 3. bale 4. bracelet	1. meat 2. machine 3. measles 4. meal	1. flavoured 2. framed 3. faded 4. forgave	1. searching 2. stirred 3. surging 4. swerve
1. hostess 2. hotel 3. home 4. hosepipe	1. square 2. scarecrow 3. share 4. staircase	1. peck 2. pestered 3. pedalling 4. pressed	1. tie 2. timetabled 3. tried 4. time
1. drum 2. dummy 3. dungarees 4. dove	1. crucifix 2. computer 3. cucumber 4. clue	1. counting 2. cowered 3. crown 4. crowded	1. besieged 2. breed 3. breathe 4. beat
1. furniture 2. fern 3. furnace 4. fertiliser	1. cloud 2. councillor 3. crown 4. couch	1. trudging 2. thumped 3. tunnelling 4. touch	1. chopping 2. cross 3. comment 4. complicate

PAGE 91	**PAGE 92**
1. polite 2. private 3. psychic 4. primary	1. Understandably 2. unconventionally 3. undoubtedly 4. underfoot
1. ravenous 2. ramshackle 3. ragged 4. Random	1. shyly 2. scientifically 3. silently 4. Surprisingly
1. toxic 2. tropical 3. toffee 4. throbbing	1. temporarily 2. technically 3. torrentially 4. terribly
1. naughty 2. normal 3. nautical 4. northern **or** north-east	1. tactfully 2. tragically 3. tyrannically 4. thankfully

Answers

SLIPPERY CHARACTERS

PAGES 109–110

1. equip
2. women
3. often
4. money
5. eight
6. reign
7. chief
8. weird
9. guide
10. lying
11. rhyme
12. group
13. scary
14. early
15. earth
16. heard
17. learn
18. occur
19. awful
20. forty
21. actual
22. harass
23. vacuum
24. breath
25. centre
26. energy
27. except
28. length
29. pigeon
30. rhythm
31. symbol
32. system
33. occupy
34. luxury
35. muscle
36. eighth
37. exceed
38. genius
39. recent
40. arrive

PAGES 111–112

41. decide
42. island
43. though
44. future
45. pursue
46. usable
47. answer
48. arctic
49. circle
50. fourth
51. absence
52. amateur
53. attract
54. average
55. grammar
56. imagine
57. natural
58. perhaps
59. tragedy
60. address
61. century
62. develop
63. mention
64. possess
65. regular
66. several
67. special
68. suggest
69. twelfth
70. weather
71. similar
72. vicious
73. foreign
74. popular
75. promise
76. strange
77. achieve
78. deceive
79. disease
80. extreme

PAGES 113–114

81. receipt
82. sincere
83. thieves
84. hygiene
85. licence
86. variety
87. suppose
88. through
89. article
90. bargain
91. bizarre
92. pharaoh
93. burglar
94. certain
95. further
96. purpose
97. awkward
98. forward
99. quarter
100. thought
101. accident
102. actually
103. apparent
104. attached
105. category
106. marriage
107. sandwich
108. cemetery
109. definite
110. exercise
111. February
112. medicine
113. pleasant
114. pressure
115. question
116. relevant
117. sentence
118. separate
119. strength
120. addition

PAGES 115–116

121. business
122. consider
123. equipped
124. horrific
125. increase
126. interest
127. mischief
128. misspell
129. omission
130. physical
131. position
132. broccoli
133. opposite
134. possible
135. thorough
136. grateful
137. occasion
138. straight
139. completely
140. material
141. describe
142. guidance
143. surprise
144. shoulder
145. although
146. humorous
147. barbecue
148. sergeant
149. tomatoes
150. forwards
151. embarrass
152. guarantee
153. sacrifice
154. desperate
155. excellent
156. necessary
157. prejudice
158. recognise
159. recommend
160. vegetable

Answers

PAGES 117–118

161. beginning
162. committee
163. criticise
164. different
165. disappear
166. equipment
167. existence
168. hindrance
169. interfere
170. interrupt
171. miniature
172. principal
173. privilege
174. religious
175. signature
176. conscious
177. knowledge
178. accompany
179. available
180. basically
181. immediate
182. recycling
183. programme
184. beautiful
185. community
186. curiosity
187. raspberry
188. therefore
189. according
190. important
191. exaggerate
192. accelerate
193. acceptable
194. aggressive
195. especially
196. experiment
197. lieutenant
198. possession
199. profession
200. vegetarian

PAGES 119–120

201. dictionary
202. disappoint
203. discipline
204. individual
205. particular
206. ridiculous
207. sufficient
208. conscience
209. correspond
210. accomplish
211. government
212. playwright
213. appearance
214. appreciate
215. experience
216. frequently
217. accumulate
218. disastrous
219. determined
220. outrageous
221. accidentally
222. fascinating
223. practically
224. explanation
225. preparation
226. remembrance
227. independent
228. mischievous
229. accommodate
230. competition
231. controversy
232. opportunity
233. pronunciation
234. unnecessary
235. acquaintance
236. maintenance
237. occasionally
238. convenience
239. immediately
240. performance